ARGUING WITH SCRIPTURE

ARGUING WITH SCRIPTURE

The Rhetoric of Quotations in the Letters of Paul

CHRISTOPHER D. STANLEY

T&T CLARK INTERNATIONAL
A Continuum imprint
NEW YORK • LONDON

T & T Clark International, Madison Square Park, 15 East 26th Street, New York, NY 10010
T & T Clark International, The Tower Building, 11 York Road, London SE1 7NX
T & T Clark International is a Continuum imprint.

Cover art: Manetti, Rutilio. Saint Paul. Museo Civico, Siena, Italy. Alinari / Art Resource, NY.

Cover design: Tom Castanzo

Library of Congress Cataloging-in-Publication Data

Stanley, Christopher D.
Arguing with Scripture : the rhetoric of quotations in the letters of Paul/Christopher D. Stanley.
p. cm.
Includes bibliographical references and index.
ISBN 0-567-02630-2 (pbk.)
1. Bible. N.T. Epistles of Paul—Relation to the Old Testament.
2. Bible. O.T.—Quotations in the New Testament.
3. Bible. N.T. Epistles of Paul—Language, style.
4. Bible. N.T. Epistles of Paul—Criticism, interpretation, etc. I. Title.
BS2655.R32S7 2004
227'.06—dc22

2003022983

Printed in the United States of America
04 05 06 07 08 09   10 9 8 7 6 5 4 3 2 1

To Jeremy and David

May they always wrestle
with the meaning of scripture

CONTENTS

Preface

This book owes its existence to two moments of insight that seem rather obvious in retrospect, though neither seemed so at the time. The first concerns methodology. While working on an article for a volume of essays several years ago, I ran across a number of studies by scholars from different fields (literary studies, philosophy of language, linguistics, and rhetorical studies) that examined the rhetorical and literary effects of the quotation process. These studies raised important methodological questions that had been neglected by scholars engaged in the study of early Christian appropriation of the Jewish Scriptures. Over time, the insights offered by these studies profoundly reshaped my understanding of the use of Scripture in Paul's letters. My initial reflections on the relevance of these materials appeared in a 1997 article entitled, "The Rhetoric of Quotations: An Essay on Method," in *Early Christian Interpretation of the Scriptures of Israel: Investigation and Proposals* (ed. Craig A. Evans and James A. Sanders; Sheffield: Sheffield Academic Press, 1997, 44–58). This article was refined and expanded to form chapter two of the present volume. My quest for a framework to integrate these new insights eventually led me to Eugene White's "configurational" model of rhetoric (described in chapter one), which serves as the methodological backbone of the present study.

The second moment of insight occurred while I was attending a conference on the use of Isaiah 53 in the New Testament. As I listened to several days of presentations and sometimes heated discussions, I was struck by the number of ungrounded historical assumptions that the various parties were making about the availability and use of Scripture in the early Christian churches. Having recently finished William Harris's magisterial work, *Ancient Literacy* (Cambridge: Harvard University Press, 1989), and Harry Gamble's equally prescient study, *Books and Readers in the Early Church: A History of Early Christian Texts* (New Haven: Yale University Press, 1995), I was keenly aware of the high levels of illiteracy in the ancient world, including the early Christian movement. Yet the participants in this conference were talking as though everyone in the early Christian community would have known and recognized the literary context of the many explicit quotations and indirect allusions to the Jewish Scriptures that fill the pages of the New Testament. This experience gave rise to the question that lies at the heart of this study: Why did Paul (and many other early Christian authors) quote so often from the Jewish Scriptures when writing to predominately illiterate Gentile audiences who would have been unable to read the biblical text for themselves? The question was fleshed out (but not answered) in a 1999 article entitled, "'Pearls Before Swine': Did Paul's Audiences Understand His Biblical Quotations?" (*Novum Testamentum* 41 [1999], 124–44). This article became the basis for chapter three of the present volume.

Some of my early attempts to piece together these new insights can be found in papers that I presented at various professional meetings. This book represents my first attempt to offer a coherent statement of the problem and my own thoughtful response.

I would like to express my appreciation to the many people who offered critical and constructive feedback after hearing some of the early papers that I presented on the issues addressed in this book. Special thanks are due to a few individuals who had the interest and patience to maintain the dialogue over longer periods of time, particularly Ross Wagner, Bruce Fisk, and Richard Hays. Their criticisms helped me to sharpen my thinking in a number of areas. I hope that I have returned the favor. Additional thanks are due to my editors at T & T Clark, Henry Carrigan and Amy Wagner, who accepted my manuscript with enthusiasm and published it with utmost professionalism. Finally, I would like to thank my wife, Laurel, and my sons Jeremy and David for their patience as I have struggled with this book over the last several years. My sons have grown to maturity along with this book. I dedicate this book to them in the hope that it will inspire them to wrestle seriously with the words of Scripture as they formulate their own adult identities.

List of Abbreviations

AB	Anchor Bible
AnBib	Analecta biblica
BECNT	Baker Exegetical Commentary on the New Testament
BFT	Biblical Foundations in Theology
BHT	Beiträge zur historischen Theologie
BIOSCS	*Bulletin of the International Organization for Septuagint and Cognate Studies*
CBET	Contributions to Biblical Exegesis and Theology
CRINT	Compendia rerum iudaicarum ad Novum Testamentum
HNTC	Harper's New Testament Commentaries
HTKNT	Herders theologischer Kommentar zum Neuen Testament
ICC	International Critical Commentary
JBL	*Journal of Biblical Literature*
JSNT	*Journal for the Study of the New Testament*
JSNTSup	Journal for the Study of the New Testament: Supplement Series
Neot	*Neotestamentica*
NICNT	New International Commentary on the New Testament
NovT	*Novum Testamentum*
NovTSup	Novum Testamentum Supplements
NTM	New Testament Message
NTS	*New Testament Studies*
SBLDS	Society of Biblical Literature Dissertation Series
SNTSMS	Society for New Testament Studies Monograph Series
SP	Sacra Pagina
TNTC	Tyndale New Testament Commentaries
WBC	Word Biblical Commentary
WUNT	Wissenschaftliche Untersuchungen zum Neuen Testament

Introduction

The apostle Paul labored for most of his adult life to establish Christian house-churches in the towns and cities of the northeast Mediterranean basin. Some of his followers were Jews, but most came from non-Jewish backgrounds. Why, then, did Paul quote so often from the Jewish Scriptures in his letters to these churches? Did he have reason to believe that his predominately Gentile audiences were capable of following his often obscure arguments from specific biblical texts? Or was he so steeped in the language of Scripture that he naturally lapsed into "Biblespeak" whenever he felt compelled to address questions of faith and practice?

A partial answer, supported by several recent studies, is that Paul remained deeply engaged with the Jewish Scriptures throughout his life, so that his thinking and mode of expression were continually shaped by the symbolic universe of the Bible and the language of specific passages.[1] As a devout and educated Jew, Paul labored mightily to convince himself and others that the Christian message was consistent with the testimony of Scripture regarding the nature and activity of Israel's God, including the prophets' assurances that God would show mercy to Israel in the "last days." When writing to his churches about matters of faith and practice, Paul simply followed his habitual practice of grounding his teaching and exhortation in specific passages of Scripture.[2]

Surely this scenario is valid as far as it goes. There is ample evidence that Paul regarded himself as a more or less faithful Jew to the end of his life, and his letters demonstrate how thoroughly his thinking was molded by his

---

1. The term "Jewish Scriptures" is used here (and throughout this study) in place of the Christian term "Old Testament" not only because the latter term is anachronistic when applied to Paul's day, but also to emphasize three points: (1) these were the holy texts of the Jewish ethnoreligious community; (2) Paul read these texts as a member of that community; and (3) people outside this community normally had little or no knowledge of the content of these texts (see chapter 3). The importance of these points will become clearer as the study progresses.

2. On the central place of Scripture in Paul's theology, see Richard B. Hays, *Echoes of Scripture in the Letters of Paul* (New Haven: Yale University Press, 1989); Dietrich-Alex Koch, *Die Schrift als Zeuge des Evangeliums: Untersuchungen zur Verwendung und zum Verständnis der Schrift bei Paulus* (BHT 69; Tübingen: Mohr, 1986); J. Ross Wagner, *Heralds of the Good News: Paul and Isaiah "in Concert" in the Letter to the Romans* (Leiden: Brill, 2002).

ancestral Scriptures. But the fact remains that Paul quotes explicitly from Scripture in only four of his assured letters (Galatians, 1 and 2 Corinthians, and Romans), and he often treats weighty issues of belief and practice without adducing any particular biblical text in support of his argument (e.g., Gal 3:19–4:7, 5:16–26; 1 Cor 7:1–8:13; 2 Cor 5:1–21; Rom 1:18–32, 5:1–8:30, 12:1–16; cf. Phil 3:1–21; 1 Thess 4:1–12; 2 Thess 2:1–12). Moreover, many of his quotations appear in contexts that bear little relation to those "central issues of the faith" that are said to have motivated Paul's studies in the Jewish Scriptures (e.g., 1 Cor 2:16, 9:9, 14:21; 2 Cor 4:1, 8:15, 9:9; Rom 14:11, 15:21). These examples suggest that we must look beyond Paul's own theological interests to understand why he chose to quote a specific verse of Scripture at a specific point in his developing argument.

Another common explanation for Paul's frequent quotations from Scripture, cited often in conjunction with the first one, is that Paul expected his Gentile converts to understand his biblical citations because he had taught extensively from the Jewish Scriptures when he was with them and had impressed upon them the importance of continuing in the Scriptures in his absence. Paul knew that the non-Jews in his churches could not fully understand the Christian message without a proper biblical foundation, so he took pains to lay such a foundation when he was with them. After he left, he expected the Jewish Christians in his churches to continue this pattern of instruction and answer any further questions that might arise. Thus, Paul could reasonably expect even the Gentiles in his churches to understand and appreciate his many quotations from the Jewish Scriptures.

This scenario, like the first one, appears plausible, though our knowledge of Paul's oral instruction of his churches remains fragmentary at best. At several points in his letters Paul alludes to biblical ideas and/or characters with the clear expectation that his audiences will understand the references, perhaps from earlier teaching (e.g., Gal 3:6–9, 16–18, 4:21–31; 1 Cor 9:13, 10:1–10, 15:45–49; 2 Cor 3:7–18, 11:3; Rom 1:3, 3:25, 4:1–22, 5:12–21, 9:4–17, 25–29, 10:16–21, 11:1–4). Moreover, some of his explicit quotations would have made little sense unless the recipients were familiar with the broader context from which the quotation was extracted. These facts have convinced most interpreters that Paul's Gentile readers were in fact conversant with the Jewish Scriptures.

But questions remain: (1) Why does Paul quote and allude to Scripture so extensively in his letter to the church in Rome, which he had never visited, when he includes no explicit quotations in his letter to the Philippians, with whom he had a long-standing relationship? How could he know what passages the Roman Christians did or did not know from the Jewish Scriptures? (2) Why does Paul so often quote the Scriptures in a way that strains any sense of "original context" (e.g., 1 Cor 14:21; 2 Cor 4:13; Rom 2:24, 9:25–26, 10:5–8, 18), if in other places he expects his audience to know and supply the original context of his quotations? Was he not concerned that his arguments might be rejected in these cases? (3) Why should we assume that the recipients of Paul's letters, particularly the non-Jews, possessed the literary capacity to understand his quotations as he intended them? Literacy levels were low in antiquity, access to books was limited, and most non-Jews had little or no prior knowledge of the Jewish Scriptures.[3] Is it not possible that Paul simply misjudged, or failed to consider, the level of biblical literacy in his churches?

Most contemporary studies of Paul's use of Scripture have focused on the way this Jewish-Pharisee-cum-Christian-apostle understood and interpreted the biblical text. These studies have enhanced our understanding of the theological beliefs and methods of the apostle Paul. However, we must also keep in mind that Paul wrote his letters not to lay out a set of theological beliefs, but to motivate specific first-century Christians to believe and/or act (or stop believing or acting) in particular ways. The significance of this point for the study of Paul's quotations has often been underestimated. To quote from an outside text in order to lend support to an argument is a rhetorical act, and it should be studied as such. Quotations are meant to affect an audience; otherwise, there is no reason to include them in a literary work. What was Paul trying to accomplish by including biblical quotations in some of his letters? How might the recipients of Paul's letters have responded to these sudden intrusions from the Jewish Scriptures? How effective was biblical argumentation as a strategy for influencing the thinking and behavior of a first-century Christian audience? These are the kinds of questions that motivate the present study.

Chapter 1 explains what is meant by a rhetorical approach to Paul's quotations. The bulk of this chapter is devoted to a description of the theoretical model that undergirds the ensuing analysis of Paul's rhetoric,

---

3. Of course, Gentile Christians who had been Jewish sympathizers (Luke's "God-fearers") would have been exposed to the Jewish Scriptures, but we have no reason to think that their literacy levels differed appreciably from their contemporaries. For more on the question, see chapter 3.

including his explicit appeals to Scripture. This model, developed by Eugene White out of Chaim Perelman's "New Rhetoric," provides a helpful framework for integrating the diverse materials on quotations that are presented in chapter 2.

Chapter 2 surveys recent studies of the quotation process from the fields of linguistics and literary studies. These materials have been broadly neglected in recent studies of Paul's use of Scripture. Taken together, these studies provide a valuable analytical perspective from which to conduct an audience-centered investigation of Paul's quotations.

Chapter 3 examines some of the assumptions that scholars typically bring to their study of Paul's biblical quotations.[4] Included here are ideas about the nature of Paul's first-century audiences (including their familiarity with the biblical text), the sources of his biblical quotations, his intentions in quoting the biblical text, and the way quotations "work" in a literary composition. Many of these assumptions will be shown to be highly questionable if not invalid. The chapter concludes with a proposal for a more historically sensitive approach to analyzing Paul's explicit appeals to Scripture.

Chapter 4 uses the insights of the first three chapters to develop a coherent method for investigating the rhetorical significance of Paul's biblical quotations. The goal here is to estimate how a first-century audience might have responded to the sudden appearance of material from the Jewish Scriptures at a particular point in Paul's developing argument. Unlike works that treat Paul's first-century audience as a monolithic entity, the method outlined here aims to imaginatively reconstruct the potential reactions of three hypothetical audience groups to Paul's biblical quotations.

Chapters 5–8 present a series of case studies that exemplify the approach set forth in chapter 4.[5] Chapters 5 and 6 examine the rhetorical effect of sev-

---

4. As used in this study, the term "quotation" refers to "any series of several words that reproduces with a reasonable degree of faithfulness the general word order and at least some of the actual language of an identifiable passage from an outside text" (Christopher D. Stanley, *Paul and the Language of Scripture: Citation Technique in the Pauline Epistles and Contemporary Literature* [SNTSMS 74; Cambridge: Cambridge University Press, 1992], 36). To qualify for inclusion in this study, a quotation must be "identifiable" not only to the modern reader, but also to ancient readers; that is, it must be marked by an explicit quotation formula (e.g., "as it is written"), an interpretive gloss, or a clear grammatical tension with the surrounding passage (see the discussion in Stanley, *Paul*, 31–39). Allusions, "echoes," "midrashic" commentaries, and other forms of reference to the biblical text are excluded from consideration in this study because it is audience-centered (see chapter 3).

5. To insure consistency, the present study is limited to the assuredly Pauline letters.

eral isolated quotations in the Corinthian correspondence. Chapter 7 looks at two key passages in Paul's letter to the Galatians. Chapter 8 investigates the role of quotations in the epistle to the Romans. Each of these chapters covers only a handful of passages; the aim is not to be comprehensive, but to exemplify how quotations "work" as rhetorical devices in a given letter. Chapter 9 sums up the conclusions of the study and offers a retrospective analysis of the rhetorical effectiveness of Paul's biblical quotations.

Scholars interested in Paul's work as a biblical theologian will find the results of this study rather meager. The following pages offer few if any new insights into the way Paul himself read and interpreted the biblical text. But for those interested in the rhetorical dimensions of Paul's letters—how Paul used language, symbols, and ideas to provoke a particular response from his first-century audiences—Paul's quotations offer a fruitful field for study.

PART I

THE RHETORIC OF QUOTATIONS

CHAPTER 1
Rhetorical Perspectives

Theology or Rhetoric?

After Rom 9–11, Gal 3:6–16 contains the most discussed series of quotations in the Pauline corpus. In the space of ten verses, Paul quotes or refers to seven different passages from the Jewish Scriptures. The result is a carefully crafted argument that commends faith, as modeled by Abraham, over obedience to Torah as the means by which Gentiles can attain righteousness before God and participate in the blessings that God promised to Abraham and his descendants.

Interpreters have been drawn to this passage for a number of reasons. Since the time of the Reformation, Protestant commentators have found in these verses a classic statement of the doctrine of "justification by faith." According to this view, the passage describes the inherent contrast between "faith" (in Christ) and "works" (human deeds) as mutually exclusive channels by which humans seek to gain forgiveness and acceptance from God. Paul's primary aim in quoting from the Jewish Scriptures is to show that the way of faith, not the way of works, has always been God's plan for human beings.

Recent interpreters have recognized that this traditional approach, whatever its theological merits, neglects the historical context of Paul's letter to the Galatians. Paul wrote to the Galatians not to argue for the primacy of "faith" over "works" as alternate means of securing God's favor, but to address the concrete question of whether non-Jews must be circumcised and obey the Jewish Torah in order to be properly related to the God of the Jews. From the nature of Paul's counterargument, most commentators have concluded that Paul was aware that someone in the Galatian churches had appealed to the story of Abraham (most likely Gen 17) to argue in favor of the circumcision of male Gentile Christians. Galatians 3 would then be understood as Paul's response to that argument. By offering an alternative reading of the Abraham story, Paul hopes to undercut his opponents' calls for circumcision and obedience to Torah and thus avoid losing the Galatian Christians to what he anxiously calls "another gospel" (Gal 1:6).

Clearly, the latter position is more sensitive to the historical context of Paul's use of Scripture in Gal 3:6–16. But when we ask how Paul's biblical argumentation might have been understood by his Galatian audience, we find little help from the commentators. Instead, they talk about Paul's own engagement with Scripture.[1] (1) In the case of vv. 6–9, most interpreters have focused on the fact that Paul found in the Abraham story a warrant for his own contention (rooted in his missionary experience) that God accepts anyone who has the kind of "faith" that Abraham did (including "Gentiles"), not just the physical descendants of Abraham (i.e., the Jews).[2] Comparisons are then made with Rom 4 to determine whether Paul's thinking has changed or remained the same between the two letters. (2) In v. 10, the discussion customarily centers on what Paul meant by his statement about the "curse of the law" and how this relates to his "Christian" understanding of the Jewish Torah. The key question about the quotation from Deuteronomy is how it relates to Paul's assertion in the first part of the verse.[3] (3) In the case of v. 11, commentators have routinely noted how Paul found in the brief Habakkuk quotation a vital support for his own theology of "justification by faith." Debate continues over whether Paul rightly interpreted the Habakkuk passage and what role it might have played in the development of his theology.[4] (4) For the quotations from Leviticus and Deuteronomy in vv. 12 and 13, the

---

1. Since Gal 3:6–14 will be treated more fully in chapter 7, the present discussion is limited to summary comments.

2. Hans Dieter Betz is more explicit about this point than most: "In opposition to Judaism, however, Paul interprets the concept of 'faith' not in the Jewish sense, but in terms of his own theology. In his view, the example of Abraham is not one that shows faithfulness and trust in the Jewish sense, but faith in the Pauline sense. Therefore his contention that Gen 15:6 proves his understanding of 'justification by faith' as opposed to 'by works of the Torah' can convince only those who share his theological and methodological presuppositions" (Betz, *Galatians: A Commentary on Paul's Letters to the Churches in Galatia* [Philadelphia: Fortress, 1979], 141).

3. According to one popular interpretation, Paul's association of God's "curse" with the Jewish Torah can be traced to a Deuteronomic theology that sees the continued dispersion of the Jews among the nations and the rule of Palestine by foreign powers as proof that God's "curse" still stands against Israel on account of its violations of Torah (N. T. Wright, *The Climax of the Covenant: Christ and the Law in Pauline Theology* [Minneapolis: Fortress, 1991], 137–56). For a review of alternative views, see Christopher D. Stanley, "'Under a Curse': A Fresh Reading of Gal 3.10–14," *NTS* 36 (1990): 481–511.

4. Included here is the intriguing suggestion that Paul saw in the expression ὁ δίκαιος a reference to Jesus, the "righteous one" par excellence. See Richard B. Hays, *The Faith of Jesus Christ: An Investigation of the Narrative Substructure of Galatians 3:1–4:11* (SBLDS 56; Chico, Calif.: Scholars Press, 1983).

usual mode of interpretation is to investigate what each verse meant in the context of the Israelite legal tradition and then to discuss how Paul's usage compares with the common Jewish understanding of both verses.[5] The central concern is to uncover how Paul's Christian theology shaped his understanding and application of the biblical text. (5) In the case of v. 16, commentators have labored to explain how Paul's admittedly idiosyncratic reading of Gen 13:15 makes sense within the context of Paul's own theology and contemporary Jewish exegetical practice. Here again the primary question is what the verse (including the brief quotation) says about Paul's view of God's saving purposes for humanity.

This brief example illustrates how recent interpreters, in an effort to avoid reading later theological concerns back into Paul's argument, have turned their attention to the hermeneutical question of how Paul understood and interpreted the biblical text. A similar methodological shift has affected the study of Pauline quotations in other letters.[6] The result has been a series of important studies that have broadened our understanding of Paul's exegetical and hermeneutical techniques and perspectives.

But something is missing here. Despite their laudable concern to elucidate Paul's engagement with the biblical text (or perhaps because of it), scholars have had little to say about the *rhetorical* aspects of Paul's biblical quotations. Why did Paul include a series of explicit quotations from the Jewish Scriptures at this point in his argument? What was he trying to accomplish? How did he expect his audiences to respond? Were they able and willing to give the desired response? In sum, was the use of explicit biblical quotations an effective strategy for influencing the beliefs and/or conduct of the original recipients of Paul's letters? Or might Paul have misjudged the ability (or willingness) of his largely Gentile Christian audience to respond to this form of argumentation? Questions such as these have been largely ignored in recent studies of Paul's use of Scripture. An adequate

---

5. Examples include Betz, *Galatians*, 147–52; F. F. Bruce, *The Epistle to the Galatians: A Commentary on the Greek Text* (Grand Rapids: Eerdmans, 1982), 162–67; and James D. G. Dunn, *The Epistle to the Galatians* (London: A & C Black, 1993), 175–78.

6. The recent move toward applying literary theories of intertextuality to the study of Paul's quotations, popularized by Richard B. Hays and pursued by many of the participants in the "Scripture in Early Judaism and Christianity Section" of the Society of Biblical Literature, is similar to the hermeneutical approach in that it focuses on the relation between the quotation and a prior text, not the role of the quotation within a developing argument. The problems that result when modern readers equate their own intertextual readings with those of Paul's first-century audiences will be explored in chapter 3.

response requires a thoroughly rhetorical analysis of Paul's appeals to the Jewish Scriptures.[7]

RHETORICAL STUDIES OF QUOTATIONS

If we want to understand how Paul's quotations "work" as rhetorical devices, the natural place to begin is with a review of what contemporary rhetorical theorists have to say about the role of quotations in advancing and sustaining an argument.[8] Unfortunately, the literature reveals very little interest in the question. Speakers and writers have been using quotations to enhance the rhetorical quality of their works for centuries, but neither the ancient handbooks nor the modern textbooks on rhetoric and speech communication have much to say about their function.[9] The subject is customarily treated rather briefly (if at all) in a section dealing with the use of evidence or testimony to lend credibility to an argument.[10] The few com-

---

7. Anders Eriksson, using language drawn from the social sciences, draws a helpful distinction between "emic" forms of rhetorical analysis that focus on the way the people of antiquity understood their own practice, and "etic" approaches that use modern categories and methods "to provide the best scientific explanation of the persuasive strategies in the text" (*Traditions as Rhetorical Proof: Pauline Argumentation in 1 Corinthians* [Stockholm: Almquist & Wiksell, 1998], 21). The present study is fundamentally "etic" in approach, since the ancient rhetorical handbooks do not say enough about quotations to support a fruitful "emic" analysis (see note 10).

8. Kenneth Burke's definition of the term "rhetoric" offers a good starting point for this study: "the use of words by human agents to form attitudes or induce actions in other human agents" (*A Rhetoric of Motives* [New York: Prentice-Hall, 1950], 41). A more nuanced definition will be given below.

9. For example, the index of the classic work by Chaïm Perelman and L. Olbrechts-Tyteca, *The New Rhetoric: A Treatise on Argumentation* (trans. John Wilkinson and Purcell Weaver; Notre Dame, Ind.: University of Notre Dame Press, 1969), lists four references (in 514 pages!) to the subject of "quotations," all of them quite brief.

10. In *Rhetorica,* Aristotle does refer briefly to the practice of citing "ancient witnesses" (defined as "the poets and all other notable persons whose judgments are known to all"; 1.15) to support an argument, but he limits their usefulness to providing analogies that can be applied to a contemporary legal case (2.23). The use of proverbs and maxims (arguably a special form of quotation) is restricted here to elderly men whose long experience gives them the credibility to cite traditional wisdom (2.21). In the right hands, says Aristotle, maxims can prove helpful to an orator "due to the want of intelligence in his hearers, who love to hear him succeed in expressing as a universal truth the opinions which they hold themselves about particular cases" (2.21). In *Institutio oratoria,* Quintilian offers similar observations in a brief section in which he recommends the use of quotations to lend authority to the orator's pronouncements (5.36–44).

Pronouncements from the past are valuable because "they form a sort of testimony, which is rendered all the more impressive by the fact that it was not given to suit special cases, but was the utterance . . . of minds swayed neither by prejudice or influence, simply because it seemed the most honourable or honest thing to say" (5.37). Maxims can also be useful because they

ments that do appear, however, are consistent enough that a brief overview of common observations can suffice for the whole.

Like other "arguments from authority," quotations are generally used to anticipate and/or close off debate regarding a statement made by a speaker/author in direct speech: "One resorts to [them] when agreement on the question is in danger of being debated."[11] This is especially true when the quotation is taken from a source that is deemed authoritative (or sacred) by the intended audience. In this case the authority of the source is implicitly transferred to the argument of the speaker/author, thereby reducing the likelihood of question or challenge. In most cases, however, the argument from authority plays only a subsidiary role for the speaker. As Chaïm Perelman observes, "More often than not, the argument from authority will not constitute the only proof, but will round off well-developed argumentation."[12]

The effectiveness of appeals to authority is also influenced by the audience's perception of the authority and/or credibility of the speaker/author.[13] Arguments from authority can be particularly effective when accompanied by power imbalances between speaker and audience, since the audience is typically inclined to accept the words of the speaker/author as valid. In cases where a favorable disposition cannot be taken for granted, "the superior participant will often choose to mask his/or her own position by exploiting the ambiguities available in the language" of the source text.[14] Such an approach can be effective as long as the audience is not in a position to question the speaker/author's interpretation of the source text.

Quotations can also serve to create or enhance a sense of communion between speaker and audience.[15] In cases where the speaker is already viewed

---

have "carried conviction of their truth to all mankind" (5.41). Similar observations can be found in other ancient rhetorical works.

11. Perelman and Olbrechts-Tyteca, *New Rhetoric,* 308.

12. Ibid., 307.

13. Robert Bostrom, in *Persuasion* (Englewood Cliffs, N.J.: Prentice-Hall, 1983), describes the detailed experiments of James McCroskey, who demonstrated that appeals to evidence could be quite effective for speakers who were perceived as having low-to-medium credibility by the audience, but were of minimal help for a high-credibility speaker (146–50). "Effectiveness" is defined here as the production of lasting changes in the beliefs and/or attitudes of the immediate audience (150–52).

14. Dick Leith and George Myerson, *The Power of Address: Explorations in Rhetoric* (London: Routledge, 1989), 124.

15. Perelman and Olbrechts-Tyteca, *New Rhetoric,* 177–78. Perelman also includes allusions, maxims, and proverbs among his "figures that relate to communion." Inexplicably, Perelman limits this "communion-building" function to times when the act of quotation "is not fulfilling its normal role of backing up a statement with the weight of authority" (177).

favorably by the audience, quotations from a source deemed reliable by both parties can serve to highlight the bond between them, thus enhancing the audience's receptivity to the speaker's message. In cases where the audience is uncertain or hostile toward the speaker, "a well-chosen quotation will suffice to create a feeling of confidence, by showing that the speaker and his audience have common values."[16] In both cases the quotation appeals to the emotions of the audience, "the emotion created by memories, or community pride."[17]

Although rhetorical studies have typically focused on the authoritative use of quotations, some theorists have recognized that quotations can be adduced for purposes other than appeals to authority. For example, quotations can be used to illustrate or exemplify a point made by a speaker using ordinary language. The effect here is less direct, and therefore less predictable. According to one popular textbook, "The value and power of any literary material quoted in a speech depends upon its relevance to the point of the message and upon its strength in saying something—with grace, felicity, and a sense of the poetic or the dramatic—that could not be said as aptly in the speaker's own words."[18] In this statement we see an acknowledgement of the poetic dimension of the quotation process: the "value and power" of a quotation can depend as much on the manner of expression as on the content or source of the statement. Yet even here the argument from authority is not far from the surface, since the very act of quotation implies that the source of the quotation is respected by the intended audience. Even quotations that look like innocent ornamental devices can be heavily "power-coded" when taken from an authoritative source, since they inevitably add an aura of respectability to the speaker/author's pronouncements.

A Model of Rhetorical Communication

From this brief overview we learn that quotations from an authoritative source can help to increase an audience's receptivity to a speaker/author's message. But not all quotations have the same effect on an audience. What

16. Ibid., 496. In other words, quotations can serve to enhance the speaker's *ethos*—a key concern of rhetoricians at least since Aristotle.

17. Ibid., 177. In classical terms, this is an appeal to *pathos*, Aristotle's second mode of persuasion.

18. Kenneth G. Hance, David C. Ralph, and Milton J. Wiksell, *Principles of Speaking* (3rd ed.; Belmont, Calif.: Wadsworth, 1989), 88.

makes some quotations more effective than others? How can we evaluate the effectiveness of quotation as a rhetorical strategy in a particular situation? To answer such questions, we need a model of the rhetorical process that is not merely descriptive, but is also evaluative.[19] We find this in the "New Rhetoric" of Chaïm Perelman and his followers, as developed especially in the work of Eugene E. White.[20]

Eugene White's definition of rhetoric is rather technical, but carefully framed: "the purposive use of symbols in an attempt to induce change in some receiver(s), thereby derivatively modifying the circumstances that provoked, or made possible, the symbolic interaction between persuader(s) and receiver(s)."[21] According to White (and Perelman before him), all rhetorical acts are situational; that is, they are grounded in what White calls a "provoking rhetorical urgency."[22] By "provoking rhetorical urgency," White means "a structured perception of ongoing events" that a speaker/author constructs out of his/her knowledge of a particular situation.[23] The presence and nature of a "rhetorical urgency" depends entirely on the perception of the speaker/author; as White puts it, "Rhetorical urgencies are not really 'out there' as sequences of objective events; they are patterns of thought and feel-

19. The evaluative side of contemporary rhetorical studies has generally been neglected by scholars of early Christian rhetoric in favor of purely descriptive approaches. This emphasis on the importance of evaluation is one of the distinctives of the present study.

20. See especially Eugene E. White, *The Context of Human Discourse: A Configurational Criticism of Rhetoric* (Columbia: University of South Carolina Press, 1992).

21. Ibid., 11.

22. White's idea of "provoking rhetorical urgency" is quite close to the concept of "rhetorical situation" developed by Lloyd Bitzer in his classic essay "The Rhetorical Situation" (*Philosophy and Rhetoric* 1 [1968]: 1–14). Bitzer defines "rhetorical situation" as "a complex of persons, events, objects, and relations presenting an actual or potential exigence which can be completely or partially removed if discourse, introduced into the situation, can so constrain human decision or action as to bring about the significant modification of the exigence." Bitzer presents a significant refinement of his ideas in "Functional Communication: A Situational Perspective," in *Rhetoric in Transition: Studies in the Nature and Uses of Rhetoric* (ed. Eugene E. White; University Park: Pennsylvania State University Press, 1980), 21–38.

23. White, *Context,* 105. This insistence on the socially constructed nature of "rhetorical urgencies" is what makes White's approach preferable to that of Bitzer, who has been criticized for the Platonic idealism that seems to be implied in his concept of "rhetorical situation." See Robert L. Scott, "Intentionality in the Rhetorical Process," in White, ed., *Rhetoric,* 56–58; Alan Brinton, "Situation in the Theory of Rhetoric," *Philosophy and Rhetoric* 14 (1981): 234–48. For a review of the debate in the years since Bitzer's essay, see Johann D. Kim, *God, Israel, and the Gentiles: Rhetoric and Situation in Romans 9–11* (SBLDS 176; Atlanta: Scholars Press, 2000), 35–40.

ing in people's heads."[24] What makes such a situation "rhetorical" is the perception by a speaker/author that things are not as they should be, and that language can be used to induce an audience to bring about a change in the situation.[25] By addressing a group of people in terms meant to win their adherence, the speaker/author hopes to induce the audience to think or act in such a way as to eliminate the rhetorical urgency that provoked the address.[26] Rhetorical speech is thus audience-centered speech; its purpose is to promote action on the part of the audience, not merely to communicate the ideas of a speaker/author.

Although rhetorical analysis normally assumes intentionality on the part of the speaker/author, critics disagree about the extent to which these intentions can be recovered. In White's view, the only way to evaluate a piece of communication is to make some form of judgment about the speaker/author's intentions: "We can't make any qualitative judgments about any human actions, including rhetorical actions, without assuming something about why those actions were taken."[27] White holds no illusion that the critic can establish with certainty the intentions behind a rhetorical work. But experience tells him that "with careful digging, one can usually form reasoned conclusions about persuaders' purposes."[28]

---

24. White, *Context*, 105. The speaker/author's perception of a situation as a "rhetorical urgency" is shaped by a broad array of factors, including the nature of the information available to the speaker/author, the speaker/author's relation to the audience, the personal beliefs and values of the speaker/author, and the broader pattern of societal influences (110–11, 146–47). As with estimates of a speaker/author's intentions (see below), the critic's judgment about a speaker/author's perception of a situation will never be more than probable (119).

25. Clearly, this way of conceiving the rhetorical process is better suited to persuasive rhetoric than to epideictic rhetoric—a fact that White seems to overlook. But even epideictic speech can be viewed as a response to a "provoking rhetorical urgency" within a particular social system: in our own society, a death requires a funeral oration, a wedding reception calls forth a toast, and a graduation ceremony evokes a final charge to the graduates. Chaïm Perelman, whose influence can be seen throughout White's study, goes so far as to argue that "the epideictic genre is central to discourse because its role is to intensify adherence to values without which discourses that aim at provoking action cannot find the lever to move or inspire their listeners" (*The Realm of Rhetoric* [trans. William Kluback; Notre Dame, Ind.: University of Notre Dame Press, 1982], 19).

26. As White observes, "The ultimate purpose of talk is *not* to induce change in readers or listeners. That is an intermediate step toward the ultimate goal of applying pressure on the urgency" (*Context*, 39). Yet even this is not the end of the matter. As White recognizes, "It is quite possible—even likely—that the changed state of the original urgency will, in turn, constitute new provoking urgencies that give rise to later rhetorical efforts toward modification" (*Context*, 35). We see this clearly in Paul's correspondence with the Corinthians.

27. Ibid., 47.

28. Ibid., 53.

White identifies five aspects of the message that can shed light on the speaker/author's intentions: (1) the basic thesis of the communication; (2) the substance of what is said; (3) the arrangement of the ideas; (4) the language with which the ideas are clothed; and (5) the paralinguistic characteristics that accompany the formal language.[29] Information about the historical and social setting of the rhetorical act can also help to illuminate the "internalized self-systems" that shaped the speaker/author's rhetorical choices.[30] The critic's judgments about the speaker/author's intentions will rarely be more than probable, but there can be no evaluation of a rhetorical work without some form of assumption about what the speaker/author was trying to achieve.

To speak of evaluation implies that the speaker/author is not invariably effective. One of the chief tasks of a rhetorical critic is to evaluate the effectiveness of the speaker/author's argumentation. The primary criterion by which the effectiveness of a rhetorical act should be judged is, according to White, the degree of "congruence" between the speaker/author's use of language and the various circumstantial forces that influence the rhetorical process.[31] As White puts it, "A communication can be based on 'good reasons,' be eloquent in style, be expressive of high moral principles, have sound documentation and helpful internal summaries, and still be *incongruent* with other forces that help to shape the configuration in which the communication occurs."[32] Such a communication can hardly be labeled "effective."

---

29. Ibid., 64. Because of his situational view of rhetoric, White insists that "in estimating rhetorical intent, it is neither necessary nor desirable to use psychoanalytical approaches" (73).

30. Ibid., 74–75. Exploring the speaker/author's "self-system" can be helpful because "self-systems (individual or collective) condition the way persuaders view urgencies, audiences, and occasions, and the ways persuaders conceptualize their relationships to these forces. Persuaders' self-systems determine their rhetorical choices, including their choices of purpose" (74–75). This recalls White's insistence on the importance of the speaker/author's *perception* of the audience's situation.

31. This criterion flows naturally out of what White calls the "master concept" of his work: "To the degree that rhetorical constraints are matched by appropriate rhetorical responses, persuasion can take place" (ibid., 36). According to White (14–15), the degree of "congruence" among rhetorical forces is a better barometer of effectiveness than are the actual "effects" of a rhetorical act, since "effects" are notoriously difficult to trace to a single cause, and even an exemplary rhetorical effort can lead to limited results due to other forces in the configuration. Moreover, "congruence" can be evaluated in terms of "degrees," whereas "effects" are an all-or-nothing enterprise.

32. Ibid., 17.

White list six constraints that impinge upon the effectiveness of a rhetorical communication:[33]

1. The potential for modification of the urgency;
2. The capacity of the readers/listeners to alter the urgency;
3. The readiness of the readers/listeners to be influenced;
4. The occasion—the immediate circumstances in which the communication takes place;
5. Relevant aspects of the persuader's self-system; and
6. The persuader's real and apparent purposes in communicating.

Chief among these rhetorical constraints, in White's view, is the audience. The success of a rhetorical communication depends in large part on the willingness of audience members to allow themselves to be influenced by the words and ideas of the speaker/author.[34] To induce a positive response, the speaker/author must be able to create a sense of coherence between the beliefs and values commended in the message and the prior convictions of the audience.[35] The recipients' experiences both prior and subsequent to encounter-

---

33. Ibid., 38–39. According to White, "It is the interrelationship—the interplay—of these factors that must be 'read' by communicators and by those who interpret and evaluate communications" (39). White sums up the critical viewpoint in the form of a question: "How congruent were the basic thrusts or theses of the communication(s) with the amount and kind of modification that such a communication could make in the urgency?" (199).

34. As White puts it, "Persuaders do not unilaterally determine the standards for judgments. . . . Readers and listeners determine *for themselves* whether they will attend to what persuaders say and what changes, if any, they will make in the ways they think and feel" (ibid., 208–9). The importance of the audience's disposition is stressed throughout White's study: "How ready the readers and listeners are to be influenced by a message conditions the way they respond to what is said and, derivatively, the way they eventually influence the urgency. Successful persuaders accept that the potential responsiveness of audiences constrains what they can successfully do and say" (63).

35. White uses the term "identification" to describe both the speaker/author's efforts to appeal to the beliefs and values of the audience and the audience's response to those appeals (ibid., 17–18, 210–19). He explains the process this way: "To begin persuading, an advocate must meet readers and listeners where they are at the outset of the communication. He or she must provide them with language and ideas that will enable them to perceive analogies between what is being said and some aspect of their own relevant knowledge, beliefs, values, attitudes, and behaviors. Without some initial identification, persuasion cannot begin. To promote further movement toward closure, the persuader must enable his or her readers/listeners to enlarge and reinforce the initial beachheads of identification and to perceive fresh areas of identification. The persuadees must continue to recognize analogies between themselves and what is being said as communication develops" (216). White's theory could be enhanced by a greater

ing the speaker/author's argumentation will also affect the way they respond to a rhetorical communication.[36] Other important influences include the recipients' opinions about the character of the speaker/author and their perception of the degree of "fit" between the message and their situation.[37]

In some cases, the audience may be either unable or unwilling to provide the response that the speaker/author desires. Audience members might harbor negative feelings about the character and/or the beliefs or values of the person who addresses them; they might view the situation in terms different from those of the speaker/author; they might be incapable of understanding the ideas and/or language used by the author; they might be divided among (or within) themselves over the issue; or they might simply be disinterested in the subject of the discourse. If the speaker/author fails to recognize and counter these potentially damaging influences, the effectiveness of the rhetorical act will be diminished. The effective communicator is one who takes full account of the capabilities and likely responses of the audience within a given rhetorical context. One of the primary goals of rhetorical analysis is to evaluate how well the speaker/author carries out this task.[38]

---

appreciation of the persuasive role of the speaker/author's depiction of the exigency. As Dennis Stamps has observed, "A text presents a selected, limited, and crafted entextualization of the situation. The entextualized situation is not the historical situation which generates the text and/or which the text responds to or addresses; rather, at this level, it is that situation embedded in the text and created by the text which contributes to the rhetorical effect of the text" ("Rethinking the Rhetorical Situation: The Entextualization of the Situation in New Testament Epistles," in *Rhetoric and the New Testament: Essays from the 1992 Heidelberg Conference* [ed. Stanley E. Porter and Thomas H. Olbricht; JSNTSup 90; Sheffield: JSOT Press, 1993], 199). For more on the way Paul's depiction of the situation affects the reception of his quotations, see chapter 9.

36. Over against static and/or unidirectional interpretations of the rhetorical process, White speaks of rhetoric as a dynamic process in which the speaker/author, the audience, and the message are shaped and reshaped by the changing configuration of their relationship. As White puts it, "Any persuasive experience is experience of a dynamic, cyclical flow of antecedents—events—consequences that, in the course of its developing, encompasses not only the particular piece(s) of persuasion that we are interested in but also all other successful and abortive attempts at modification that are relevant to experiencing that rhetoric" (*Context,* 13; cf. 34–36, 208–10).

37. Ibid., 252–63.

38. White describes the critic's task this way: "In all cases, the degree of congruence between rhetors' proffered satisfactions and the readiness of audiences [to be persuaded] must be located by looking at the basic thrusts of the communication, at the degrees to which conceptions of provoking urgencies were shared, at the status or ethos of the communicator(s), and at the situational acceptability of remedial actions proposed. . . . We cannot 'measure' the potentialities of rhetoric in this way, but we can *estimate* how wise the communicator's choices were and why what was done worked (in whole or in part) or did not work. We can also explain why this degree of achievement came into being" (ibid., 262–63).

Quotations as Rhetorical Acts

So what does all of this mean for the study of Paul's biblical quotations? At the heart of a rhetorical approach to Paul's quotations is a concern to explore how the quotations "work" as part of the unfolding surface structure of Paul's letters. Quotations will be studied as rhetorical devices designed to influence the thoughts, feelings, and actions of a first-century audience, not as windows to the theology or interpretive activities of the author.[39] Primary attention will be given to the way quotations advance (or fail to advance) the author's rhetorical strategies in a given passage. Questions will be raised about why Paul introduced a biblical citation at this particular point in his argument, what he might have hoped to accomplish by it, and how a first-century audience from diverse social and religious backgrounds might have viewed this sudden intrusion of material from a Jewish religious text. Consideration will be given to the affective and poetic elements as well as the intellectual effects of such an encounter with the holy Scriptures of Israel. The primary evaluative question will not be "How effectively does Paul integrate the text of Scripture into his theology?" but "How well do Paul's quotations cohere with his own rhetorical aims and the needs and capabilities of his first-century audience?" In short, a rhetorical study will focus on what quotations *do* as part of a developing argument, not just on what they *say*.

But why do we need a rhetorical analysis of Paul's biblical quotations? What might we gain from such an approach?

First, we gain a better understanding of Paul's argumentation. Most of Paul's quotations from the Jewish Scriptures were introduced to commend his views to first-century audiences. The better we understand the role that biblical quotations played in his argumentative strategy, the better we can trace and evaluate the effectiveness of his argumentation.

Second, we gain new insight into the historical relation between Paul and his churches. Rhetorical analysis includes an investigation of the way a

39. This is the chief point that distinguishes a rhetorical approach from other recent studies of Paul's use of Scripture, virtually all of which seek to explicate how Paul interpreted the biblical text prior to the composition of his letters. Because of their focus on Paul's hermeneutics, most scholars have failed to ask how much of Paul's prior reflection on the biblical text would have been evident to the recipients of his letters. As we will see, the bulk of Paul's interpretive activity would have been hidden to his audiences, and thus devoid of rhetorical effect, unless they knew the Jewish Scriptures well enough to identify the original passage and retrace Paul's interpretive activity. In light of what we know about literacy levels in antiquity and the makeup of Paul's churches, it seems unlikely that Paul's audiences were in such a position. See the discussion in chapter 3.

speaker/author perceived the intended audience and how well that perception corresponds to what we know about the audience from other sources. This attention to the audience raises questions about many of the assumptions that interpreters have commonly held concerning the historical context of Paul's quotations.

Third, we gain a deeper appreciation for the many ways in which Paul's first-century audiences might have responded to his biblical quotations. Rather than simply assuming that Paul's first-century addressees understood and accepted his repeated appeals to the Jewish Scriptures, rhetorical analysis raises questions about the effectiveness of biblical quotation as a persuasive strategy within the social and rhetorical contexts of Paul's churches.

There are many reasons to pursue a rhetorical analysis of Paul's quotations from Scripture. But since Paul's letters also belong to the domain of literature, we would do well to ask whether there is anything useful to be learned from contemporary literary studies about the art of quotation. Fortunately, a number of important studies have appeared in recent years in the fields of linguistics and literary studies that explore the way quotations "work" as part of a literary communication. These studies affirm that the meaning and/or effect of a quotation arises out of its secondary literary and rhetorical context, regardless of how this relates to the "original sense" of the quoted passage. The next chapter will examine some of these studies and discuss their implications for the analysis of Paul's quotations.

CHAPTER 2

Literary Perspectives

Laying the Foundation: Speech-Act Theory

The publication in 1955 of J. L. Austin's *How to Do Things with Words*[1] signaled a paradigm shift in the study of language by philosophers and linguists. According to Austin, language does more than simply make a statement or pass on information. Words are spoken or written with the aim of *doing* something to the hearer(s)—that is, evoking some sort of response. This is true even when the response is limited to accepting the speaker's words as "fact."

Austin identified three distinct components of the speech process: (1) the *locutionary act*, the vocalization (or inscription) of a series of words that carry a more or less definite sense and reference in a given language; (2) the *illocutionary act*, the construction of words into a specific form of communication (informing, questioning, commanding, promising, etc.) according to the linguistic conventions of a particular society or context; and (3) the *perlocutionary act*, the effect (intended or not) that these words have on the thoughts, feelings, or conduct of the audience (e.g., convincing, persuading, deterring, surprising, or misleading them).[2] Even the simplest of statements will produce some sort of perlocutionary effect in the person who experiences (hears or reads) an utterance.[3] As Austin puts it, "Once we realize that what we have to study is *not* the sentence but the issuing of an utterance in a speech situation, there can hardly be any longer a possibility of not seeing that stating is performing an act."[4] Every meaningful use of language is in reality a "speech-act," the term that gives this theory its name.

---

1. J. L. Austin, *How to Do Things with Words* (2nd ed.; Cambridge: Harvard University Press, 1962).

2. Ibid., 94–120.

3. Ibid., 133–40. Rhetorical speech is thus no different in principle from any other form of speech; it is simply more self-conscious about the perlocutionary effects that it seeks to produce.

4. Ibid., 139. John R. Searle, who studied with Austin, makes a similar point: "The unit of linguistic communication is not, as has generally been supposed, the symbol, word or sentence, or even the token of the symbol, word or sentence, but rather the production or issuance of the

The idea of an "illocutionary act" assumes that speakers have a purpose that they wish to achieve through speaking. To achieve this purpose, the speech-act must satisfy certain "felicity conditions" that arise from the social context of the utterance. If it fails in this regard, the act must be regarded as, at least to some extent, a failure.[5] The perlocutionary effects of the speech-act, on the other hand, need not be intended or even anticipated by the speaker. For instance, in the illocutionary act of "arguing," the speaker's intention is achieved if the audience grasps the point of the argument. The audience's response of agreement or rejection, along with such emotional reactions as happiness, anger, and frustration, constitute the perlocutionary effects of the speech-act.

Unfortunately, Austin did not include quotations among the speech-acts that he chose to examine for his study. But his groundbreaking work on the nature of language laid the foundation for subsequent studies of quotation in the fields of philosophy, literary studies, and linguistics. Most of these studies have focused on issues other than the rhetorical aspect of quotations. Philosophers of language, for example, have raised theoretical questions about the meaning and reference of quotations and what it means to place quotation marks around words in a sentence. Such questions lie beyond the limits of the present study.[6] The same can be said for the many literary studies that explore the theoretical distinctions between direct, indirect, and "free indirect" quotations in fictional literature.[7] Even linguists, typically

---

symbol or word or sentence in the performance of the speech act" (*Speech Acts: An Essay in the Philosophy of Language* [Cambridge: Cambridge University Press, 1969], 16).

5. For example, even the simple communication of information requires that the recipients grasp the meaning and sense of the locution. Austin calls this response "uptake." At a higher level, a speaker who pronounces a couple married must be duly authorized to perform weddings if the act is to achieve its purpose. In still other cases, the illocutionary act must be understood as inviting a particular kind of response in order to be deemed effective (e.g., eliciting obedience to a command) (*Words*, 116–18). For more on felicitous and infelicitous speech, see ibid., 12–52.

6. See Searle, *Speech Acts*, 72–76; Donald Davidson, *Inquiries into Truth and Interpretation* (Oxford: Clarendon, 1984), 79–92; Nelson Goodman, *Ways of Worldmaking* (Indianapolis: Hackett, 1978), 41–56. One insight from the philosophical approach that might prove useful in analyzing biblical quotations is the recognition that "in quotation, the normal referential function of words is suspended, because the words that we utter when we quote are not our own" (Florian Coulmas, "Reported Speech: Some General Issues," in *Direct and Indirect Speech* [ed. Florian Coulmas; Trends in Linguistics: Studies and Monographs 31; Berlin: de Gruyter, 1986], 12). This observation is confirmed by several of the linguistic studies reviewed later in this chapter.

7. For example, Barbara Hall Partee, "The Syntax and Semantics of Quotations," in *A Festschrift for Morris Halle* (ed. Stephen R. Anderson and Paul Kiparsky; New York: Holt,

attuned to the rhetorical dimensions of language, have devoted the bulk of their attention to the role of quotations in ordinary conversation, not their function in written texts.[8] But among the handful of scholars who have studied the role of quotations in written compositions, Austin's work is cited again and again as a seminal resource.

How Does a Quotation Mean?

In recent years several scholars have put forward theories to explain how quotations "work" as part of a literary communication. Because these scholars work in different disciplines, most of them have developed their ideas independently.[9] A careful review of their findings can enhance what we have learned from our survey of contemporary rhetorical theory in chapter 1. The most important of these models are the "Dramaturgical Theory" of Anna Wierzbicka, the "Proteus Principle" of Meir Sternberg, the "Demonstration Theory" of Herbert Clark and Richard Gerrig, and the "Parodic Approach" of Gillian Lane-Mercier.

The Dramaturgical Theory (Anna Wierzbicka)

The dramaturgical theory of Anna Wierzbicka[10] was developed primarily to answer a series of theoretical questions about the relation between direct, indirect, and "free indirect" quotations in literature.[11] Behind all quotations, says Wierzbicka, lies a concern to "dramatize" the words of an earlier speaker/author to a later audience. As Wierzbicka puts it, "The per-

---

Rinehart & Winston, 1973), 410–18; Ann Banfield, "Narrative Style and the Grammar of Direct and Indirect Speech," *Foundations of Language* 10 (1973), 1–39; Yukio Hirose, "Direct and Indirect Speech as Quotations of Public and Private Expression," *Lingua* 95 (1995): 223–38. On the meaning of "free indirect" quotation, see note 11.

8. For example, Deborah Tannen, *Talking Voices: Repetition, Dialogue, and Imagery in Conversational Discourse* (Cambridge: Cambridge University Press, 1989); Herbert Clark, *Using Language* (Cambridge: Cambridge University Press, 1996).

9. Exceptions to this pattern are indicated in notes 18, 19, and 51.

10. Anna Wierzbicka, "The Semantics of Direct and Indirect Discourse," *Papers in Linguistics* 7 (1974): 267–307.

11. The term "free indirect" quotation is one of several used by linguists to refer to a form of speech, found primarily in fictional literature, in which the identity of the speaker shifts subtly between the characters and the author throughout the passage. As Florian Coulmas puts it, "The stylistic veil covers the speaker, leaving it up to the reader to determine whether the speaker of a given section of a narrative is the hero or the author" ("Reported Speech," 7). For examples, see Banfield, "Narrative Style," 10–13, 25–33; Wierzbicka, "Semantics," 294–97; Herbert H. Clark and Richard R. Gerrig, "Quotations as Demonstrations," *Language* 66 (1990): 786–88.

son who reports another's words by quoting them, temporarily assumes the role of that other person, 'plays his part,' that is to say, imagines himself as the other person and for a moment behaves in accordance with this counter-factual assumption."[12] At the moment of quotation, says Wierzbicka, the quoting author takes on the *persona* of the original speaker/author, dramatically reenacting the original speech-event so that the two voices merge into one.[13]

The reason for such an imaginary exercise (the "illocutionary purpose" of the quotation) is to convey not only *what* the original speaker/author said, but also *how* it was said.[14] The task of communicating what was said can be fulfilled through the use of an indirect quotation ("He or she said that . . . "). The use of a direct quotation therefore signals a concern to lead the audience into a brief, imaginary reenactment of the original speech-event.[15] When a written text is quoted, the reenactment is limited to hearing the words of the original author. In the case of observed speech, the quoting speaker can also mimic the tone of voice, facial expressions, gestures, and other nonverbal elements of the communicative process.[16]

Unfortunately, Wierzbicka has little to say about why a later speaker would want to create such a momentary reenactment of the original speech-event. The closest she comes is her suggestion that "a person who quotes another's speech may feel unable to separate the meaning from the form and to state it in his own words. . . . Quoting directly one undertakes to portray the meaning *together* with the form, thus avoiding the responsibility for a correct representation of the meaning as such."[17] In other words, the speaker

---

12. Wierzbicka, "Semantics," 272. Wierzbicka's more complicated discussion of the role of dramatic reenactment in indirect quotations (ibid., 283–300) is put aside for now because it contributes nothing to the present study.

13. Ibid., 273.

14. Ibid., 274–77. According to Wierzbicka, the words "I want to cause you to know . . ." are always implied in the quotation process.

15. This is the "perlocutionary effect" of the direct quotation. Wierzbicka's discussion is laced with references to speech-act theory.

16. The latter point is developed more fully by Charles N. Li in "Direct Speech and Indirect Speech: A Functional Study," in Coulmas, ed., *Direct and Indirect Speech*, 38–40.

17. Wierzbicka, "Semantics," 279. Wierzbicka says that this is only "one of the reasons why people sometimes prefer to quote rather than to paraphrase the speech of others" (p. 279), but she fails to mention any others. Chaïm Perelman makes a similar point concerning the presentation of evidence, where quotation can have a distancing effect: "If (except in a historical work) a speaker quotes the source from which the information is derived, he often seems to suggest that he does not necessarily stand behind the information himself" (*The Realm of Rhetoric* [trans. William Kluback; Notre Dame, Ind.: University of Notre Dame Press, 1982], 139).

who chooses direct quotation purposely leaves to the reader the tasks of interpretation, evaluation, and response.

Wierzbicka's insistence on the imaginative or "dramatical" quality of direct quotation has found broad support among subsequent investigators.[18] Much of this approbation can be traced to the fact that other scholars have found her model helpful for explaining some of the similarities and differences between direct, indirect, and "free indirect" quotations. Its usefulness for the study of ancient biblical quotations, however, is less apparent. Perhaps the greatest value of Wierzbicka's theory lies in its stress on the dynamic interplay between the voice of the quoting author and the quoted text. According to Wierzbicka's model, an author who quotes from Scripture temporarily lays aside his or her own speech and allows the biblical text to speak directly to the audience. In this way the members of the audience are enabled (in theory) to hear for themselves what the quoting author heard in an earlier encounter with the biblical text. But Wierzbicka overlooks the fact that direct quotation also empowers the audience by opening up the possibility that they could hear something in the text that is different from what the quoting author intended. To preclude this possibility, authors of argumentative texts routinely embed their quotations in an interpretive context that points the reader toward a particular understanding of the quoted text.[19] Thus, quotation does not offer the kind of unmediated reenactment of the original speech-event that Wierzbicka thought. Instead, the voice of the original is muffled in varying degrees by the voice of the quoting author.

In summary, Wierzbicka is correct in insisting that quotation brings the audience into forceful contact with the voice of the original text. In the case

---

18. The validity of Wierzbicka's theory is assumed by Florian Coulmas ("Reported Speech," 2, 6), and is affirmed, with qualifications, by Clark and Gerrig ("Quotations," 801–2). The term "dramaturgical" theory as a label for Wierzbicka's approach actually comes from Clark and Gerrig's study, not from Wierzbicka herself.

19. In the premodern world, including Greco-Roman antiquity, it was also common to reshape the wording of the quotation to reflect the quoting author's understanding of the original text. For a review of the evidence, see Christopher D. Stanley, *Paul and the Language of Scripture: Citation Technique in the Pauline Epistles and Contemporary Literature* (SNTSMS 74; Cambridge: Cambridge University Press, 1992), 338–360. The same phenomenon occurs routinely in oral quotations, as is shown by the experiments of Elizabeth Wade and Herbert H. Clark, "Reproduction and Demonstration in Quotations," *Journal of Memory and Language* 32 (1993): 805–19. According to Clark and Gerrig, the common assumption that quotations strive for verbatim reproduction can be traced to "the written language bias of linguistics and philosophy" ("Quotations," 800). Clark and Gerrig criticize Wierzbicka for her implicit acceptance of this view ("Quotations," 802).

of Jewish and Christian quotations from Scripture, this is a voice that speaks with profound authority. But Wierzbicka, along with many contemporary students of biblical quotations, fails to observe that quotations can also be used to advance a speaker/author's rhetorical agenda. By claiming the voice of Scripture as one's own, a speaker/author can increase the chances that an audience of Christians or Jews will adopt or reject the set of beliefs and/or practices that the speaker/author recommends or opposes. This important effect of quotation is neglected in Wierzbicka's analysis.

The Proteus Principle (Meir Sternberg)

The question that concerns Meir Sternberg[20] is what happens to the meaning of a statement when it is extracted from its original setting and embedded into a new context in the form of a quotation. Unlike Wierzbicka, Sternberg is keenly aware of the many ways in which a quoting author can shape the meaning of a quotation. According to Sternberg, "Quotation brings together at least two discourse-events: that in which things were originally expressed (said, thought, experienced) by one subject (speaker, writer, reflector), and that in which they are cited by another."[21] Whereas the original statement was grounded in the subjective experience of an individual speaker, the quotation makes the words themselves (the "world of discourse") the object of reflection and interpretation.[22] The original statement becomes, in functional terms, "an *inset* within the surrounding *frame* of the context-of-quotation."[23] This recontextualization invariably has a profound effect on the meaning of the statement.

Sternberg's analysis merits quotation here:

> What this new mode of existence involves is not just formal restructuring but manifold shifts, if not reversals, of the original meaning and significance. For regardless of the formal relations between inset and frame . . . the framing of an element within a text entails a

20. Meir Sternberg, "Proteus in Quotation-Land: Mimesis and the Forms of Reported Discourse," *Poetics Today* 3 (1982): 107–56.

21. Ibid., 107.

22. Ibid. Cf. Coulmas: "The speaker does not claim authorship for a part of his utterance which he ascribes to another speaker or unspecified source. This part of his utterance does not serve a regular referential function such that words refer to things. Rather, they refer to words, not to any arbitrary words, but purportedly to those words that some other speaker uttered at some other time" ("Reported Speech," 12).

23. Sternberg, "Proteus," 108.

> communicative subordination of the part to the whole that encloses it. However accurate the wording of the quotation and however pure the quoter's motives, tearing a piece of discourse from its original habitat and reconstructing it within a new network of relations cannot but interfere with its effect.[24]

This happens because

> the very extraction of a part from a speech-event must, to a certain degree, modify, if not misrepresent, its role and import within the original whole, where it is qualified and supplemented, defined and substantiated, by a set of other components relating to the various parameters of context. And the resetting of the part within a different whole widens the distance still further by exposing it to the pressure of a new network of relations.[25]

A shift in meaning is inevitable:

> Whatever the units involved, to quote is to mediate, to mediate is to frame, and to frame is to interfere and exploit. Autonomous, non-narrated, reporter-free, single-voiced quotation: each of these is a contradiction in terms.... Charged with a different significance and assigned a new role by the whole, the recontextualized discourse proportionately moves away from the original string of words or thoughts.[26]

In the final analysis, says Sternberg,

> each act of quotation serves two masters. One is the original speech or thought that it represents, pulling in the direction of maximal accuracy. The other is the frame that encloses and regulates it, pulling in the direction of maximal efficacy. Reported discourse

---

24. Ibid.

25. Ibid., 131. As Sternberg explains further, "The inset's configuration of point of view must be different and more complex than the original's, even when composed of the same words in the same order, for the perspectives of the global speaker and his audience are superimposed on those of the original participants" (131).

26. Ibid., 145, 150.

> thus presents a classic case of divided allegiance, between original-oriented representation (with its face to the world) and frame-oriented communication (with its face to the reader).[27]

In sum, every quotation, no matter how faithfully it follows the wording of the original, is a complex speech-event in which "the quotee always subserves the global perspective of the quoter, who adapts it to his own goals and needs."[28] In cases where the members of the later audience have no independent access to the quoted text, this "embedded" form of the quotation is the only form of the original that they will encounter, and thus the sole basis for their construction of its meaning.[29] In this setting, it is the context-of-quotation, not the original context, from which the audience obtains the necessary cues for interpreting the text.

The importance of Sternberg's work for the study of biblical quotations should be obvious. Although there is much to be gained from looking at the way Jewish and Christian authors read and interpreted the biblical text, modern investigators have been slow to ask how much of this interpretive activity would have been apparent to a first-century audience.[30] Questions about how the recontextualization of the quotation might have advanced the rhetorical purposes of the quoting author have also been neglected. As Sternberg observes, the effect of a quotation "depends not so much on the makeup of the inset vis-à-vis the original as on the strategy informing the frame."[31] Unless the members of the audience were familiar with the original passage (which was unlikely for most Gentile Christians in antiquity, and for many Jews as well), their experience with the words of Scripture would have been filtered through the interpretive and rhetorical lens of the quoting author.[32]

---

27. Ibid., 152.

28. Ibid., 109. It is from this "many-to-many relationship between linguistic form and contextual function," the result of a complex interplay between rhetorical, contextual, and functional forces, that Sternberg's "Proteus Principle" gets its name (154).

29. Ibid., 140–44.

30. Chapter 3 will treat this question at length.

31. Sternberg, "Proteus," 153.

32. For an estimate of the level of biblical knowledge in Paul's churches, see chapter 3. Some of Paul's quotations clearly presuppose a degree of familiarity with the biblical text, including his unexplained references to Abraham and his family in Rom 9:7–13 and Gal 3:6, 8, 16. In most cases, however, Paul includes enough cues in the surrounding verses to indicate what meaning he expects his audience to get from the quoted material, which may or may not correspond to its "original meaning."

The Demonstration Theory (Herbert Clark and Richard Gerrig)

The work of Herbert H. Clark and Richard R. Gerrig seeks to explain how quotations work from a linguistic perspective.[33] Like Wierzbicka, Clark and Gerrig insist that a person who quotes the words of another intends not only to report (or "describe") what the other person *said,* but also to show (or "demonstrate") what the person *did* in the act of speaking.[34] To "demonstrate" (i.e., to selectively repeat an action to show how it was done) is a qualitatively different mode of communication than to "indicate" (refer to an event still in progress) or to "describe" (report on an event using a verbal narrative). "Demonstrations," according to Clark and Gerrig, "work by enabling others to experience what it is like to perceive the things depicted"; this includes showing "what in part it looks, sounds, or feels like to a person for an event, state, process, or object to be present."[35]

But no demonstration can reproduce every detail of an earlier action, and no demonstrator attempts to do so. Rather, all demonstrations are selective; that is, they focus on certain parts of the action that are deemed important in the eyes of the demonstrator. Subsidiary elements may be added to round out the demonstration, but these must be distinguished from the intended point of the demonstration.[36] An effective demonstrator will signal to the observer (using explicit commentary or implicit cues) which parts of the demonstration are intended to be primary, and which are supportive or incidental.[37]

---

33. Clark and Gerrig, "Quotations," 764–805.

34. Ibid., 764. Clark and Gerrig make it clear that they are using the term "demonstrate" here "in its everyday sense of 'illustrate by exemplification' and not in its technical linguistic sense of 'point to' or 'indicate' (as in demonstrative reference)" (764 n. 2). As with Wierzbicka, the theory propounded by Clark and Gerrig is explicitly grounded in speech-act theory (778–80, 785).

35. Ibid., 765, 766 (cf. 793).

36. Ibid., 767–68, 774–78, 782–85. Clark and Gerrig label those features that serve as the focal point of the demonstration "depictive aspects," while the less central features are divided into "supportive aspects," "annotative aspects," and "incidental aspects" (768). This inherent selectivity of the quotation process helps to explain why quotations are rarely rendered verbatim in common speech. Clark and Gerrig mount a sustained and effective attack against the widespread assumption that speakers (or writers) who incorporate direct quotations into their work are committed to verbatim reproduction of the original source (795–800). Cf. Wade and Clark: "Speakers who remember the exact wording but produce a quotation that is not verbatim aren't lying. They are merely choosing to depict aspects of the original other than its wording" ("Reproduction," 808). See also the comments and materials cited in note 19.

37. Clark and Gerrig, "Quotations," 768–69. Features that can be "marked" for audience attention in a written quotation include the language/dialect/register of the original speaker, the

How does this relate to written quotations? According to Clark and Gerrig, the standard assumption that speakers employ direct quotations only when they feel that they can reproduce the wording of the original is wrong.[38] The decision to include direct quotations in a written work depends entirely on the rhetorical aims of the quoting author.[39] Direct quotations can advance an argument in a variety of ways.

First, direct quotations lend vividness and drama to a discourse, since they "give the audience an experience of what it would be like in certain respects to experience the original event."[40] The inclusion here of the phrase "in certain respects" reveals the key difference between Clark and Gerrig's theory and that of Wierzbicka. What the audience experiences in this approach (contra Wierzbicka) is not a full reenactment, but an edited version of the original speech-event. The quoting author ultimately decides which aspects of the original event will be reexperienced by the audience. This rhetorical strategy is typically hidden from the view of the audience.

Second, direct quotations serve to insulate the quoting author from negative reactions to a particular statement or viewpoint. In direct quotation, the quoting author takes responsibility only for those parts of the original speech-act to which he or she calls attention (i.e., what the author "depicts"). The remainder is implicitly charged to the original source. But the reverse may also be true: the author may rely on the "undepicted" elements of the quotation "to convey information implicitly that it might be more awkward to express explicitly."[41] This strategy allows the author to bring a word of challenge to an audience with less risk to the author's rhetorical *ethos*.

Third, direct quotations help to create a sense of solidarity between speaker and audience. Where both parties are familiar with the original text, a well-chosen quotation can dispose the audience to respond more favorably

---

original style of delivery (rare), and the linguistic acts of the original (propositional content, illocutionary point, etc.) (782–86).

38. Alternative theories of quotation are summarized and refuted in Clark and Gerrig, "Quotations," 795–802; Wade and Clark, "Reproduction," 806–8. See also note 36.

39. Cf. Wade and Clark: "The wording and demonstration theories contrast, then, in their emphasis on memory versus rhetoric. . . . By the demonstration theory, a speaker's choice is a matter of rhetorical purpose" ("Reproduction," 808).

40. Ibid. Cf. Clark and Gerrig: "When we hear an event quoted, it is as if we directly experience the depicted aspects of the original event. We perceive the depicted aspects partly as we would the aspects they are intended to depict" ("Quotations," 793).

41. Clark and Gerrig, "Quotations," 792, citing Ronald K. S. Macaulay, "Polyphonic Monologues: Quoted Direct Speech in Oral Narratives," *International Pragmatics Association Papers in Pragmatics* 1 (1987): 2.

to the speaker's message.[42] As Clark and Gerrig put it, "When speakers demonstrate only a snippet of an event, they tacitly assume that their addressees share the right background to interpret it the same way they do. In essence, they are asserting, 'I am demonstrating something we both can interpret correctly,' and that implies solidarity."[43]

Clark and Gerrig's proposal contains a number of important insights for the study of biblical quotations. In particular, it helps us to understand why authors include direct quotations in their texts, and why quotations affect readers the way they do. For Jewish and Christian audiences in antiquity, biblical quotations spoke more powerfully than many modern interpreters have recognized. Direct appeals to a community's sacred Scripture do more than simply reinforce a point or settle a dispute. Quotations increase the likelihood of a favorable response to the speaker's message by recalling the common bond that unites speaker and audience while at the same time insulating the speaker from negative reactions to certain parts of the message. Quotations also allow the speaker to influence the audience's response by calling attention to certain aspects of the authoritative text and minimizing others. Most importantly, quotations lead the audience into a mediated encounter with the original text, where a second, more powerful voice speaks on behalf of the quoting author. In short, biblical quotations bring the audience into the presence of God, who is shown standing firmly on the side of the speaker.

The chief weakness of Clark and Gerrig's study is that it says little about the kinds of "markers" that an author might use to signal which aspects of a quotation are meant to be "depicted" (i.e., made the basis of a response) and which are merely supportive or incidental. More clarity is also needed regarding how one is to know whether the "undepicted" aspects of a quotation are serving an implicit rhetorical purpose. Finally, more guidance is needed concerning the many ways in which quotations can advance the rhetorical strategies of a quoting author. Nonetheless, Clark and Gerrig's analysis offers many useful insights for the study of biblical quotations.

---

42. The problem of how to create a well-disposed audience has been a central concern of rhetoricians at least since Aristotle's treatment of the subject (*Rhetorica* 1.2; 2.1–17; 3.14–15, 19).

43. Clark and Gerrig, "Quotations," 793. Chaïm Perelman makes a similar point in Chaïm Perelman and L. Olbrechts-Tyteca, *The New Rhetoric: A Treatise on Argumentation* (trans. John Wilkinson and Purcell Weaver; Notre Dame, Ind.: University of Notre Dame Press, 1969), 177–78, 496.

The Parodic Approach (Gillian Lane-Mercier)

Where other scholars have looked at quotations through the lens of a particular discipline, Gillian Lane-Mercier's study is purposely interdisciplinary.[44] Her analysis pulls together insights from the fields of linguistics, philosophy, literary studies, and rhetoric. Lane-Mercier's approach is also "postmodern" in the sense that she identifies and critiques the fundamental assumptions (social and intellectual) that underlie the quotation process.

Lane-Mercier identifies two primary reasons why an author might want to quote from the work of another. The first, the "authoritative" use of quotations, aims to establish proof for a statement made by the quoting author. This approach is grounded in a particular philosophy of language: the belief "that words are endowed with a stable meaning, adhere directly to reality, can be used to reproduce the already said, and, in this way, enable one to attain a preexisting Truth . . . embodied in a preexisting utterance spoken by an identified other."[45] Since these assumptions are typically left unstated, the speaker's role in crafting the quotation is obscured, so that the truth-value of the quotation appears to be self-evident.

The second, the "parodic" use of quotations, employs the words of the source text as a vehicle for the thoughts and ideas of the quoting author. As Lane-Mercier puts it, "The words of the other are used as a springboard for the words of the self, [so that] 'originality' shifts from the quoted utterance to the framing utterance."[46] In this mode of quotation, the quoting author feels free to recast both the ideas and the language of the source text, producing "an ambiguous mingling of voices" within the quotation.[47] This second type of quotation, like the first, presupposes a philosophy of language: it treats language "as a form of play, whereby quotation allows for the emergence of a discursive space within which . . . true parodic creativity is deployed."[48]

According to Lane-Mercier, scholars have favored the "authoritative" use of quotations over the "parodic" use because of the broad cultural influence

44. Gillian Lane-Mercier, "Quotation as a Discursive Strategy," *Kodikas* 14 (1991): 199–214.

45. Ibid., 201.

46. Ibid., 201–2.

47. Ibid., 202.

48. Ibid., 201. Lane-Mercier states in her summary, "The underlying principle, in this case, resides in the refusal of sameness (imitation) and of the already said in favour of difference and the as-yet-unsaid (innovation), through the use of conscious semantic deformation and the polysemic nature of the linguistic sign" (201).

of the Platonic philosophy of language that is presupposed in the former view. But this judgment ignores the dynamic tension between reproduction (faithfulness to the text) and construction (subservience to the purposes of the author) that characterizes all acts of quotation.[49] A more suitable approach would treat the "authoritative" use of quotations as a subset of the "parodic." As Lane-Mercier explains,

> If, on the one hand, one accepts the existence of a parodic space within which quotation as play is permitted to flourish, and if, on the other hand, quotation is redefined in terms of a logic of reproduction and construction, it follows that quotation as play becomes the prototype of reported speech, while quotation as proof is simply the result of a conventional bracketing of any factor liable to discredit the truth-value of the utterance.[50]

This understanding of quotations highlights the role of the quoting author, who in both cases draws on the language of an outside text in order to achieve a particular rhetorical and/or ideological goal. This activity of the author is masked by the seemingly objective nature of the quotation process. Although it appears that the quoting author is momentarily stepping aside and letting the source text speak for itself, the author's act of selecting and embedding a quotation into a new rhetorical context actually amounts to a substantial deconstruction and reconstruction of the original text.[51] The ultimate goal of this deconstructive-reconstructive process is to reinforce the authority and/or reputation of the quoting author in the eyes of the audience so that they will respond more favorably to the quoting author's message.[52]

At the heart of the quotation process is a covert attempt by the quoting author to assert power over both the source text and the audience. Lane-Mercier goes to great lengths to highlight both sides of this equation. In its relation to the source text, quotation represents "an act of specious discur-

49. Ibid., 203.

50. Ibid.

51. Ibid., 205. Lane-Mercier cites Meir Sternberg's work with approval at this point.

52. Ibid., 204, 207. As Lane-Mercier puts it, "To cite is not only to position oneself grammatically, discursively, and ideologically with respect to another, it also represents an unavowed attempt to exert control over the other, which leads both to a transgression of the boundaries imposed by syntax and to a subtle combining of voices ultimately intended to strengthen the voice of the quoted self" (206).

sive altruism whereby one 'allows the other to speak' without relinquishing one's own right to speak."[53] As a rhetorical strategy, quotation brings about "the metaphorical death of the quotee, whose utterance, apparently intact, has nonetheless been decontextualized, severed from its 'origin,' and subsumed by the utterance of the quoter."[54] On the audience's side, quotation can be described as "a discursive strategy designed to manipulate the listener and, as such, to program the listener's response," as well as "a pretext for the reaffirmation of the self and the exploitation of the other."[55] Quotation, therefore, is a duplicitous process:

> Reported speech operates on two distinct planes, setting up an essentially democratic, unambivalent, non-interactive status quo between the self and the other which in fact masks a sliding toward a hierarchized, ambiguous relationship based on the insidious (re)establishment of dominating/dominated positions and an implicit unbalancing of the superficial linguistic, pragmatic, and ideological status quo. The quoter is able to surreptitiously regulate this duplicity either by perpetrating the myth of literality . . . or by accentuating the parodic dimension.[56]

Despite her strong language, Lane-Mercier does not place the blame for the duplicity of the quotation process entirely upon the quoting author. Quotation is one of many tools that a society offers to those in power to help them dominate and manipulate others in order to insure the continuation of society.[57] By appealing to a revered text from the society's past, quotation serves to uphold the homogeneity/sameness of a society against moves toward difference/otherness, especially in contexts where "the listener's individuality is seen as menacing."[58] Quotation can achieve its intended effect as long as the audience believes in the truth-value of the source text and the literalness of the quotation. Since the act of quotation clearly presupposes this belief, "the listener is thus manipulated into tacitly recognizing and sanc-

53. Ibid., 206.
54. Ibid.
55. Ibid., 207, 206.
56. Ibid., 206.
57. Ibid., 207, 209.
58. Ibid., 201, 211.

tioning the authenticity of the quote."[59] Lane-Mercier finds it troubling that this implicit trust in the veracity of quotations is routinely violated by the very mechanics of the quotation process.[60]

Lane-Mercier's sweeping critique of the quotation process has much to offer the study of biblical quotations. Especially helpful is her concern to take seriously both the individual and institutional aspects of the practice. By highlighting the power issues at stake in the use of quotations, Lane-Mercier reminds us not to overlook the social context within which quotations are offered. It is perhaps no accident that all of Paul's explicit quotations appear in letters to churches in which power relationships were being contested.[61]

Lane-Mercier also underlines the importance of an audience-centered approach to quotations in her insistence that even quotations that do not explicitly appeal to authority (the "parodic" use) are meant to affect an audience in some way. When analyzing Paul's quotations, we need to ask about the rhetorical purpose not only of quotations that are offered as "proofs," but also of those that seem to play a more "ornamental" role.

Lane-Mercier also challenges us to ask critical questions about the way Paul uses the power of quotations, coupled with his explicit claims to apostolic authority, to advance his rhetorical goals. Lane-Mercier probably goes too far in her criticism of the "duplicitous" nature of the quotation process—not all quotations are meant to be taken seriously—but her insistence that quotations invariably seek to manipulate both the source text and the audience can help us to look beyond the apparent innocence of Paul's

---

59. Ibid., 209. Elsewhere Lane-Mercier observes, "Like clichés and commonplaces, quotation represents a powerful tool for ensuring rapid consensus and persuading a given listener, with the result that differences between the quoting self and the listening other are potentially levelled out by way of a unifying process that presupposes the latter's recognition of and adherence to the truth value/authenticity/literality of the cited utterance" (208).

60. Lane-Mercier speaks of "the insidiousness of the various intersubjective and ideological (re)positionings (between quotee and quoter, quoter and listener, quotee and listener) this rhetorical dimension permits, all of which, reinforced by reported speech's semiotic potential, occur under the aegis of a discourse centered on truth and often backed by one or more powerful institutions" (ibid., 208). Taken to its extreme, this mode of discourse can lead to totalitarianism (in a hierarchical society) or anarchy (in a more egalitarian society) (211–13).

61. Although Paul's claims to authority are not being directly challenged in Rome as they are in Galatia and Corinth, his letter to the Romans contains several oblique attempts to establish a favorable balance of power with the Roman Christians prior to his impending visit. On Paul's letter to the Romans, see chapter 8.

appeals to Scripture in order to ask questions about his underlying motives. Lane-Mercier's critical study adds to our stock of tools for understanding and analyzing Paul's rhetorical use of quotations.

Taken together, the rhetorical and literary models described in chapters 1 and 2 provide a useful framework for analyzing and evaluating Paul's frequent appeals to the Jewish Scriptures. The value of these models will become apparent in the discussions of particular passages in chapters 5–8. First, however, there is another question that must be addressed. A rhetorical analysis of Paul's quotations seeks to determine not only how Paul used quotations to further his argument, but also how effective this rhetorical strategy might have been when addressing a first-century audience. For this task, we need to know more about the literary capabilities of Paul's audiences. This is the subject of the next chapter.

CHAPTER 3

Paul and His Audience(s)

Framing the Question

Paul's letters show clearly that he regarded direct quotations from the Jewish Scriptures as an effective tool for motivating various first-century Christian audiences to accept his ideas and follow his recommendations. But was he correct in this view? For a piece of rhetoric to be effective, careful crafting alone is not enough; the work must also be appropriate to the audience. This means that the audience must be capable of following the argument sufficiently to grasp the speaker's point and willing to seriously consider the course of action proposed by the speaker. If problems are anticipated in either of these areas, an effective speaker will take the problem into account and craft the speech accordingly. Otherwise the effectiveness of the work will be compromised.[1]

Was Paul an "effective speaker" in this sense? The answer depends on how we view his first-century audience. As we will see, Paul routinely assumes that his audience not only accepts the authority of the Jewish Scriptures but also knows the biblical text well enough to supply the background and context for many of his quotations. In some cases he requires the audience to infer how a quotation fits into his broader argument as well. This evidence had led most scholars to conclude that Paul's first-century addressees must have been reasonably familiar with the text of the Jewish Scriptures, whether from Paul's earlier teaching or their own study, since Paul would not have made impossible demands upon his audience.[2]

---

1. This does not mean, of course, that the entire work will be rendered ineffectual, but merely that this particular rhetorical strategy will fall short of the speaker's goals. Eugene White speaks about "degrees of congruity" between the speaker's aims and the audience's capacity to respond; the effects of a failure in one area can be mitigated by strengths in other aspects of the work (*The Context of Human Discourse: A Configurational Criticism of Rhetoric* [Columbia: University of South Carolina Press, 1992], 14).

2. Richard B. Hays shows more sensitivity than most when he distinguishes between the "implied readers" and the real first-century readers of Paul's letters (*Echoes of Scripture in the Letters of Paul* [New Haven: Yale University Press, 1989], 29). According to Hays, "The implied

But is this a fair assumption? Is it possible that Paul might have misjudged the literary capacities of his audience? To put the matter bluntly, did Paul's first-century audiences really understand his biblical quotations? The question is not insignificant. One of the chief benefits of a rhetorical approach to Paul's letters lies in the questions that it raises about the accuracy and reliability of the way in which the author and audience are portrayed within the text. Rhetorical analysis reminds us that we are hearing only the author's side of the story. The characterizations of the situation, the audience, and the author that we meet in the text are not objective reality, but the author's constructions. Paul's letters serve as primary sources regarding his *perception* of the situations of his churches, but only as secondary sources regarding their *actual* conditions.[3] To draw conclusions about the actual situation of either author or audience from these characterizations is a perilous enterprise to be pursued with great caution.

What we need, then, is some way to test the validity of the picture of Paul's audience that emerges from his letters. Unfortunately, we have no direct testimony concerning the level of biblical knowledge in Paul's congregations. But through a careful sifting of the evidence we can determine what counts as a reasonable assumption concerning the capabilities of Paul's audience.

Examining Our Assumptions

The best place to begin our study is with an investigation of the availability and use of written texts in the ancient world. A survey of the evidence

readers of these letters appear to be primarily Gentile Christians with an extensive knowledge of the LXX and an urgent interest in its interpretation." But as Hays points out, we cannot simply assume that this is an accurate portrait of the original recipients of the letters: "Whether the actual original readers of the letters fit this description is a question that must be distinguished carefully from the literary question about the implied reader as an intertextual phenomenon." In the end, however, Hays dodges the implications of these statements with the comment that "some such characterization of Paul's actual readers … is not implausible" (201 n. 92). Ross Wagner (*Heralds of the Good News: Isaiah and Paul "in Concert" in the Letter to the Romans* [NovTSup 101; Leiden: Brill, 2002]), 33–36) also discusses this problem briefly, concluding that "there is no way to be certain that the theoretical construct of the ideal hearer actually represents any of the first real empirical hearers of the letter [to the Romans]" (35). His solution is to assert that Paul meant for his audiences to read and study his letters and thus to develop the biblical literacy that they needed to understand his many references to the Jewish Scriptures (*Heralds*, 36-39). As we will see later, this view of Paul's audience simply does not fit the evidence of the letters (see note 46). Wagner's proposal also does not address the question of how Paul meant for his quotations to be understood (if at all) when the letters were initially read aloud in the gathered congregations, a question that Wagner regards as unimportant (*Heralds*, 39).

3. For more on this point, see chapter 4.

reveals a number of questionable assumptions that scholars have traditionally made about the way in which Paul and his churches interacted with the biblical text. A critical examination of these assumptions will point the way toward a more historically sensitive evaluation of the effectiveness of Paul's quotations.

Assumption #1: *Paul's audiences acknowledged the authority of the Jewish Scriptures as a source of truth and a guide for Christian conduct.* From the way Paul refers to the Jewish Scriptures in his letters, it seems clear that he not only accepted the sacred text as authoritative for his own life but also expected a similar response from his audiences, whether they were Jews or Gentiles. Many of his quotations appeal explicitly to the authority of Scripture in order to ground an argument or settle a dispute. For these reasons scholars have routinely assumed that the members of Paul's churches shared his high regard for the Jewish Scriptures.

But can we be sure that this was the case? The fact that Paul's "opponents" sometimes appealed to Scripture in support of their positions seems to imply that biblical proofs were an effective strategy in Paul's churches. But the fact that not everyone accepted their teaching could be taken as a sign that some of the members of Paul's churches, like Marcion and the gnostics in a later period, had questions about this procedure. We know that non-Jews frequently disparaged the Jewish Scriptures, and many of them had rather strange ideas about their content.[4] The idea of a single normative holy text also had no clear precedent or parallel in the Greco-Roman world.[5]

Since we hear only Paul's side of the argument, we cannot be sure how a predominately Gentile audience would have responded to his repeated appeals to the Jewish Scriptures. But in view of the broad acceptance of the Jewish Scriptures in other sectors of the Christian church, it seems fair to assume that the bulk of Paul's audience would have acknowledged the authority of the biblical text. If so, they would have granted a measure of respect to anyone who could quote and interpret its words.[6]

---

4. On non-Jewish attitudes to the Jewish Scriptures, see note 24.

5. The only texts that approached normative status in the Greco-Roman world were the epics of Homer, and even they were criticized by many philosophers. For a comparison of the relative status of Homer and the Jewish Scriptures within their respective communities, see Christopher D. Stanley, "Paul and Homer: Greco-Roman Citation Practice in the First-Century CE," *NovT* 32 (1990): 48–56.

6. In addition to the obvious influence of Jewish respect for the Scriptures, the very fact that texts were written gave them an aura of authority in a world in which most people were unable to read. As Joanna Dewey puts it, "In a world in which most people were nonliterate,

Assumption #2: *Paul and his audience(s) had relatively free access to the Greek version of the Jewish Scriptures (the "LXX") and could study and consult them whenever they wished.* Scholars routinely speak of "the Septuagint" as though it were a single-volume text that could be pulled down from the shelf of an ancient library or purchased for study by anyone with the time and inclination to do so. In reality, what we call "the Septuagint" did not exist as a fixed collection under a single cover until the invention of the codex, which occurred no earlier than the late first century C.E.[7] In Paul's day, "the Septuagint" was a diverse collection of scrolls containing Greek translations of individual biblical books prepared over the course of two centuries or more in a wide variety of times and circumstances.[8] When and how these diverse scrolls were united into a fixed collection remains shrouded in mystery.[9]

Whatever their origins, it seems highly unlikely that anyone, including Paul and the members of his churches, had access to a full complement of

---

writing was both an instrument of power and a symbol of power. . . . Nonliterates would honor reading and writing as symbols of culture and status; they would also fear them as instruments of social and political oppression" ("Textuality in an Oral Culture: A Survey of the Pauline Traditions," *Semeia* 39 [1994]: 44, 47).

7. The ambiguity surrounding the term "Septuagint" (and its abbreviation, "LXX") in modern scholarship has led many investigators to adopt the designation "Old Greek" to refer to the (theoretical) original translation of a given biblical book. The label "Septuagint" is then reserved either for the Greek Pentateuch (so Leonard Greenspoon, "The Use and Misuse of the Term 'LXX' and Related Terminology in Recent Scholarship," *BIOSCS* 20 (1987): 21–29) or for that collection of translations represented in the great codices of the fourth and fifth centuries C.E. (so Emanuel Tov, "The Septuagint," in *Mikra: Text, Translation, Reading, and Interpretation of the Hebrew Bible in Ancient Judaism and Early Christianity* [ed. Martin Jan Mulder; CRINT 2.1; Assen: Van Gorcum; Philadelphia: Fortress, 1988], 161). On the nature and use of books in the ancient world (including the rise of the codex in the early Christian era), see C. H. Roberts and T. C. Skeat, *The Birth of the Codex* (London: Oxford University Press for the British Academy, 1983); E. G. Turner, *Greek Manuscripts of the Ancient World* (Princeton, N.J.: Princeton University Press, 1971); idem, *The Typology of the Early Codex* (Philadelphia: University of Pennsylvania Press, 1977); Harry Y. Gamble, *Books and Readers in the Early Church: A History of Early Christian Texts* (New Haven: Yale University Press, 1995); Allan Millard, *Reading and Writing in the Time of Jesus* (Biblical Seminar 69; Sheffield: Sheffield Academic Press, 2000); and the various entries s.v. "Buch" in volume 2 of *Reallexicon für Antike und Christentum* (ed. T. Klauser et al.; Stuttgart: Hiersemann, 1954).

8. Emanuel Tov sums up the situation well: "As a result of recent finds and studies in early recensions, the heterogeneity of the canon of the LXX has become increasingly evident. It has been recognized that 'the LXX' contains translations of different types, early and late, relatively original and significantly revised, official and private, literal and free" ("Septuagint," 225).

9. For a review of recent scholarship on the origins and history of the Septuagint, see Christopher D. Stanley, *Paul and the Language of Scripture: Citation Technique in the Pauline Epistles and Contemporary Literature* (SNTSMS 74; Cambridge: Cambridge University Press, 1992), 41–51.

"Septuagint" scrolls in the middle of the first century C.E.[10] Whether they would have been able to consult *any* biblical scrolls on a regular basis remains uncertain. Books (i.e., scrolls) were expensive in antiquity, and few people in Paul's day could have afforded to purchase a single book from the Jewish Scriptures, much less an entire collection.[11] The same can be said for Paul. The state of his financial resources was often precarious, and it seems unlikely that he would have attempted to carry a bulky collection of scrolls along with him on his arduous travels.[12] If the book of Acts is any indication, the tensions that existed between the synagogue and the church in many of the places that Paul visited would have further limited Christian access to the Jewish Scriptures. Though it is possible that some of the wealthy patrons of Paul's churches may have purchased copies of individual books for use in their churches, we have no firm evidence of such a practice in Paul's day.[13]

---

10. Although it seems reasonable to suppose that a wealthy Diaspora synagogue might have owned copies of all the scrolls that we call "the Septuagint," we have no evidence to that effect. The possibility of such a collection depends on the existence of a standard collection of texts that a synagogue would want to own—a notion that many scholars reject for this period.

11. On the costliness and relative scarcity of books in antiquity, see William Harris, *Ancient Literacy* (Cambridge: Harvard University Press, 1989), 193–96, 224–25; Millard, *Reading,* 164–65; Gamble, *Books,* 83–93. As Gamble observes, "The Scriptures of Judaism comprised not a single book but a collection of scrolls, five of the Torah and more of the prophetic books. These books were relatively costly, and their availability even to all synagogues cannot be taken for granted" (*Books,* 214).

12. The quotations themselves tell against the possibility that Paul carried with him a collection of scrolls from which he excerpted his quotations (despite the obscure reference in 2 Tim 4:13). In his reexamination of textual evidence, Dietrich-Alex Koch (*Die Schrift als Zeuge des Evangeliums: Untersuchungen zur Verwendung und zum Verständnis der Schrift bei Paulus* [BHT 69; Tübingen: Mohr, 1986], 48–57) essentially confirmed the century-old findings of Hans Vollmer (*Die alttestamentlichen Citate bei Paulus: text-kritisch und biblisch-theologisch gewürdigt: nebst einem Anhang über das Verhältnis des Apostels zu Philo* [Freiburg: Mohr, 1895], 20–21) regarding the diversity of text-types employed in Paul's quotations. A similar lack of consistency is evident within the individual letters: repeated quotations from a single book of Scripture show divergent textual affinities even within the same letter. Ross Wagner's suggestion (*Heralds,* 24 n. 86) that Paul may have known multiple versions of some passages, offered in support of his thesis that Paul had memorized most of the book of Isaiah from a single textual tradition, is purely speculative. The fact that the bulk of Paul's quotations in Romans stand close to the "Alexandrian" textual tradition only indicates that this tradition was present in many of the manuscripts consulted by Paul, as it was elsewhere in the ancient world. For more on the subject, see Stanley, *Paul,* 67–69, 254–55.

13. The likelihood that local Christian leaders owned biblical scrolls for use within their congregations would be greater, of course, for churches with a wealthy patron. On the social status of house-church leaders in the Pauline congregations, see Gerd Theissen, *The Social Setting of Pauline Christianity* (ed. and trans. John H. Schütz; Philadelphia: Fortress, 1982); Wayne Meeks, *The First Urban Christians* (New Haven: Yale University Press, 1983); Abraham

We do know, however, that Paul and other early Christian authors studied regularly in the Greek text of the Jewish Scriptures, so the educated elite must have had at least sporadic access to the major biblical scrolls.[14] During times when access was limited, Paul and other educated Christians probably relied on personal notebooks into which they had copied key verses from the Jewish Scriptures, as well as their memories.[15] For the ordinary person in Paul's churches, a firsthand encounter with a biblical scroll was probably an unusual event.[16]

Assumption #3: *Paul's audiences routinely read and studied the Jewish Scriptures for themselves in his absence.* In at least some of his quotations, Paul clearly assumes that his audience is familiar with the background and context of specific verses from the Jewish Scriptures (e.g., Rom 4:9–22, 9:10–13, 11:1–4; Gal 3:6–9, 4:21–31).[17] To explain this assumption, scholars have asserted that the members of Paul's churches routinely studied the

---

Malherbe, *Social Aspects of Early Christianity* (2nd ed.; Philadelphia: Fortress, 1983). For more on private libraries among aristocratic Greeks, Jews, and Christians in antiquity, see Gamble, *Books,* 188–202; Jocelyn Penny Small, *Wax Tablets of the Mind: Cognitive Studies of Memory and Literacy in Classical Antiquity* (London: Routledge, 1997), 160–69.

14. Careful studies of the apostle Paul's references to Scripture have repeatedly shown that his practice of quoting from the Greek version of the Jewish Scriptures derives from his own use of the Greek text in his studies. See the discussion under "Assumption #6" below.

15. For evidence concerning the common practice of note-taking in antiquity and its significance for the apostle Paul, see Stanley, *Paul,* 73–78. Individuals for whom we have evidence of note-taking while reading include Socrates (according to Xenophon), Aristotle, Cicero, Pliny the Elder, Seneca, Plutarch, and Aulus Gellius. Several techniques were available: copying the texts directly onto a papyrus scroll; using one of the sturdier parchment notebooks that were already becoming available by this time; or taking notes onto a wax tablet (using a stylus) and then transferring them later to a more permanent repository. According to William Harris (*Literacy,* 194), codices of up to ten wax tablets were common, with each tablet able to hold fifty or more words per side. Jocelyn Penny Small (*Wax Tablets,* 149) calls attention to a third-century C.E. relief of a boy holding a writing case containing his writing equipment (pens, ink, and knife), and remarks that "anyone doing research in a library, public or private, would carry such a writing case as well as tablets or papyri for taking notes." For more on the technology of note-taking, see Gamble, *Books,* 50–53; Millard, *Reading,* 63–69; Small, *Wax Tablets,* 149–50, 169–74, 177–81; Roberts and Skeat, *Codex,* 18–29; B. M. W. Knox and P. E. Easterling, "Books and Readers in the Ancient World," in *Cambridge History of Ancient Literature* (ed. B. M. W. Knox and P. E. Easterling; 2 vols.; Cambridge: Cambridge University Press, 1985), 1.18; Frederic Kenyon, *Books and Readers in Ancient Greece and Rome* (Oxford: Clarendon, 1932), 91–92.

16. Even if the words of Scripture were read aloud when Paul's churches gathered for worship (cf. 1 Tim 4:13), this need not imply that the actual biblical scrolls were present. Notebooks filled with biblical excerpts would have served the same purpose (see Gamble, *Books,* 214).

17. As we will see in chapters 5–8, virtually all of the passages in which Paul expects his audience to know the original context of his quotations are narratives.

Bible for themselves, whether individually or in their corporate gatherings.[18] But this convenient solution overlooks the many practical obstacles that stood in the way of such a practice. The limited availability of biblical scrolls, discussed under "Assumption #2" above, raises serious problems for this hypothesis. Further difficulties arise from the fact that ancient scrolls had no chapter or verse divisions or other textual markers that would allow the reader to easily locate and examine specific texts.[19] But the greatest obstacle by far is the fact that few people in Paul's churches would have been able to read the scrolls even if they had been available. In his acclaimed study of ancient literacy, William Harris concluded that no more than 10–20 percent of the populace would have been able to read or write at any level throughout the classical, Hellenistic, and Roman imperial periods.[20] In a subsequent investigation of early Christian literacy, Harry Gamble concluded that even if the early church had a disproportionate number of craftspeople and small-business workers among its numbers, the literacy level in the earliest churches still would not have exceeded the upper end of the range specified by Harris.[21] As Gamble observes,

---

18. For a careful discussion of the subject, see Gamble, *Books,* 212–14. The question of how much Scripture Paul's addressees might have known must be distinguished from the question of how Paul himself engaged with the biblical text. Many otherwise careful scholars have jumped to faulty conclusions about the biblical literacy of Paul's audiences due to their failure to distinguish these two points. All scholars would agree that Paul's quotations offer insight into his own understanding of the Jewish Scriptures, and that at least some of his quotations reflect a deep engagement with the broader context from which they were taken. But it is a logical fallacy to conclude from this that Paul expected his audiences to know the original context of his quotations. The question of how much biblical literacy Paul assumes on the part of his audiences must be handled on a case-by-case basis. See the discussions in chapters 5–8.

19. For a discussion of the problems associated with locating and retrieving specific passages in ancient books, see Small, *Wax Tablets,* 14–25.

20. Harris, *Literacy,* 272, 284, 328–30. Of course, literacy levels were lower for women than for men throughout the ancient world; see Susan Guettel Cole, "Could Greek Women Read and Write?" in *Reflections of Women in Antiquity* (ed. Helene P. Foley; New York: Gordon & Breach, 1981), 219–45. The general validity of Harris's findings is affirmed (with some reservations) by the scholars who examined his work in the series of essays in J. H. Humphrey, ed., *Literacy in the Ancient World* (Ann Arbor, Mich.: Journal of Roman Archaeology, 1991). Allan Millard (*Reading,* 154–84) offers a more optimistic assessment of the data, but nearly all of his examples pertain to the practices of upper-class and "professional" writers (i.e., scribes), not ordinary working people. The same is true of the recent study by John F. A. Sawyer, *Sacred Languages and Sacred Texts* (London: Routledge, 1999), 44–58. Sawyer compounds the problem by conflating materials from different periods.

21. Gamble, *Books,* 2–11. On the social composition of Paul's churches, see the sources cited in note 13.

> It cannot be supposed that the extent of literacy in the ancient church was any greater than that in the Greco-Roman society of which Christianity was a part. . . . This means that not only the writing of Christian literature, but also the ability to read, criticize and interpret it belonged to a small number of Christians in the first several centuries, ordinarily not more than about 10 percent in any given setting, and perhaps fewer in the many small and provincial congregations that were characteristic of early Christianity.[22]

We have no reason to think that Paul's churches were any exception to this rule. The inevitable conclusion is that not more than a few individuals in Paul's churches, those recruited from the educated elite, would have been capable of reading and studying the Scriptures for themselves.[23]

The implications of this observation are far-reaching indeed. All of Paul's letters were written to predominantly Gentile congregations. We can assume that except for the few people who had attended the synagogue as Jewish sympathizers, no one in Paul's churches had any significant knowledge of the Jewish Scriptures before entering the Christian church.[24] If the bulk of these Gentile converts were illiterate, and if biblical scrolls were not readily available in the churches, then the common belief that Paul's audiences engaged in regular personal study of the Jewish Scriptures would

---

22. Ibid., 5–6. As Gamble rightly notes, "We must assume, then, that the large majority of Christians in the early centuries of the church were illiterate, not because they were unique but because they were in this respect typical" (5). Pieter J. J. Botha ("Greco-Roman Literacy as Setting for New Testament Writings," *Neot* 26 [1992]: 195–215) comes to a similar conclusion: "If early Christianity reflects a fair cross section of society, it would follow that a rather small percentage within those groups were literate. What is probably true in any case is that we have a completely disproportionate impression of an extremely small group of Christians" (211).

23. Joanna Dewey holds a similar view ("Textuality," 47–54). For more on the subject, see Pieter J. J. Botha, "Greco-Roman Literacy"; idem, "The Verbal Art of the Pauline Letters: Rhetoric, Performance and Practice," in *Rhetoric and the New Testament: Essays from the 1992 Heidelberg Conference* (ed. Stanley E. Porter and Thomas H. Olbricht; JSNTSup 90; Sheffield: JSOT Press, 1993), 409–28.

24. Of course, non-Jews were familiar with Jewish beliefs and practices, including their reverence for a collection of holy texts, but they did not (so far as we know) read the Jewish Scriptures for themselves. Even the literati of Greco-Roman society had wild ideas about the content of the Jewish Scriptures; see the citations in Menahem Stern, ed., *Greek and Latin Authors on Jews and Judaism* (3 vols.; Jerusalem: Israel Academy of Sciences and Humanities, 1974–84), and the discussion in Louis H. Feldman, *Jew and Gentile in the Ancient World* (Princeton, N.J.: Princeton University Press, 1993). The earliest non-Jewish source that reveals a familiarity with the content of the Jewish Scriptures is Pseudo-Longinus's *On the Sublime* (late first century C.E.), which praises the "sublime" quality of Gen 1.

appear to be unfounded. Whatever knowledge they had concerning the content of the Jewish Scriptures would have come to them via oral instruction from the few literate and/or Jewish members of the congregation.[25] What form this instruction might have taken remains unclear, since we do not know how new converts were trained or how the Jewish Scriptures were used in the corporate meetings of the Pauline congregations, if they were used at all.[26] As far as we can tell, only the educated few possessed the requisite background and skills to critically assess Paul's handling of the biblical text.[27]

Assumption #4: *Paul's audiences were able to recognize and appreciate all of his quotations, allusions, and "echoes" from the Jewish Scriptures.* The question of what constitutes a "quotation" has received various responses from scholars who have examined Paul's use of the Jewish Scriptures. Since most scholars have been concerned with the way Paul understood and interpreted the biblical text, they have usually defined "quotation" as broadly as possible to include any series of words that reproduces with some measure of accuracy the wording of a particular passage of Scripture. In this "author-centered" approach, quotations need not be marked for audience recogni-

---

25. Harry Gamble makes a strong argument that literacy was a key factor in determining who was recognized as a leader in the early Christian community. In Gamble's words, "Given that texts were important to Christianity from the beginning, though only the Jewish Scriptures at first, it is difficult to imagine any Christian community where either no one could read or no authority accrued to those who could. In a community in which texts had a constitutive importance and only a few persons were literate, it was inevitable that those who were able to explicate texts would acquire authority for that reason alone" (*Books,* 9–10).

26. Despite recent scholarly work highlighting the role of memory in the ancient world, we have no evidence that non-Jews were taught to memorize specific passages of Scripture in the Pauline churches. Evidence is scanty for the common scholarly presumption that the illiterate members of Paul's churches absorbed much of the content of the Jewish Scriptures from their regular recitation in Christian worship. In the few passages in which Paul speaks about corporate worship (1 Cor 11:17–34, 14:1–40; cf. Eph 5:19–20), there is no mention of the public reading of Scripture. Harry Gamble issues a similar warning against the uncritical assumption "that scripture reading belonged from the outset to specifically Christian worship or, if it did, that it played the same role that it did in the synagogue" (*Books,* 212). Like others, however, he eventually concludes that Paul's expectations concerning his readers' familiarity with Scripture imply that the Jewish Scriptures were regularly read and taught in the Pauline congregations (212–13). Joanna Dewey, after a careful survey of the evidence, concludes, "There is no evidence that Scripture readings were important in the worship of Paul's communities and it seems unlikely that they occurred at all" ("Textuality," 52).

27. Because Gamble assumes that the Jewish Scriptures were read aloud in Christian worship, he can argue that "the limited extent of individual literacy . . . had little adverse effect on the ability of Christians generally to gain a close acquaintance with Christian literature" (*Books,* 8–9). This may have been true for the second century and later, but we cannot retroject this situation into Paul's first-century churches without supporting evidence.

tion; the focus is on what the author was doing with the biblical text, not whether the audience was aware of the author's activity. The identification of allusions and echoes is important in this approach, since these indirect references offer additional clues to the author's interpretive activity.

When, on the other hand, the question is framed in terms of audience understanding, the definition of "quotation" must be drawn more narrowly. The only quotations that Paul's first-century audience definitely would have recognized are those marked as such within the text. These include (1) those introduced by an explicit quotation formula, such as "as it is written" (the bulk of the texts); (2) those accompanied by a clear interpretive gloss (e.g., 1 Cor 15:27); and (3) those that stand in demonstrable syntactical tension with their present Pauline surroundings (e.g., Rom 9:7, 10:18; Gal 3:12).[28] In light of all that has been said thus far about the literary capabilities of Paul's first-century audience, we should not assume that the original recipients of his letters would have recognized even a verbatim quotation from Scripture unless it was marked as such within the text.

This is all the more true for Paul's allusions and echoes of Scripture. Unless it can be shown that the audience was familiar with a particular passage, the evidence discussed thus far cautions against the presumption that Paul's first-century audience recognized and appreciated his many unmarked references to the biblical text.[29] There may have been individuals

28. For a discussion of the methodological problems surrounding the definition of the term "quotation," see Stanley, *Paul,* 33–37.

29. Richard B. Hays's otherwise exemplary study on this topic, *Echoes of Scripture in the Letters of Paul,* is seriously flawed at this point. Hays proposes a "common sense hermeneutics" that assumes a basic continuity between ancient and modern responses to Paul's allusions and echoes of Scripture (27–28). As Hays puts it, "If I, having learned something about Paul's historical circumstances and having read the same Scripture that Paul lived in so deeply, discern in his language echoes of that same Scripture, it is not improbable that I am overhearing the same echoes that he *and his earliest readers* might have been able to hear" (28 [italics added]). Like most modern investigators, Hays fails to consider the profound differences in the literary capabilities of ancient and modern readers; as a result, he slides too quickly from literary analyses into historical judgments, despite his contentions that "claims about intertextual meaning effects are strongest where it can credibly be demonstrated that they occur within the literary structure of the text and that they can plausibly be ascribed to the intention of the author *and the competence of the original readers*" (28 [italics added]). Ross Wagner, whose approach is patterned on that of Hays (*Heralds,* 9–19), shows more sensitivity to the limited biblical competency of Paul's original audiences when he suggested that Paul's audiences might have learned to recognize his biblical allusions and echoes under the tutelage of the more literate members of the congregation (see note 2). But the ease with which Wagner can mimic Hays's practice of referring to "those who have ears to hear" when referring to the purported echoes of biblical passages in Paul's letters (including references to the original context of his quotations) suggest that he has not wholly freed himself from Hays's ahistorical understanding of Paul's audiences.

in Paul's churches (mostly educated Jews and an occasional educated Gentile) who were capable of appreciating these references, but most of Paul's allusions and echoes, along with his unmarked citations, would have gone unnoticed by the bulk of his first-century audience.[30] Their presence reveals the literary capabilities not of the audience, but of Paul himself, whose engagement with the Jewish Scriptures was such that his thinking and mode of expression were shaped and reshaped by the symbolic universe of the Bible and the language of specific passages. Such expressions came so naturally to Paul's mind that he might never have stopped to think about how well they might be understood by his audience.

On the other hand, it is possible that Paul thought that his displays of biblical erudition would commend him to the Jewish-Christian members of his audience by emphasizing his faithfulness to the biblical tradition.[31] In this case his many unmarked references to Scripture would have been directed toward the Jewish members of his audience. Perhaps he hoped that such a display would reinforce their loyalty to him and allay their fears about the "law-free" gospel that he preached to the Gentile majority in his churches. In any event, the idea that Paul expected his Gentile audiences to recognize and appreciate his many allusions and other unmarked references to the Jewish Scriptures appears to be mistaken.

Assumption #5: *Paul composed his letters with the expectation that the recipients would know and supply the background and context for his many quotations, allusions, and other references to the Jewish Scriptures.* Judging from the way Paul handles the Jewish Scriptures in his letters, many scholars have concluded that he was intentionally playing on the prior biblical knowledge of his audiences. Yet a careful historical analysis suggests that the majority of Paul's addressees would have been unable to read and study the

---

30. Joanna Dewey ("Textuality," 44) cites several studies that suggest that literacy levels were no greater for Jews than for non-Jews in the first century C.E. As Dewey observes, "To be a good Jew … did not require the ability to read the sacred texts" (42). Of course, literacy is not a prerequisite for recognizing biblical allusions; an illiterate but devout Jew might have absorbed enough Scripture from the oral readings in the synagogue to recognize the cadences of a fleeting reference to the biblical text. But we have no reason to think that the Gentile members of Paul's congregations (clearly the majority) possessed such a store of prior knowledge.

31. If so, he might have been following the course recommended later by Gregory of Nazianzus (*Epistula* 51.4): "The best and most beautiful letter is written so that it is persuasive to both the educated and the uneducated, appearing to the former as written on the popular level and to the latter as being above that level, and being immediately understandable" (cited in a different context by Jeffrey T. Reed, "Using Ancient Rhetorical Categories to Interpret Paul's Letters: A Question of Genre," in Porter and Olbricht, eds., *Rhetoric*, 311).

biblical text for themselves. How are we to explain this discrepancy? Several answers are possible.

(1) Paul, or the local leaders of his congregations, routinely instituted a rigorous program of Scripture study and memorization in his churches, so that he could reasonably expect even the illiterate members of his audience to have enough background knowledge to understand his quotations and allusions, and perhaps even his echoes of the Jewish Scriptures. The problem is thus illusory: the people to whom Paul wrote were simply unlike other ancient Gentile audiences in their knowledge of the biblical text.

(2) Paul grossly misjudged the capacities of his audience. As an educated Jew who was accustomed to thinking and arguing in biblical terms, Paul slipped naturally into biblical modes of discourse in the heat of his most argumentative letters without stopping to consider whether his audience, which was mostly Gentile and illiterate, could have understood his many references to the Jewish Scriptures. The bulk of Paul's audience was probably befuddled by most of these references.

(3) Paul addressed his letters primarily to the literate members of his churches, who because of their prior history (in the case of Jews and "Judaizing" Gentiles) and/or personal study were reasonably familiar with the Jewish Scriptures. Paul knew that he could count on these people to read and explain his letters, including his biblical references, to the less educated members of the church. Thus, Paul did not anticipate that everyone in his churches would be capable of following his arguments from the Jewish Scriptures.

(4) Paul was aware of, and at times even counted on, the relative ignorance of his first-century addressees concerning the content of the Jewish Scriptures, but he expected them to accept the validity of his arguments nonetheless due to their deep respect for the authority of the Jewish Scriptures. At most, Paul expected his audience to know the broad outlines of a few key biblical stories; in most instances the force of his quotations can be appreciated with little or no knowledge of the biblical text. The many allusions and echoes of Scripture in Paul's letters reflect his own habit of using biblical modes of expression. Paul did not expect his audiences to recognize and/or appreciate these references, with the possible exception of those who came from Jewish backgrounds.

Weighing the merits of these four explanations is difficult in view of our lack of information concerning Paul's intentions and expectations. But we should be careful about jumping too quickly into explanations that presume that Paul was thoroughly aware of how his quotations would be received.

Although Paul says that he tried to be "all things to all people" (1 Cor 9:22), his stormy relationships with some of his churches suggest that he was not always adept at anticipating how an audience would respond to his words. On the other hand, Paul grew up in a Greek city and spent most of his life among non-Jews, so we cannot easily accuse him of ignorance concerning Gentile familiarity with the Jewish Scriptures.

Of the four positions outlined above, only the first can be ruled out with any degree of confidence, since the proposed program of study is entirely hypothetical and does not, in any case, explain the extensive use of quotations in Paul's letter to the Romans. But all four proposals contain elements of truth that can help us to understand why Paul appeals to Scripture so often in letters addressed to predominately illiterate audiences.

1. Clearly, illiteracy did not prevent the Gentiles in Paul's congregations from knowing something about the Jewish Scriptures. The Christian gospel was accompanied by scriptural "proofs" from the earliest days of the movement, and Christian moral instruction was likewise grounded partly in biblical injunctions. A few key biblical texts (e.g., the Decalogue) and stories about important biblical figures (Abraham, Moses, Elijah, David) were so well known that Paul could refer to them in his letters without explanation. The same might have been true for texts that could assist the members in defending their faith before a hostile world.[32] But this is a far cry from the level of biblical knowledge needed to grasp the significance of a string of quotations such as Paul offers in Gal 3:6–14 or Rom 9–11, especially when the letter was being read aloud before a gathered congregation. The frequent appeals to Scripture in Romans, addressed to a church that Paul had not yet visited, stand in stark contrast to the absence of explicit quotations in Philippians, written to a church with which Paul had a long-standing relationship. From this we see that the frequency and the content of quotations are unreliable indicators of the extent to which Paul had trained his churches in the Jewish Scriptures.[33]

---

32. This is the central thesis of Barnabas Lindars in his book, *New Testament Apologetics: The Doctrinal Significance of the New Testament Quotations* (Philadelphia: Westminster, 1961). See also Donald Juel, *Messianic Exegesis: Christological Interpretation of the Old Testament in Early Christianity* (Philadelphia: Fortress, 1988).

33. Adolf von Harnack made this observation one of the cornerstones of the famous article in which he argued that Paul referred to the Jewish Scriptures only when he was compelled to do so by the need to confront what he calls "the judaizing error" ("Das Alte Testament in den paulinischen Briefen und in den paulinischen Gemeinden," *Sitzungsberichte der Preußischen Akademie der Wissenschaften* [1928]: 124–41; ET, "The Old Testament in the Pauline Letters and

2. Paul's letters leave no doubt that his patterns of thought and expression were heavily molded by the Jewish Scriptures. We should be careful, therefore, about assuming that he expected his audience to grasp all or even the majority of his biblical references. Though it is unlikely that Paul was wholly ignorant of the literary capabilities of his churches, we have no reason to think that he was aware of precisely which passages they did or did not know from the Scriptures.[34] On various occasions he may well have misjudged what his audience knew.

3. It is a truism that literate people wrote for other literate people in antiquity, but the significance of this observation for interpreting Paul's letters has often been overlooked. To put it simply, we may be asking too much of Paul if we expect him to speak in a way that even the illiterate members of his churches could understand everything that he said. As an educated person in antiquity, Paul would naturally be concerned about how the literate people in his audience would respond to what he was saying, including his biblical quotations. The fact that his letters were written to be read aloud might have mitigated this concern somewhat, but the written format of the letter would have exercised an irresistible pull toward more literate modes of expression. In other words, Paul may have been directing his argument primarily to the literate members of his churches (or more precisely, to those who were familiar with the Jewish Scriptures) when he penned his biblical quotations.[35]

---

in the Pauline Churches," in *Understanding Paul's Ethics: Twentieth Century Approaches* [ed. Brian S. Rosner; Grand Rapids: Eerdmans; Carlisle: Paternoster, 1995], 27–49). Harnack called attention to the absence of biblical quotations and references in Paul's letters to the Thessalonians, Colossians, Philemon, Ephesians, and Philippians ("Old Testament," 28–33). From this observation he drew the rather far-reaching conclusion that "the apostle has not given the Old Testament simply as the book of edification to the churches and the Gentiles; he has not fed them out of Scripture from the beginning, nor later on; he has been very reticent to pass on the meaning which the Old Testament held for himself and concerning any appreciation of the history of salvation one might gain from it" (33). Most subsequent interpreters have recognized that Harnack placed too great a burden on the argument from silence.

34. The question of how Paul could have known which passages of Scripture were familiar to the Christians in Rome has been consistently overlooked by those who believe that Paul framed his quotations to take advantage of the prior biblical knowledge of his audiences.

35. It is likewise possible that Paul expected that these people would explain his biblical references to those whose biblical knowledge was more limited, as suggested by Ross Wagner (*Heralds*, 36–37). But it is worth observing that Paul says nothing about this in his letters. Was the practice so common that Paul could take it for granted? Or was this not Paul's expectation? For more on this point, see the comments in notes 2 and 46 and the extended discussion in chapter 9.

4. When Paul quotes from the Jewish Scriptures in his letters, he invariably has a rhetorical purpose. Usually this means drawing on the authority of the biblical text to extend or seal an argument. In these cases the biblical quotation carries weight regardless of whether the recipients fully understand the reference, since the quotation shows the God of Israel standing firmly on the side of the speaker. The ability to quote and interpret Scripture is a potent weapon within a religious community, especially when the skill is limited to a few practitioners, and Paul did not hesitate to wield this weapon in his letters. Neither literacy nor familiarity with the original context is required for people to be moved by a quotation from a text deemed authoritative by a religious group.

Assumption #6: *Paul himself knew and took into account the original context of his biblical quotations.* As a Pharisaic Jew who took his faith seriously, Paul would obviously have been well versed in the Jewish Scriptures. But in what form? Most scholars have assumed that Paul knew and studied the Hebrew text, but his quotations offer no support for this position. Paul drew his quotations exclusively from the Greek text (usually, but not always, the "Septuagint"), even in places where it diverged significantly from the Hebrew, and even when the Hebrew would have better supported his argument.[36] Paul's manner of expression was also heavily molded by the vocabulary, diction, idioms, and thought-forms of the Greek translation of the Jewish Scriptures.[37] The inevitable conclusion is that Paul's use of the Greek text in

---

36. For the evidence, see the sources cited in note 12. Using a very different approach than the present study, Ross Wagner has once again confirmed Paul's reliance on a Greek version of the Jewish Scriptures (*Heralds*, 16–17, 344–45). This is not surprising, since virtually every Diaspora Jew whose writings have survived from Paul's day used the Greek text (see Stanley, *Paul*, 292–337). Passages in which Paul follows the Greek text despite its divergence from the known versions of the Hebrew text include Gal 3:17 (= Exod 12:40) and 1 Cor 10:8 (= Num 25:9). A notable instance in which the Hebrew text would have been more congenial to Paul's argument is 1 Cor 2:16 (= Isa 40:13). All three passages are noted by Otto Michel, *Paulus und seine Bibel* (1929; repr., Darmstadt: Wissenschaftliche Buchgesellschaft, 1972), 68.

37. A helpful listing of numerous parallels can be found in Vollmer, *Citate*, 10–13. Decisive for Vollmer is the frequency with which even Paul's allusions to the biblical narrative reproduce the language of the Septuagint; he notes Rom 4:4, 5, 13, 19, 7:8, 10, 11, 8:32; 1 Cor 10:6, 9, 10; 2 Cor 3:3, 7–11, 13, 16, 18, 4:4, 6; Gal 4:22–23, 24 (13). Otto Michel (*Paulus*, 59–60) points out echoes of the Septuagint version of the Psalms in texts such as Rom 1:23, 3:4, 5:5, 10:6–7, 11:1; 1 Cor 10:1. More recently, Dietrich-Alex Koch has stressed the significance of such data as evidence for Paul's intensive labors in the Greek text: "Je stärker Paulus sich veranläßt sieht, seine eigene Position theologisch zu klären, desto intensiver wird zugleich auch die Beschäftigung mit der Schrift und ihre Verwendung in seinen Briefen" ("The more Paul feels obliged to clarify his

his letters is no mere concession to the ignorance of his Greek-speaking audience, but reflects his own pattern of study in the Greek version of the Jewish Scriptures. When we ask about Paul's familiarity with the original context of his biblical quotations, it is the Greek version that we should consider, not the Hebrew.[38]

So why should there be any question about Paul's knowledge of the original context of his quotations? The question arises in part from the fact that Paul often quotes from Scripture in a way that bears little evident relation to the apparent sense of the original passage.[39] But an even larger problem arises from the inaccessibility of biblical scrolls in the ancient world. Though there is ample evidence that Paul drew his quotations from some form of written text, the improbability of his either owning or having easy access to scrolls has led many scholars to suggest that Paul drew at least some of his quotations from a "testimony book" containing verses of Scripture that had proven useful in the early church.[40] A more recent hypothesis sees Paul relying on a papyrus or parchment notebook into which he had copied verses of Scripture at times when he had access to bib-

---

own theological position, the more intense becomes his engagement with Scripture and its application in his letters") (*Schrift,* 101; cf. 98-99). So also Richard B. Hays: "The vocabulary and cadences of Scripture—particularly of the LXX—are imprinted deeply on Paul's mind, and the great stories of Israel continue to serve for him as a fund of symbols and metaphors that condition his perception of the world, of God's promised deliverance of his people, and of his own identity and calling. His faith, in short, is one whose articulation is inevitably intertextual in character" (*Echoes,* 16).

38. Recent studies have shown that earlier scholars were wrong in thinking that Paul had occasionally altered the Greek text of his quotations to coincide with the Hebrew. The few places where this appears to be the case can be traced to Paul's use of earlier "Hebraizing" revisions of the Greek text. The evidence is discussed in Koch, *Schrift,* 57–81, and summarized in Stanley, *Paul,* 67–68 (cf. 44–48). Ross Wagner's recent careful study of Paul's quotations in the book of Romans comes to the same conclusion (*Heralds,* 16–17, 126–36, 170–74, 344–46).

39. Among the many examples that could be cited are the quotations from Ps 19:4 in Rom 10:18; Isa 28:11–12 in 1 Cor 14:21; and Ps 116:10 in 2 Cor 4:13. Recently, Ross Wagner has argued that even quotations such as these reflect Paul's intense engagement with the broader context of the biblical passage (e.g., his treatment of Rom 10:18 in *Heralds,* 180–86). Some of his analyses lend a measure of credence to his thesis, but others are either too speculative or too tendentious to be credible (e.g., the links that he attempts to draw between Rom 10:19 and the broader context of Deut 32 in *Heralds,* 187–201). See the discussion of individual passages in chapters 5–8.

40. Martin C. Albl (*"And Scripture Cannot Be Broken": The Form and Function of the Early Christian Testimonia Collections* [NovTSup 96; Leiden: Brill, 1999]) offers a helpful review of scholarship on the "testimony book" hypothesis, including a thorough survey of the ancient evidence.

lical scrolls.[41] In either case, the only link between the quotation and its "original context" at the time the letter was being dictated would have been in the author's mind (i.e., his memory). This link would have been fairly substantial in the case of passages to which Paul refers often in his letters (e.g., Deut 32; Isa 28).[42] But at least some of his more fanciful interpretations of the biblical text could have arisen from the fact that the original context was no longer available to him when he was reflecting on the individual verses and incorporating them into his letters.[43] It seems fair to say that we should be careful about assuming that Paul was aware of the "original context" of every passage that he cites in his letters.

Assumption #7: *Paul expected his audiences to evaluate and accept his interpretations of Scripture.* Implicit in most scholarly treatments of Paul's biblical quotations is the presumption that Paul expected his audiences to refer back to the original context of his quotations, whether in printed form

---

41. For a discussion of the evidence that Paul relied on some kind of written text containing excerpts from Scripture rather than quoting entirely from memory, see Stanley, *Paul,* 16–17, 69–79, 257–58 (cf. Small, *Wax Tablets,* 177–90). This does not imply the obviously anachronistic notion that Paul looked up each verse in a written source and copied it down (or read it aloud to a secretary) in the moment of dictation (rightly criticized by Wagner, *Heralds,* 25). All that is being suggested here is that Paul used some kind of written collection of biblical excerpts as the basis for his regular reflection on the words of Scripture and that this collection in turn shaped his understanding and use of the verses that it contained. Wagner's caricature of this model as "a modern-day 'Bible verse memory program'" (*Heralds,* 25) reveals a fundamental misunderstanding of this point. The fact that Paul regularly incorporates interpretive elements into the wording of his quotations could be taken to suggest that he relied on his memory in the moment of dictation, though we should be careful about assuming that Paul would have been unwilling to make such modifications when copying from a written text. The issue is discussed more fully in Stanley, *Paul,* 338–60.

42. As argued most recently by Ross Wagner, *Heralds,* 62–65, 98–106, 126–57, 168–70 (on Isa 28), 191–205, 216–17, 265–71, 315–17, 354–56 (on Deut 32).

43. This assumes, of course, that Paul was interested in the "original context" of his quotations—a view that often has been disputed. The same conclusion could be drawn from the traditional view that Paul quoted biblical verses from memory, though this seems less likely in light of recent studies. See the discussions of Stanley, *Paul,* 16–17, 69–71; Small, *Wax Tablets,* 177–85. Ross Wagner finds it "incredible . . . that once Paul expended the labor to find and excerpt a passage, he promptly forgot all about its original context" (*Heralds,* 25). But this is because Wagner thinks that Paul made a habit of memorizing large chunks or even whole books of Scripture—in fact, that he knew the entire book of Isaiah by heart (*Heralds,* 21–27). If Paul had an entire book memorized, why did he copy at least some of his quotations from a collection of excerpts, as Wagner freely admits (*Heralds,* 22)? As we will see in chapters 5 through 8, some of Paul's appeals to Scripture, including quotations from the book of Isaiah, diverge so far from any natural reading of the original context that even an audience that was familiar with the biblical text might have had difficulty identifying any link between the two.

or via memory, in order to grasp the full significance of his repeated appeals to Scripture. This presumption implies the further belief that Paul's audiences were capable of retracing his reading of the biblical text and uncovering for themselves the mostly unstated links that modern scholars have posited between Paul's quotations and their original biblical contexts. At an even deeper level, this approach assumes that Paul's audiences found his interpretations of Scripture to be perfectly reasonable and supportive of his argument. All of these assumptions must be called into question.

First, the idea that Paul's audiences either knew the Jewish Scriptures well enough to supply the context of his quotations or had ready access to the written text overlooks the historical realities of illiteracy and the relative scarcity of texts in the ancient world. Nor is it likely that Paul was ignorant of his addressees' limited access to and knowledge of the biblical text. A careful reading of his biblical argumentation suggests that Paul made a serious effort to frame his quotations so that individuals with a relatively low level of biblical literacy could grasp the rhetorical point of his quotations.[44] The bulk of Paul's prior interpretive engagement with the text of Scripture would have been invisible to most of the people in his audiences.

Second, even if the original audiences knew the original context of some of Paul's quotations, there is no reason to suppose that they were capable of reconstructing the reasoning behind Paul's appeals to Scripture when contemporary scholars, with all of their training and expertise, still disagree about what Paul was doing in many cases.[45] In reality, the original addressees' estimations of Paul's intent would probably have been as diverse as those posited by contemporary scholars. Even some of the more literate people in the early church found Paul's argumentation hard to follow (cf. 2 Pet 3:15–16). To think that Paul expected his audiences to figure out and agree with his many unexplained interpretations of the biblical text strains credulity.

Third, although we must be careful about assuming that first-century readers shared our modern notion of "original context," some of Paul's appeals to Scripture diverge so far from any obvious contextual reading that

44. This point will be developed in the discussions of individual passages in chapters 5–8.

45. The common presumption that Paul's audiences were interested in tracing the logic behind his use of quotations sounds anachronistic in light of what we know about the way texts were read and understood in antiquity. The examples of the rabbis and the Qumran community are not germane here, since both groups were made up entirely of Jews who had heard the Jewish Scriptures recited since childhood, and both groups trained their members to read and interpret the Scriptures for themselves. Neither of these points applies to Paul's audiences.

audience members who were familiar with the quoted text would have found it difficult if not impossible to follow his line of reasoning.[46] This in turn could have led them to question his entire argument. Either Paul was rhetorically inept in these cases, or he did not expect his audiences to engage in this kind of evaluative exercise. The latter option finds support in the fact that Paul frames most of his quotations with enough interpretive comments to insure that a person who knows nothing about the original context can grasp the rhetorical point of the quotation.[47] Even when he assumes that the audience will recognize a particular biblical character or story, the level of knowledge that he presupposes is actually quite limited.[48] Only rarely does Paul offer an extended commentary on a specific passage of Scripture.[49]

Although it is certainly possible that Paul thought that his readings of Scripture were so obvious as to require no justification, it seems more likely that he was aware that any serious effort at justification would have been useless because of the limited biblical knowledge of his intended audience. In other words, instead of assuming that his audience knew the context of his quotations and could evaluate his interpretations accordingly, Paul seems

---

46. Notable examples include Rom 2:24 (Isa 52:5), 9:25–26 (Hos 2:23, 1:10), 10:5–8 (Deut 30:12–14), 10:18 (Ps 18:5), 1 Cor 14:21 (Is 28:11–12), 2 Cor 4:13 (Ps 116:10), Gal 3:10 (Deut 27:26). The point is not that Paul wholly neglects the original context in these cases, but rather that he quotes verses in such a way that their relation to the source text would have been difficult, if not impossible, for a knowledgeable reader to figure out. Ross Wagner rightly calls attention to Paul's "radical rereading" of Scripture (*Heralds*, 25, 82, 154, 271) that includes numerous "misreadings" of Scripture that Wagner labels "shocking" (82), "tendentious" (185, 212), "stunning" (205), and "brazen" (211), along with at least one passage where Paul "brazenly contradicts the scriptures, certainly as they were read by most of his contemporaries" (159). These observations pose serious problems for Wagner's presumption (*Heralds*, 36–37) that Paul expected the literate members of his congregations to retrace, approve, and explain the intricacies of his biblical argumentation to the majority who had little or no formal education and little free time to devote to the task. If this was Paul's intention, his decision to include so many "brazen misreadings of Scripture" in his letters must be judged a major rhetorical miscalculation.

47. See the discussions of individual passages in chapters 5–8.

48. Examples include Rom 4:6–8 (David), 9:14 (Moses), 9:16 (Pharaoh), 10:5 (Moses), 11:2–4 (Elijah). For more on this point, see the discussions of individual passages in chapters 5–8. Verses that simply mention the name of a prophet (e.g., Rom 9:25, 27, 29) require no prior knowledge of a specific passage or story on the part of the audience.

49. Among the few places where Paul does this are his comments on the Abraham story in Rom 4:1–22, 9:6–13, and Gal 3:6–18, 4:21–31, as well as the midrashic exposition of the exodus story in 1 Cor 10:1–10 (cf. 2 Cor 3:7–18, which contains no explicit quotations).

to have crafted his quotations for an audience with relatively little knowledge of the biblical text.[50]

Assumption #8: *Paul expected everyone in his churches to have an equal appreciation of his biblical quotations.* Paul was keenly aware of the diversity within the early Christian movement. In several of his letters he refers directly or indirectly to the differences in socioeconomic level, religious background, ethnicity, gender, and other categories of social status within his churches.[51] In other words, Paul did not think of his churches as undifferentiated masses of Christian believers. Paul lived in a world in which social differences were highly significant, and he often sought to mitigate those differences in his letters. Thus, Paul would have been aware that the members of his churches differed widely in their ability to understand his biblical quotations, with educated Jewish males comprehending the most and illiterate Gentile women the least. Paul set himself a demanding rhetorical task when he undertook to write a letter that would prove both understandable and persuasive to such a diverse audience, and he used a variety of rhetorical tools and strategies to do so. Direct quotation from the Jewish Scriptures was but one of those tools.[52]

But to whom were his quotations directed? It is natural to think that Paul appealed to the Jewish Scriptures to sway those who were most familiar with the biblical text—that is, educated males, especially those with a background in Judaism.[53] Because of their high status within the group, these individuals were in a position to influence others to accept Paul's arguments and to follow his instructions. But these people were also capable of evaluating and challenging Paul's interpretations of Scripture, and some of them might have had political motivations for resisting the intrusion of an

50. Of course, Paul's letter carriers would have been present to answer questions about the content of his letters when they were read aloud to the initial audience (see Botha, "Verbal Art," 415–20). But it seems improbable that the illiterate members of Paul's churches would have been motivated to raise questions about Paul's use of Scripture, and it is even more unlikely that they would have been able to understand and critique the answers if they were offered. Questions of this sort arise from a literate (and print-oriented) audience; Paul's first-century audiences would have had more pressing questions about the contents of his letters.

51. Examples include 1 Cor 1:18–31, 7:17–24, 8:4–8, 9:19–23, 11:3–22; 2 Cor 8:1–15; Gal 3:26–28. For more on the subject, see the studies listed in note 13.

52. The use of multiple lines of argumentation is a standard recommendation of rhetoricians as far back as Aristotle.

53. Questions remain as to how many (if any) of the people in Paul's churches actually fit this description; see Dewey, "Textuality," 48–50.

outside authority, even a respected one such as Paul, into the life of their churches.

Among the illiterate masses, on the other hand, a person who could read and quote from the authoritative Scriptures would have been greeted with considerable respect. Paul's facility in interpreting the holy Scriptures would have cast him in the role of a hierophant dispensing the sacred mysteries of God. His numinous pronouncements would have appeared to many as incontrovertible, since they were backed by the authority of the one true God. To people such as these, Paul's quotations from the Jewish Scriptures would have seemed the strongest of all his arguments, the trump card against all merely human argumentation.

But there is no reason for us to limit this attitude to the illiterate masses. The Enlightenment distinction between the "superstitious masses," who take things on authority, and the "intelligentsia," who test all things by reason, simply does not hold for the ancient world. Arguments from authority carry great weight at all levels of a hierarchical society, especially when they are couched in religious language. In the ancient world, when the gods spoke, people listened. Though the gods commonly spoke in oral form (through oracles, dreams, etc.), written texts were also important modes of communication from the divine realm.[54] Typically these messages from the gods took the form of written oracles—short enigmatic sayings that offered the recipients guidance concerning the will of the deity or spells to be recited to secure divine protection. These written oracles were especially valued by the literate members of society, who consulted them in times of trouble and even made them into objects of cultic veneration. The diviners who had charge over these written oracles were held in high esteem by the literate and the illiterate alike.[55]

---

54. See Harris, *Literacy*, 218–21, and the supplementary material provided by Mary Beard, "Ancient Literacy and the Function of the Written Word in Roman Religion," in Humphrey, ed., *Literacy*, 35–58. Equally relevant here is the evidence collected by Pieter van der Horst ("*Sortes:* Sacred Books as Instant Oracles in Late Antiquity," in *The Use of Sacred Books in the Ancient World* (ed. L. V. Rutgers et al.; CBET 22; Leuven: Peeters, 1998], 143–73) regarding the ancient practice (followed by Greeks, Romans, Jews, and Christians) of using sacred books as "instant oracles," whether by opening the book at random, asking a child to recite the last verse he or she had memorized in school, consulting a line of text based on the rolling of dice, or some similar randomizing practice.

55. See Beard, "Literacy," 49–53. In addition to the well-known *Sibylline Oracles*, which were tended by special officials in Rome, Beard cites written responses from a variety of oracular sites. According to Beard, "Oracular books in the hands of private diviners could circulate widely, reaching where the spoken word of God was rarely or never heard" (53). Harris traces

As an expert in the "oracles of God" (Rom 3:2), might Paul have been regarded as a sort of "diviner" in his use of quotations from the Jewish Scriptures? The short, pithy sayings that he cites in his letters certainly have an oracular quality to them. As written oracles, they would have been venerated as revelations of the divine will, to be acknowledged and obeyed whether their meaning was clear or not. And the one who could produce such oracles on demand would invariably share in their luster.

It is no wonder that Paul resorted regularly to quoting from the Jewish Scriptures when addressing the most contentious issues in his churches. Paul knew that only the more literate members of his audience could grasp the full sense of his quotations, but he also knew that full comprehension was not required for his quotations to achieve their rhetorical purpose. As long as the recipients acknowledged the authority of the Jewish Scriptures, direct quotations from the holy text would be greeted with respect and (Paul hoped) submission. Who would dare to argue with the mouthpiece of God?

Assumption #9: *The best way to determine the "meaning" of a Pauline biblical quotation is to study how Paul interpreted the biblical text.* Although there is much to be gained from looking at the way Paul read and interpreted the biblical text, this process does not lead us to the "meaning" of a Pauline quotation. One of the central canons of contemporary literary criticism is that the "meaning" of a text resides not in the mind or intentions of the author, but in the dynamic interplay among author, text, and audience.[56] In other words, we cannot investigate the "meaning" of a quotation without taking the audience into account. The whole purpose of introducing a quotation into a piece of discourse is to affect an audience in some way. To analyze quotations without taking the audience into account is to neglect the author's primary purpose in adducing an outside text.

---

the popularity of written oracles to "some special quality that was thought to be inherent in a written text" (*Literacy,* 219). A somewhat similar attitude can be seen in the widespread use of written charms and magical spells (see Harris, *Literacy,* 218–19). Joanna Dewey ("Textuality," 41–42) also remarks on the power of written texts in the Greco-Roman religious world, comparing their force to that of the public posting of civil laws.

56. Literary scholars differ markedly in the way they conceive this interplay, with some placing more stress on the role of the reader, some on the author, and some (most?) on the process itself. A number of helpful surveys of the differing approaches are available; see Elizabeth Freund, *The Return of the Reader: Reader Response Criticism* (London: Methuen, 1987); Susan R. Suleiman and Inge Crosman, eds., *The Reader in the Text: Essays on Audience and Interpretation* (Princeton, N.J.: Princeton University Press, 1980); Jane Tompkins, ed., *Reader Response Criticism* (Baltimore: Johns Hopkins University Press, 1980).

But which audience? The answer depends on the goal of the interpreter. If the goal is to explain how contemporary readers make sense of Paul's quotations, then the interpreter will focus on the reading experience of a contemporary audience. For this task, the literary capacities of Paul's first-century audience are irrelevant.[57] But if the goal is to determine how Paul's original audience might have responded to his quotations, then the issue of audience capability becomes highly germane. Any analysis that focuses on the first-century recipients of Paul's letters must take seriously both the diversity and the limitations of Paul's intended audience. Such an analysis will produce not one but many possible "meanings" for Paul's biblical quotations, reflecting the diverse literary capabilities and experiences of the many people in his churches.[58]

No amount of historical investigation can tell us how the recipients of Paul's letters actually viewed and responded to his quotations. But careful historical study can help to guard us against simplistic and one-dimensional interpretations of the evidence. Literary analysis can tell us what Paul assumed about the recipients of his letters, but it cannot tell us whether those assumptions were well grounded. Only social history can do that.

From what we have seen in this chapter, it seems unlikely that many of the people in Paul's congregations knew the Jewish Scriptures well enough to evaluate his handling of the biblical text. It seems equally implausible that Paul expected them to do so. As we will see later, Paul normally embeds his quotations in an interpretive framework that signals to the audience how he intends the biblical text to be understood. In these cases little or no knowledge of the original context is required; the quotation achieves its rhetorical effect as long as the audience acknowledges the authority of the Jewish Scriptures and accepts Paul's reputation as a reliable interpreter of the holy text. In some cases Paul may have purposely targeted the more literate mem-

57. This is the approach that governs Richard Hays's investigation of the many "echoes" of Scripture in Paul's letters. Hays describes his goal as "to produce late twentieth-century readings of Paul informed by intelligent historical understanding" (*Echoes,* 27). His method is grounded in "a style of interpretation that focuses neither on the poet's psyche nor on the historical presuppositions of poetic allusions but on their rhetorical and semantic effects" (29). For a critical view of Hays's approach, see note 29.

58. The implications of this observation will be spelled out more fully in chapter 4.

bers of the congregation (especially those with more exposure to Judaism) on the assumption that they would explain to the illiterate majority the significance of the verses that he cites. In still other cases he might have gotten caught up in the flow of an argument and failed to consider whether his mostly Gentile audience would be able to comprehend his references to the Jewish Scriptures. No single answer can be posited for every passage; each text must be evaluated on its own merits.

But is it possible after twenty centuries for us to even approximate the way Paul's first-century audience might have responded to a particular quotation from the Jewish Scriptures? This is the question to be addressed in the next chapter.

CHAPTER 4

Analyzing Paul's Quotations

Real and Implied Audiences

The remainder of this book is devoted to an examination of the rhetorical function of Paul's biblical quotations. Before we proceed, however, we should pause to review the results of our methodological inquiries and spell out more precisely the method that will be used in the following chapters to analyze Paul's quotations.

Chapter 1 discussed the need for a rhetorical approach to Paul's biblical quotations. Instead of focusing on the way Paul read and interpreted the biblical text, a rhetorical approach asks what Paul was seeking to accomplish when he introduced a quotation from the Jewish Scriptures at a particular point in his developing argument. The aim of such an approach is twofold: to gain a better understanding of Paul's argumentation and to evaluate the effectiveness of quotations as a rhetorical strategy for shaping the beliefs and conduct of Paul's intended audience. The rhetorical model developed by Eugene White offers a useful framework for analyzing the goals and effectiveness of Paul's biblical argumentation. White's model calls for close attention to the way Paul's perceptions of his audience may have influenced the development of his arguments.

Chapter 2 looked at several recent studies of quotations from the fields of literary studies and linguistics. From these studies we learned that quotation is a complex speech-act in which the quoting author seeks to use the voice of an earlier text to enhance his or her status and to commend his or her ideas and proposals to a later audience. Like other rhetorical acts, the quotation process is heavily power-coded. The quoting author asserts power over both the source text, whose language and ideas are made to serve the rhetorical purposes of the author, and the audience, for whom the quotation serves as an inducement to listen to the author and follow his or her recommendations. To improve the likelihood that the quotation will achieve its purpose, the quoting author typically embeds the quotation in an explanatory framework that signals to the audience how the quotation is to be understood. Whether this meaning corresponds to the "original sense" of the passage is irrelevant as long as the audience is willing to accept the quoting author's interpretation of the passage. Quotations are most effective in contexts in which the audience holds both the source text and the quoting author in high regard, though quotations can also be used to build bridges with an indifferent or hostile audience as long as they respect the source text.

Chapter 3 explored what we can know or presume about the first-century audience of Paul's biblical quotations. There we discovered a discrepancy between the level of biblical knowledge that Paul seems to assume in his letters and external data that suggest a much lower level of biblical literacy among Paul's addressees. This finding raises questions about the effectiveness of Paul's strategy of quoting from the Jewish Scriptures in his letters. The issue was not resolved in chapter 3, but it was suggested that external evidence regarding literacy levels in antiquity should take precedence over evidence derived from a "mirror-reading" of Paul's quotations because the letters give us only a partial and one-sided picture of the intended audience.

This last point requires further elucidation. Why should we give more credence to evidence gleaned from general studies of texts and literacy in the ancient world than to the specific information embedded in Paul's letters? The answer once again is that Paul's letters are rhetorical works, not objective depictions of reality. What we encounter in Paul's letters is not the "real" Paul or the "real" audience, but Paul's momentary construction of both himself and his intended audience.[1] To use the language of reader-response criticism, Paul's letters present us with the "implied author" and the "implied audience," whose relation to the actual author and recipients of the letter can be uncovered only (if at all) through careful historical investigation.

But why would Paul construct an audience that was both literate and familiar with the Jewish Scriptures if his actual audience was mostly illiterate and possessed only limited knowledge of the biblical text? The answer is more complex than the question implies.

First, we cannot always be sure how much Paul knew about the recipients of his letters. At times (as in Galatians) Paul seems to have lacked vital information about the circumstances of his audience (e.g., Gal 1:7, 4:17, 5:7–12), while at other times (as in the Corinthian correspondence) he

---

1. The title of Walter Ong's famous article says it well: "The Writer's Audience Is Always a Fiction," in *Interfaces of the Word* (Ithaca, N.Y.: Cornell University Press, 1977), 53–81. For a discussion of some of the ways in which recent interpreters have sought to correlate the rhetorical and historical situations of Paul's letters, see Johann D. Kim, *God, Israel, and the Gentiles: Rhetoric and Situation in Romans 9–11* (SBLDS 176; Atlanta: Scholars Press, 2000), 40–50.

actively misrepresents what he knows as part of a broader rhetorical strategy (e.g., 1 Cor 1:4–9, 4:8–10; 2 Cor 7:6–16).[2] In the case of Romans, scholars have debated whether the letter reveals any specific knowledge about the situation in Rome.[3] We should not assume that Paul had either the knowledge or the intention to depict his audience accurately in every case.

Second, even where Paul had taught his audiences personally from the Jewish Scriptures (as in Galatia and Corinth), he could not be certain how much they would recall from his earlier instruction, and he had no way of knowing precisely which passages they had discussed in his absence. Romans poses an even greater problem: how could Paul have known which biblical texts the Roman churches would recognize when he decided to include so many quotations in the letter that he addressed to them? Even if he was aware that the Roman church had its roots in the Jewish synagogue and would therefore know something about the Jewish Scriptures, he could not have known which biblical passages were studied and used in the Roman churches. Yet he still chose to quote repeatedly from Scripture to buttress his arguments. Here we see clear evidence that Paul's quotations cannot be taken as reliable indicators of the level of biblical literacy in his congregations.

Third, the common impression that Paul's letters presuppose extensive knowledge of the Jewish Scriptures is inaccurate. As we will see in chapters 5–8, Paul expected his audiences (even the Romans) to know the broad story line and some of the major characters of the Jewish Scriptures (e.g., Abraham, the exodus), as well as the Decalogue and a few other key passages. In most cases, however, Paul surrounded his quotations with enough explanatory comments that someone with little or no familiarity with the biblical text could follow his argument, even if the full extent of his interaction with the biblical text remained elusive.

Fourth, the materials presented in chapter 3 do not imply that everyone in Paul's churches was illiterate and ignorant of the Jewish Scriptures. Some of Paul's congregants came from Jewish backgrounds and had therefore heard the Scriptures recited in the synagogue from their youth, even if they were incapable of reading the text for themselves. Others had visited the synagogue from time to time out of a personal interest in Judaism; they, too,

---

2. For a discussion of Paul's familiarity with the situation in Galatia, see Christopher D. Stanley, "'Under a Curse': A Fresh Reading of Gal 3.10–14," *NTS* 36 (1990): 488–91, and the discussion in chapter 7 of the present volume.

3. The alternatives are spelled out in the essays in Karl Donfried, ed., *The Romans Debate* (rev. ed.; Peabody, Mass.: Hendrickson, 1991).

could have learned something about the Jewish Scriptures from their experience. Still others (probably the majority) entered the church with no prior knowledge of the Jewish Scriptures. Unless they were able to read, their familiarity with the biblical text would have been limited to whatever they were able to pick up via oral instruction and/or informal discussions within the church. Still others were new converts with little practical awareness of the Bible. And some (a tiny minority) could have deepened their knowledge of Scripture by reading the text for themselves.

In sum, we should avoid sweeping generalizations about what "Paul's audience" did or did not know about the Jewish Scriptures. If our goal is to assess the effectiveness of quotations as a rhetorical strategy in Paul's letters, we must take seriously the diverse literary capacities and backgrounds of the people in Paul's churches. In the case of the Galatians and Corinthians, whom he knew firsthand, we can assume that Paul was aware of the audience's diverse capabilities and attempted to frame his quotations accordingly. In the case of the Romans, on the other hand, Paul had to make an educated guess about the biblical knowledge of his audience. From what we have learned thus far, we should be careful about assuming that he guessed correctly.

Framing a Method

The remainder of this book is devoted to an exploration of the rhetorical effectiveness of Paul's strategy of using explicit biblical quotations to support the arguments of his letters. The investigation will revolve around two interrelated questions: (1) how do Paul's quotations serve to advance the developing arguments of his letters? and (2) how well does Paul's strategy of biblical argumentation cohere with what we can surmise about the capabilities and inclinations of his audiences?[4] The first question can be answered only by a careful rhetorical analysis of specific passages in which Paul quotes from the Jewish Scriptures. This analysis will focus on the surface structure of the argument, not the interpretive activity that preceded the composition of the argument. Aspects of Paul's argumentation that do not relate directly to his use of the Jewish Scriptures will receive, at most, cursory treatment. The second question requires an investigation of the level of biblical literacy that Paul presupposes in each of his letters. Given this information, we can

4. As explained in chapter 2, this is the key evaluative question in Eugene White's configurational model of rhetoric which serves as the theoretical framework for the present study.

use our imaginations to estimate how audience members with varying degrees of biblical literacy might have responded to Paul's biblical argumentation. The pluriformity of both "audience" and "meaning" must be given full weight in this reconstruction.

The first part of this task is fairly straightforward; the second is not. How do we avoid equating our own responses with those of the original recipients of Paul's letters? The key is to admit our limitations: we simply cannot place ourselves into the mind of a first-century Christian in Galatia, Corinth, or Rome. We can never reconstruct with confidence the actual response of any "original recipient" of Paul's letters, regardless of the level of biblical knowledge that we assume.

But the kind of study envisioned here does not require such a venture into historical psychoanalysis. All that is needed is a typology of the major interpretive strategies that might have been available to various hypothetical members of Paul's congregations. Eugene White's model of rhetoric highlights a number of variables that would have influenced how individuals in Paul's churches responded to his biblical quotations. These variables include their degree of familiarity with the biblical text, their attitude toward the Jewish Scriptures, their attitude toward Paul, and their ability to follow Paul's nonbiblical argumentation. By combining these variables into different configurations, we can construct a typology of possible audience reactions to Paul's biblical quotations.

On one side is a series of (hypothetical) audience members who would have been unable or unwilling to interact seriously with Paul's biblical quotations. Included under this heading are (1) people who did not accept the authority of the Jewish Scriptures and thus would have resisted Paul's efforts to reinforce a point by appealing to a biblical passage; (2) people who opposed Paul's personal claims to authority and therefore would have been unwilling to accept his arguments with or without the support of biblical texts; (3) people who disagreed with Paul on a particular point and consequently would have rejected any biblical evidence that he claimed would support his position; and (4) people who were unable to follow the underlying argument of Paul's letters and therefore had no framework for making sense of his quotations.[5] None of these (hypothetical) audience members would have given Paul's biblical quotations a fair hearing, since

5. All of these categories are hypothetical positions that may or may not have been held by the members of Paul's churches. But there is at least implicit evidence in Paul's letters that he encountered all four types from time to time.

they would have rejected (or failed to understand) his arguments on other grounds. Their responses, though perhaps valid on their own terms, are useless for addressing our questions about the rhetorical effectiveness of Paul's quotations.[6]

On the other side is a series of equally hypothetical audience members who would have taken a more charitable stance toward Paul's biblical quotations. The views of these people would have been the opposite of those in the first group: they accepted and respected the authority of the Jewish Scriptures; they took seriously Paul's claims to apostolic authority over his churches; they agreed with Paul's ideas, or at least were willing to give him a fair hearing; and they were able to follow the main lines of Paul's arguments as spelled out in his letters. These are the people Paul had in mind when he wrote his letters (i.e., the "implied audience").

The narrative sections of Paul's letters suggest that there were many people in his churches that matched this second profile.[7] But it is also clear that the actual members of Paul's churches varied widely in their degree of familiarity with the biblical text. An idealized typology of their capabilities might include (1) people who knew the original context of every verse that Paul quoted and agreed with all of his interpretations of Scripture (clearly an ideal type);[8] (2) people whose knowledge of Scripture was broad enough, whether from prior experience in the synagogue or personal study, to enable them to recognize most but not all of Paul's references to the biblical text; (3) people who possessed precisely the level of biblical literacy that Paul

---

6. Of course, if the number of people in any of these categories was significant, an effective rhetor would have crafted a rhetorical product that addressed their concerns. The point is simply that quotations from the Jewish Scriptures would not have been an effective strategy for addressing people with these kinds of problems.

7. Clearly, Paul was aware that there were people in his churches who did not agree with his views on every issue. He seems to have assumed, however, that his audiences would be charitable enough to take his arguments seriously. Otherwise, there would have been no reason for him to write (i.e., no "provoking rhetorical urgency," to use White's term).

8. Stanley Fish terms this audience the "optimal reader" (defined as "the reader whose education, opinions, concerns, linguistic competence, etc., make him capable of having the experience the author wished to provide") in "Interpreting the Variorum," in *Reader Response Criticism* (ed. Jane Tompkins; Baltimore: Johns Hopkins University Press, 1980), 174. Fish's term is more helpful in this case than the more generic "implied reader," since it implicitly calls attention to the diversity of "readers" that Paul may have had in mind when he penned his letters. For a helpful overview of the various kinds of "readers" and "authors" that populate the literature of reader-response criticism, see Robert Fowler, "Who Is 'the Reader' in Reader Response Criticism?" *Semeia* 31 (1985): 6–20. Additional resources are listed in chapter 3 note 56 of the present volume.

presumed in his letters, but no more; and (4) people who were generally ignorant of the content of the Jewish Scriptures. The value of such a typology is that it calls attention to some of the major options on the spectrum of audience competencies. The evidence presented in chapter 3 suggests that most of the people in Paul's churches would have fallen into one of the last two categories, with an indeterminate minority (those from Jewish backgrounds and some of the Gentiles who had been Christians for a long time) qualifying for the second category. This, at any rate, is the working assumption of the present study.

The next four chapters will explore the implications of defining Paul's audience in this way. Each chapter will focus on one of the four letters in which Paul quotes explicitly from the Jewish Scriptures (1 Corinthians, 2 Corinthians, Galatians, and Romans).[9] From each letter a handful of quotations will be selected for study. For each passage an effort will be made to estimate how three different idealized audience groups might have responded to Paul's biblical argumentation.

The first reading of each passage will adopt the vantage point of a person who knows the original context of every one of Paul's quotations and is willing to engage in critical dialogue with Paul about his handling of the biblical text. (To facilitate the discussion, this perspective will be termed the "informed audience."[10]) This is the vantage point from which most contemporary scholars analyze Paul's quotations. From what we have learned thus far, it appears that few people in Paul's churches would have had the time, ability, or inclination to interact with his quotations in this way. The responses generated by this model are best viewed as a counterbalance to the readings proposed for the other two categories.

The second reading of the passage (labeled the "competent audience") will attempt to trace the reactions of a hypothetical person who knows just enough of the Jewish Scriptures to grasp the point of Paul's quotations in their current rhetorical context.[11] This idealized response can be imagined by bracketing out of our reading all knowledge of the Scriptures except what is

9. As noted in the introduction, the present study covers only the assuredly Pauline letters in order to maximize the consistency of the data.

10. The term "audience" is used to identify the three types of audience responses instead of the more common "reader" terminology in order to highlight the fact that most of the people in Paul's churches would have experienced his letters as oral recitations before a gathered congregation, not as readers of a written text.

11. As the following chapters will show, this category tells us more about what Paul assumed regarding his audience's familiarity with the biblical text than about their actual capabilities.

specifically assumed in the letter at hand. For example, one cannot follow the argument of Rom 9:6–13 without knowing something about the patriarchal narratives in the book of Genesis. But one need not know the precise location of the quoted verses or other details of the stories to understand how the quotations relate to Paul's argument. Real-world individuals who approximated this description may or may not have been literate, but they would have known at least the broad parameters of the Jewish Scriptures as a result of instruction that they had received in Jewish or Christian circles prior to their encounter with Paul's quotations.[12]

The third reading (called the "minimal audience" in this study) will look at the passage from the standpoint of a person with little specific knowledge about the content of the Jewish Scriptures. This approach will require us to lay aside all prior knowledge of the Jewish Scriptures and attempt to make sense of Paul's quotations on this basis. Most of the real-world people who fit into this category would have been illiterate Gentiles, though literate recent converts might also be found here. Despite their general ignorance of the content of the Jewish Scriptures, we can assume that people in this category were aware of the high degree of respect given to the Scriptures in Christian circles. As a result, they would have been inclined to take seriously any argument that claimed to be grounded in the biblical text. But their ability to follow the argument of a passage laced with quotations would have been limited.

This summary of the method to be followed here leaves a crucial question unanswered: how do these three models relate to the actual interpretive experiences of Paul's first-century audiences? The answer to this question is by no means obvious. On the one hand, the task of making sense of a text is a highly individualized activity. The most that any typology can do is approximate the interpretive experience of a representative sample of the actual audience. The interpretive process also takes place much more automatically (i.e., non-reflectively) than these idealized models would suggest. Whether any first-century reader would have been conscious of the interpretive decisions involved in making sense of Paul's letters (including his quotations) is highly doubtful. To put it simply, the depiction of the interpretive process in the following chapters is inherently artificial.

Nonetheless, this does not mean that the typology is divorced from reality. The process of making sense of a text is not an arbitrary enterprise; it

---

12. Included here are individuals who were literate but had little or no access to the written text, as well as people who knew the text only through the mediation of others.

involves a dialogue between the reader and the grammatical, literary, and rhetorical codes embedded in the text, whether intended by the author or not. By slowing down and analyzing the reading process from a variety of angles, a typological approach calls attention to some of the ways in which the structures of the text might have conditioned the responses of Paul's actual first-century audiences. In short, the typology reminds us that understanding is shaped by what the audience brings to the text.

By allowing for diversity in the audience's prior knowledge of Scripture, we can explore how variations in this single element of the first-century audience's preunderstanding might have enhanced or limited the audience's ability to make sense of Paul's letters. The readings proposed by such an approach will clearly be artificial, since the whole purpose of a model is to impose a measure of order onto a complex reality in order to focus on those features of the phenomenon that are of interest to the investigator. The interpretive experiences of Paul's actual first-century audiences would have been influenced by a variety of factors, including their personal and family histories, their intellectual capacities, their gender, and their prior knowledge of Judaism and Jewish interpretive traditions.[13] But variations in biblical literacy would have been one of the more important factors—perhaps even the most important factor—shaping the way they understood Paul's quotations, and Paul would have courted rhetorical failure if he did not take this into account when crafting his quotations.

Thus, while it would be foolhardy to think that this typological approach can give us a reliable portrait of the interpretive experiences of Paul's actual first-century audiences, there is reason to think that such an

---

13. Throughout this study nothing has been said about possible influences from Jewish interpretive traditions on the way in which Paul's audiences might have understood his quotations. The primary reason for this omission is that it overcomplicates the model by introducing additional variables into the equation. This aspect of the model is not as far from reality as it might seem, however, since we have reason to question how much of this tradition would have been available to Paul's mostly Gentile and illiterate audiences. Paul seems to have been aware of this problem, since he includes almost no references to extra-biblical interpretive traditions in his letters. Among the few examples are his reference to the giving of the Torah "through angels" in Gal 3:19, the statement that Ishmael "persecuted" Isaac in Gal 4:29, and the naming of Jesus as the "spiritual rock" that "followed" the Israelites through the desert in 1 Cor 10:4. It is certainly possible—even likely—that a few individuals in Paul's churches might have known a Jewish interpretation of one of the verses that Paul quoted in his letters and that they would have interpreted Paul's quotations in light of this alternate reading. But there is no evidence to indicate that this kind of knowledge would have been widespread in Paul's churches. Even if it were, it would only mean that the present study has oversimplified the interpretive process, which is precisely what every model does.

approach can sharpen our sensitivity to some of the interpretive problems (and solutions) that might have occurred to Paul's first-century audiences as they tried to make sense of Paul's letters, including his biblical quotations. With this information, we can make a more informed judgment about the identity of the audience that Paul had in mind when he crafted his quotations. This kind of judgment is necessary for any effort to evaluate the effectiveness of Paul's biblical argumentation.

This brings us to the fundamental task of the present study: to examine the wisdom of Paul's strategy of quoting from the Jewish Scriptures in letters addressed to predominately Gentile Christian audiences. According to Eugene White, the most important factor to consider when evaluating the effectiveness of a piece of rhetoric is how well the speaker/author tailors the message to the needs and limitations of the intended audience. The kind of rhetorical analysis envisioned by White cannot be satisfied with merely describing how various hypothetical audience members might have responded to Paul's quotations; we must also attempt to judge whether quoting from the Jewish Scriptures was a wise rhetorical strategy for Paul to pursue in light of what we can determine about the audiences to whom the letters are directed. The final chapter of this study will propose an answer to this question.

PART II
CASE STUDIES

CHAPTER 5
First Corinthians

Biblical Literacy in Corinth

The Corinthian correspondence is addressed to a group of Christians whom Paul had taught personally over an extended period of time (a year and a half, according to Acts) and with whom he maintained regular contact (as witnessed by the many letters and messengers that passed between them). If Paul had a habit of teaching his churches from the Jewish Scriptures during his visits, we would expect to find evidence of this in his letters to the Corinthians.

How can we know what kind of biblical instruction Paul had given to the Corinthians? The only evidence that we have comes from the letters themselves.[1] But this is not a counsel of despair. At certain points in both letters Paul inserts an argument that presupposes that his audience is familiar with a particular passage from the Jewish Scriptures. Though it is certainly possible that Paul was mistaken about what the Corinthians knew, we should probably give him the benefit of the doubt unless the evidence indicates otherwise. Thus, when Paul refers in passing to a biblical story or character without explanation, we can presume that he is relying on earlier teaching that he expects them to recall.[2] In most cases the point of the argument would be lost without this knowledge. A clear example of this can be seen in 1 Cor 10:1–10, where Paul cites a number of specific lessons that he wants the Corinthians to learn from various episodes of the exodus story.

---

1. The common solution to this problem is to assume that Paul's audiences were familiar with the broader context of any biblical passage to which Paul refers in his letters. Behind this "solution" lies the additional assumption that Paul would not have quoted or alluded to a passage unless he knew that his addressees could retrace and approve his interpretation of the biblical text. This "mirror-reading" approach to the question is flawed in two areas: (1) it ignores evidence from outside the letters that suggests a much lower level of biblical literacy in Paul's churches, and (2) it employs an anachronistic model of the way quotations "work" as part of a developing argument. For more on these points, see the discussions in chapters 3 and 4.

2. Of course, he may have given them additional instruction from the Scriptures that he does not mention in his letters, but we have no way of verifying or denying this possibility. The argument from silence can be cited on either side.

Paul simply assumes that the Corinthians are familiar with the stories to which he refers; if they had never heard of the exodus story, his brief allusions would have made no sense. The same is true for 2 Cor 11:3, where Paul refers without comment to the negative example of Eve, who was "deceived by the serpent's cunning." If the Corinthians had never encountered the Genesis creation story, this passing reference to Eve's conduct would have been pointless.

A careful review of Paul's letters to the Corinthians reveals a number of passages in which Paul assumes prior knowledge of the content of the Jewish Scriptures, though the evidence is rather sparse.

1. In several places Paul refers to the Genesis creation story in a manner that presumes that the Corinthians are familiar with the story. Among the details that he mentions without explanation are that God created everything that exists (1 Cor 8:6, 11:12); God made light out of darkness (2 Cor 4:6); the first man, Adam, was created out of dust (1 Cor 15:44–45); the first woman was made after (and for) the man (1 Cor 11:8–9); the first woman, Eve, was deceived by a serpent (2 Cor 11:3); and death came into the world through Adam's sin (1 Cor 15:21–22). References such as these presuppose a fairly detailed knowledge of at least the second section of the creation narrative (Gen 2–3).

2. Paul also assumes that the Corinthians are familiar with certain aspects of the exodus story. In 1 Cor 10:1–10 he refers without explanation to "our forefathers" who "passed through the sea" and traveled through the desert "under the cloud" while eating "spiritual food" and drinking "spiritual drink" that flowed from a "rock that accompanied them."[3] He also alludes to several specific episodes of divine punishment that left the Israelites' bodies "scattered over the desert" (v. 5), including the stories of the golden calf (Exod 32), the Midianite women (Num 25), the bronze serpent (Num 21), and the rebellion of Korah (Num 16). In 2 Cor 3:3–12 he assumes that the Corinthians know the story of the giving of the law in Exod 34, including the facts that the Torah was written on "tablets of stone" and that Moses wore a special veil after the event. The breadth and brevity of Paul's references suggest that he expected the Corinthians to have a fairly broad knowledge of the exodus story, though these are the only episodes that he mentions.

3. In a few places Paul assumes that the Corinthians are familiar with specific commands or prohibitions from the Torah. Among the laws that he

---

3. On this point, see note 25.

presumes they know are the Passover regulations, including the sacrifice of the Passover lamb, the cleansing of leaven from the house, and the use of unleavened bread (1 Cor 5:7–8); the injunction against muzzling a treading ox (1 Cor 9:8–9); the prohibition against marrying one's father's wife (1 Cor 5:1); and an unidentified passage that (according to Paul) enjoins women to keep quiet and occupy a submissive role (1 Cor 14:34).

4. In two places Paul refers back to christological interpretations of Scripture that he had passed on to the Corinthians while he was with them. In 1 Cor 15:3–4 he reminds them of his earlier teaching about Jesus' death and resurrection having taken place "according to the Scriptures," though he never identifies the verses upon which his teaching was based. In 1 Cor 15:27 he quotes a brief snippet from Ps 8:6 (without marking it as a quotation) and then appends a clarifying comment that seems to presuppose that the audience is aware of a christological interpretation of the psalm.

5. In several places Paul assumes that the Corinthians are familiar with Jewish ideas and practices derived from Scripture, including "the day" (of the Lord) (1 Cor 3:13); circumcision and keeping God's commandments (1 Cor 7:18); priests eating from the altar in the Jerusalem temple (1 Cor 8:13); and the festival of Pentecost (2 Cor 16:8). But in these cases the language is too general for us to conclude that Paul is alluding to earlier biblical teaching. Whatever knowledge the Corinthians possessed about these matters probably came to them via the passing comments of other Christians (without reference to any particular biblical passage) or common cultural experience with Judaism. The same is true for Paul's appropriation of such biblical concepts as "covenant" (2 Cor 3:6, 14), "righteousness" (1 Cor 1:30; 2 Cor 5:21), and "wisdom" (1 Cor 2:1, 6–7), as well as his many appeals to biblical moral standards (e.g., 1 Cor 5:9, 6:9–10; 2 Cor 9:6–7, 12:14). In every case we are dealing with terms and ideas that were already so thoroughly "Christianized" that no specific knowledge of Scripture would have been required to understand them.

From this brief survey we can conclude that Paul expected the Corinthians to have a fairly good knowledge of the biblical creation stories and the exodus story, along with a couple of christological passages and a handful of Torah injunctions. Whether this was all that Paul expected them to know cannot be determined from the evidence. As we will see below, the great majority of Paul's explicit quotations can be understood with no prior knowledge of the context from which they were extracted; that is, they presume no familiarity with the biblical text. This suggests that there may have been limits to what Paul expected the Corinthians to know about the content of the Jewish Scriptures—key stories and important christological passages, yes; precise literary contexts for specific quotations, no.

The Rhetoric of Quotations in 1 Corinthians

Paul's "first" letter to the Corinthians contains eleven quotations that are marked by introductory formulae (1 Cor 1:19, 31, 2:9, 3:19, 20, 4:6, 6:16, 9:9, 10:7, 14:21, 15:54–55),[4] one that could be recognized by other means (1 Cor 15:27),[5] and five that are unmarked and would therefore have been unrecognizable to the Corinthians unless they happened to be familiar with the original passage (1 Cor 2:16, 5:13, 10:26, 15:32, 33).[6] Quotations are scattered throughout the letter; they are not limited to a particular part of the argument. The quotations in 1 Cor 1:19 and 3:19–20 function as an *inclusio* for the intervening argument,[7] but the rest of the quotations seem to have been chosen for their relevance to the point at hand rather than for any broader structural reasons. The decision to include a quotation from the Jewish Scriptures seems to have been motivated in every case by the rhetorical needs of the developing argument.

The following examples illustrate how Paul uses quotations to advance his argument in 1 Corinthians and how his quotations might have been understood by the various hypothetical audiences described in chapter 4.[8]

---

4. The source of the quotations in 1 Cor 2:9 and 4:6 is unknown, but the Corinthians had no way of knowing this. They would have assumed that both verses came from the Jewish Scriptures like the rest of Paul's quotations. The combined quotation in 1 Cor 15:54–55 (Isa 25:8 followed by Hos 13:14) is introduced by a single formula (τότε γενήσεται ὁ λόγος ὁ γεγραμμένος), and so would have been heard as a single quotation whose ending-point was uncertain (v. 54? v. 55? v. 56?).

5. First Corinthians 15:27 would have been identifiable as a quotation because of the interpretive comment (including requotation) that follows the initial (unmarked) citation of Ps 8:6.

6. None of the verses in this latter group qualifies as a quotation under the audience-centered definition that guides the present study. See the discussion in chapter 3 under "Assumption #4."

7. As noted, for example, by Raymond F. Collins, *First Corinthians* (Collegeville, Minn.: Liturgical Press, 1999), 87. Collins also notes a higher incidence of quotations in the first section of the argument (1:18–3:23), but it is hard to discern any rhetorical purpose behind such a minor concentration.

8. As explained in chapter four, the "audiences" whose interpretive experience is depicted below are imaginary constructs representing three different levels of biblical literacy in Paul's first-century congregations. The descriptions of their possible reactions to Paul's rhetoric, including his quotations, have been artificially "slowed down" for critical analysis. The actual recipients of the letters would have varied widely in their ability to follow and understand Paul's rhetoric, including his quotations. But these idealized types can give us a sense of how biblical (il)literacy might have affected their reactions to Paul's arguments.

1 Corinthians 1:19

The "provoking rhetorical urgency" that Paul faces as he begins his letter to the Corinthians is described in part in the *narratio* in 1:11–17, though the situation is actually more complex than Paul chooses to depict at this point in his letter.[9] Paul is aware that the audience is divided in its attitude toward him. On the one side are those who have remained loyal to him, including "Chloe's household" (1:11), those who say, "I follow Paul" (1:12, 3:4), and perhaps those who sent him the letter that he begins to answer in 7:1.[10] On the other side are those who reject or challenge his authority over the church, including some whom Paul describes as "arrogant" and in need of correction (4:18–21), some against whom he defends his conduct in 9:1–18, and some who claim to follow other leaders, such as Apollos, Cephas, and even Christ (1:12, 3:4, 22). From these verses we can deduce that there were a number of parties in the church that disagreed with one another about a broad range of concerns. Paul's authority was only one of many issues being debated by the Corinthians.

Paul could have chosen to attack his challengers head-on at the beginning of his letter, as he does in Galatians. Instead he opted to portray the situation in more neutral terms as a matter of disunity within the church. In a surprising move, he even goes so far as to implicitly disclaim authority over those who claim to be his followers (1:13–17). This risky strategy enabled him to argue against his opponents without appearing to be self-serving, thereby enhancing his own image (*ethos*) with the audience. The irony of these opening verses is deep indeed. Though there were many things about the Corinthian church that displeased him (as evidenced by the stinging rebukes that he issues later in the letter), he chose to veil what he knew and paint the situation in a positive light (including the surprisingly affirmative thanksgiving in 1:4–9) in order to secure a hearing for the more critical message that he planned to offer later in the letter.

---

9. Margaret M. Mitchell makes a forceful case for viewing the entire letter as a response to the situation depicted in these opening verses; see *Paul and the Rhetoric of Reconciliation* (Louisville: Westminster John Knox, 1991).

10. The relation between these groups is unclear from the letter, though it would make sense to see Chloe as one of the leaders of those who "followed Paul." The letter to which Paul responds starting at 7:1 could have been either a joint document crafted by opposing parties or the work of a single party seeking to enlist Paul's support for its views. Most scholars believe that it was delivered to Paul by the delegation of Stephanas, Fortunatus, and Achaicus, whom Paul commends at the end of the letter (16:17).

Verse 18 stands as the thesis statement for the argument that Paul intends to pursue in the first few chapters of the letter.[11] The relevance of this statement to the situation described in vv. 10–12 is not immediately apparent. In fact, it is not until chapter 3 that Paul begins to explain how the points that he raises in chapters 1–2 might relate to the immediate problem of divisions within the Corinthian church. By refusing to explain where he is going with his argument, Paul draws the attention of the audience away from the question of his authority and toward the logic of his argumentation, which centers on what he sees as the underlying principles involved.

The proposition statement in v. 18 is followed by a quotation from Isa 29:14 in v. 19. The γάρ at the beginning of the citation formula indicates that Paul means for this verse to be taken as a ground for his initial statement. Precisely how it relates to the proposition statement is not spelled out—the audience members are left to deduce the link for themselves. Since the link is by no means obvious, the audience members would have had to draw their own conclusions about its meaning in this context. Several questions would have arisen in the process. Who is the "I" who speaks in the quotation? Is it God, or Jesus, or Paul, or someone else? Who are "the wise" and "the intelligent" who the verse says will suffer at the hands of the speaker? Are they the same as the people who are said to be "perishing" in v. 18? Do they represent one or more of the Corinthian parties identified in v. 12? Is the reference to "destruction" to be taken literally, as suggested by the opposing reference to being "saved" in v. 18? Or is it hyperbole, as suggested by the parallel verb "annul" in the second half of the quotation and the reference to "foolishness" in v. 19? How might the audience have attempted to resolve these questions?

1. For the "informed audience," the answer could be found by recalling the original context of the Isaiah quotation. There, the speaker is clearly the God of Israel, and the terms "wise" and "intelligent" are applied sarcastically

---

11. Ben Witherington identifies 1:18–4:21 as the first argument of the letter, with 1:18–31 constituting the first division of the argument (*Conflict and Community: A Socio-Rhetorical Commentary on 1 and 2 Corinthians* [Grand Rapids: Eerdmans; Carlisle: Paternoster, 1995]). But he, like most scholars, sees 1:10 as the primary proposition statement of the letter (*Conflict*, 94–97). Anthony Thiselton offers a judicious critique of the recent move toward using ancient rhetorical categories to analyze Paul's letters, with special attention to 1 Corinthians (*The First Epistle to the Corinthians: A Commentary on the Greek Text* [Grand Rapids: Eerdmans, 2000], 41–52, 111–13).

to those in Israel who believe that they can hide their evil deeds from God and deceive the deity by their outward forms of worship.[12] The description of the coming invasion and siege of "Ariel" in Isa 29:1–12 would have pointed them toward a literal reading of the word "destruction" in the Pauline quotation.[13] But the informed audience still had to figure out how these points pertained to the proposition statement in v. 18 and the Corinthian parties described in v. 12. The most natural solution (by no means obvious to everyone in the category) would have been to correlate "the wise" and "the intelligent" in v. 19 with those who are said to be "perishing" in v. 18—that is, those who reject the message of the cross as "foolishness" (confirmed in vv. 20–21). But this kind of language did not apply to any of the parties mentioned in v. 12, so the informed reader would have been left without an explanation for how the quotation relates to the issue of divisions within the church. Such a reading also stands in tension with the original context, where "the wise" and "the intelligent" are members of the people of Israel, not outsiders. Thus, it seems that a familiarity with the original context might have confused the audience at this point rather than aiding their understanding. A sympathetic audience would have had no choice but to suspend judgment and await the further development of Paul's argument. A less sympathetic audience might have begun to question Paul's rhetoric at this point.

2. The "competent audience" would have been unfamiliar with the original context of the quotation in v. 19, since Paul makes no obvious reference to any other features of the original passage. Paul does assume that the audience knows enough about the Jewish Scriptures to recognize that the voice

---

12. Richard B. Hays (*First Corinthians* [Interpretation; Louisville: John Knox, 1997], 29) suggests that Paul may have been drawn to this passage by the reference in the prior verse (Isa 29:13) to people who honor God in their speech but not in their actions (cf. 1 Cor 1:17, 20). But even this association would not have helped the informed audience to figure out how the quotation pertained to the problem mentioned in 1:12.

13. The informed audience might also notice that Paul has adapted the wording of the quotation by replacing the somewhat ambiguous κρύψω, "I will hide," with ἀθετήσω, "I will annul," at the end of the verse. The significance of the change is unclear, but it could be taken as strengthening the description of what God will do and thus reinforcing a more literal understanding of the "destruction" promised in the first half of the verse. See the discussion in Christopher D. Stanley, *Paul and the Language of Scripture: Citation Technique in the Pauline Epistles and Contemporary Literature* (SNTSMS 74; Cambridge: Cambridge University Press, 1992), 185–86.

speaking in the quotation is that of the God of Israel, and he probably assumes at least a minimal awareness of the biblical depictions of God bringing judgment upon the people for their sins. With this limited biblical knowledge, the competent audience could have reasoned to the same conclusions about the relation of the quotation to v. 18 as the informed audience had. In fact, their ignorance of the original context might have given them an advantage in understanding the passage because they would not have been misled by the way Paul shifts the reference of the terms "wise" and "intelligent" from insiders to outsiders. They still would not have understood how the verse relates to the parties mentioned in v. 12, but they would have had no reason to distrust Paul's use of the verse.

3. For members of the "minimal audience," the meaning of the quotation would have remained fairly puzzling until they encountered the interpretive keys that Paul provides in v. 20. The reference to "the power of God" in v. 18 might have cued them to understand the "I" in the quotation as "God," but not until v. 20, where God is the subject of the verb, would that conjecture have been confirmed. Like the competent audience, they could have used the language of v. 18 to help them guess how Paul understood the words "wise" and "intelligent" in the quotation, but not until they reached the explanation in v. 20 could they have known that Paul was applying these terms to "the scholar" (γραμματεύς) and "the debater of this age" (συζητητὴς τοῦ αἰῶνος τούτου). Since the minimal audience would have known little or nothing about the biblical prophets and their pronouncements of judgment against Israel, the language about God "destroying" and "annulling" the wise and intelligent would have made sense in only the most general of terms. If anything, they might have interpreted such statements through the lens of Greco-Roman myths about gods who bring down humans possessed by hubris or who destroy people and places without cause. How any of this related to "the message of the cross" would have remained a mystery to them until Paul began explaining what he meant in vv. 21–25. In other words, the inclusion of such a poorly explained quotation at this point in his argument would likely have confused the minimal audience more than it enlightened them.

In summary, none of the proposed audiences would have been capable of grasping the meaning and significance of the quotation from Isa 29:14 as Paul himself seems to have understood it. Their understanding of the verse would have been tempered by their own judgments about its relation to the proposition statement in v. 18. None of them would have possessed sufficient information at this point to discern how the verse related to the immediate problem of divisions within the church.[14] Apparently, Paul was aware of this, since he proceeds to unpack the meaning of the statement (and implicitly of the associated quotation) in the verses that follow.[15]

So why introduce a quotation at all? What does Paul gain from such an obscure appeal to Scripture at this point in his argument? Although we can never be sure about Paul's motives, the studies surveyed in chapter 2 draw our attention to the fact that God is the speaker (the "I") in the quotation. If Paul did not choose to give an immediate explanation of his quotation, perhaps it is because his goal was more strategic. By introducing his argument with a quotation in which God is the speaker, Paul implicitly claims that the God of Israel endorses the argument that he plans to offer in the following verses. Rather than making the claim directly, he brings his audience into a firsthand encounter with the voice of God speaking through the words of Scripture.[16] For an audience that reveres the God of Israel and his Scriptures, the effect of such a quotation could be profound.

But why take this approach? Perhaps Paul knew that he could not appeal to his own authority at this point in the letter without arousing objections from those who questioned his authority. Since his rhetorical strategy required him to adopt a conciliatory tone at the beginning of the letter, he had to find another way to lend authority to his argument. His solution was to cite a verse from the authoritative Jewish Scriptures that showed the God of Israel speaking on his side. From there, he could proceed to unpack the meaning of the quotation, albeit in a rather roundabout way, in the ensuing verses.

1 Corinthians 10:7

Though 1 Cor 10:1–14 can be read as an independent rhetorical unit, the γάρ at the beginning of the section links it to the materials at the end of

---

14. This is not entirely correct if Margaret Mitchell is right in seeing an implicit reference to the Corinthians' factionalism in the phrase συζητητὴς τοῦ αἰῶνος τούτου in v. 20 (*Rhetoric,* 87–88). But since the word συζητητής is unattested elsewhere in Greek (*Rhetoric,* 87), it probably is unreasonable to expect that the Corinthians could have made the connection with v. 12 based their knowledge of the cognate verb συζητέω.

15. By the time the argument reaches 3:19–20, the various audiences would probably have gained enough familiarity with Paul's language and arguments to arrive at a common (Pauline) understanding of the two similar-sounding quotations that round off the section.

16. F. W. Grosheide seems to have an inkling of how the quotation works here: "Paul is here warning the Corinthians, who believed in the Holy Scriptures, against the world and he does so by appealing to those Scriptures. Thus God himself speaks in the world. He will thwart all wisdom of man" (*Commentary on the First Epistle to the Corinthians* [NICNT; Grand Rapids: Eerdmans, 1953], 45).

chapter 9. By this point, the highly charged rhetoric of self-defense that dominated the bulk of chapter 9 has been left behind in favor of a stylized description of the motives and strategies that shaped Paul's missionary activities.

The "provoking rhetorical urgency" in this section of the letter is still the divided nature of the Corinthian church,[17] but the discussion has now shifted to matters of conduct. As a result of a letter that he has received from the Corinthians (7:1), Paul is aware that the church at Corinth is wracked with disagreements over a wide range of questions pertaining to life in a non-Christian society. The bulk of Paul's rhetoric in 1 Cor 7–15 is designed to address these problems.[18] For the most part, his answers consist of reasoned argumentation rather than bald assertions of authority, though his tone does become rather heated at times.[19] But by the time they reached this part of the letter, the Corinthians would have already encountered several passages in which Paul bluntly asserts his authority over the church at Corinth (3:1–3, 4:18–21, 5:3–5). These passages would have cast a long shadow over the remainder of the letter, especially for those who had declared their allegiance to leaders other than Paul (1:12, 3:4, 22).

Behind all of Paul's reasoning lies the assumption that he is the Corinthians' spiritual "father" (4:14–15), that he speaks for God (2:4–7, 12–13), and that they should do as he says. The fact that this remains largely hidden in 1 Cor 7–15 is the result of a strategic decision on Paul's part to mask his authority in favor of rational argumentation. Only when he has reason to think that someone might challenge his argument does he allow this presumption of authority to flash to the surface (7:10–12, 9:1–6, 11:16 [?], 14:36). We must remember that however calm the tone, Paul's arguments represent the views of one who thinks of himself as "God's coworker" and of the Corinthians as the "field" or "building" (3:9; cf. 4:1) where his service to God takes place.[20]

---

17. See the discussion in Mitchell, *Rhetoric,* 138–40, 250–54.

18. The focus on issues of audience conduct is suspended temporarily in 9:1–23, but Paul returns to the Corinthians' problems in 9:24.

19. Passages in which Paul adopts a more challenging tone include 11:16, 20–22, 14:36, and 15:12. The only lengthy passage of this type is 9:1–18, where Paul shifts away from questions of audience conduct to a defense of his pattern of ministry. Of course, Paul speaks in the imperative voice on many occasions in these chapters. The point is simply that these commands are consistently embedded in arguments that appeal to the audience's understanding instead of simply insisting on obedience and threatening those who hold a different view.

20. Though she does not mention Paul's appeals to the Jewish Scriptures, Elisabeth Schüssler Fiorenza would no doubt include this practice in her indictment of Paul for his excessive reliance on arguments from authority in 1 Corinthians. As Schüssler Fiorenza puts it, "Paul

In 1 Cor 9 Paul's presumption of superior status comes to the fore as he engages in a spirited defense of his pattern of ministry against some who had voiced concerns about his method (9:1–23). Toward the end of this argument he begins to steer the discussion back toward the Corinthians' internal problems. In 9:24–27 he cites the familiar image of a runner training for a race in order to underline the rigorous self-discipline that he practices in his service of Christ. The use of the first-person singular in 9:26–27 links these verses to the prior section (9:19–23), but the rhetorical focus has now shifted from description (of Paul's missionary strategy) to prescription (of proper conduct for the Corinthians), as the imperative in v. 24 makes clear. The first-person references in 9:26–27 are therefore exemplary; that is, Paul sets himself up as a model for the Corinthians to imitate. By combining a depiction of his own heroic example with a popular image from ordinary life (the runner at the games),[21] Paul constructs an argument that would appeal to the Corinthians on two rhetorical levels at once.

The same pattern can be seen in chapter 10. As the argument develops, it becomes clear that Paul intends to return to the issue of "idol meat," which he had addressed in chapter 8 (cf. 10:14–11:1). Thus, the "provoking rhetorical urgency" that called forth the rhetoric of 1 Cor 10:1–14 is the same as in chapter 8.[22] But the Corinthians had no way of knowing where Paul's argument was going as he moved into an extended allegorical commentary on the exodus story. All they could do was follow along and see where the argument led.

In the first fourteen verses Paul uses a variety of verbal strategies to reinforce his bond of friendship with the Corinthians (a necessity after his defensive outburst in chapter 9) and to entice them to accept his arguments, including his prescriptions for their conduct. Some of these strategies are

---

introduces the vertical line of kyriarchal subordination not only into the social relationships of the *ekklesia,* but into its symbolic universe as well by arrogating the authority of God, the 'father,' for himself. . . . [His] rhetoric does not aim at fostering independence, freedom, and consensus, but stresses dependence on his model, order, and decency, as well as subordination and silence" (*Rhetoric and Ethic: The Politics of Biblical Studies* [Minneapolis: Fortress, 1999], 119, 121.

21. According to Eugene's White model of rhetoric, this strategy of appealing to beliefs and values (and culture) that are shared by both author and audience (White's term is "identification") is a crucial element in any successful rhetorical work. See chapter 1, note 35.

22. Gordon Fee argues that all four of the problems that Paul mentions in vv. 7–10 (idolatry, sexual immorality, testing God, and complaining) are related to the issue of "idol meat," but he admits that the evidence for sexual immorality in the pagan temples at Corinth is weak (*The First Epistle to the Corinthians* [NICNT; Grand Rapids: Eerdmans, 1987], 451–58).

fairly explicit, as when he refers to the Corinthians as "brothers" (10:1) and "my beloved (friends)" (10:14). Others are less obvious, such as his repeated use of the first-person plural to create an atmosphere of solidarity with the Corinthians (10:1, 6, 8, 9, 11). The rhetorical nature of these inclusive references becomes apparent when we encounter them in places where a literal reading of the pronoun would be inaccurate, as with the reference to "our forefathers" in v. 1 (not literally true for non-Jews)[23] and the inclusion of himself among those who might be tempted (along with the Corinthians) to commit *porneia* (v. 8) or "test the Lord" (v. 9). Especially notable in this regard is his twice-repeated assertion (10:6, 11) that the biblical stories to which he alludes were written as "examples" to keep "us" (not "you") from committing these kinds of acts. By using inclusive language in conjunction with his appeal to a common sacred text, Paul aims to create a sense of solidarity between himself and his audience. His goal, of course, is to motivate the Corinthians to accept his ideas about proper Christian conduct. Here again we see Paul playing on the authority of Scripture instead of appealing directly to his own authority, which was being questioned by some in the Corinthian church.

First Corinthians 10:1–11 is the only place in the letter where Paul interacts extensively with the Jewish Scriptures. His rhetoric presupposes a fairly broad familiarity with the exodus story, as evidenced by his unexplained references to various details of the desert narrative (vv. 1–5) and especially his allusions to specific episodes in the story (vv. 7–10). Only once does he quote explicitly from the words of Scripture (v. 7); the rest of the time he assumes that his audience will recognize and supply the background of the stories to which he refers.[24] How might the Corinthians have reacted to this sudden shift to a biblical mode of argumentation?

1. The "informed audience" would have had little trouble recognizing the stories to which Paul refers or grasping the points that he was trying to make. The use of terms such as "baptized into Moses," "spiritual food," and "spiritual drink" (vv. 3–4) to describe the events in the desert might have

---

23. Gordon Fee reads too much into this expression when he states, "This language is sure evidence of the church's familiarity with the OT as their book in a very special sense" (ibid., 444).

24. As we saw in chapter 3, there is no historical basis for Gordon Fee's "mirror-reading" assertion that Paul's allusions to the exodus story "indicate that these early Christians knew their Bible better than most moderns do, so that the allusion itself was enough to give them recall of the biblical context" (ibid., 454.)

sounded rather odd at first, but the allusions to the Christian practices of baptism and communion were obvious enough for them to recognize the parallels despite the lack of explanation. The identification of Christ as the "spiritual rock" that followed the Israelites in the desert (v. 4) might have been more puzzling,[25] but the eucharistic understanding of "spiritual drink" implied in the first part of the verse would have pointed them toward a similar interpretation of this reference: Christians are nourished by the God-given wine of the Eucharist as the Israelites were nourished by God-given water in the desert.[26] But identifying the parallels is not the same as understanding them. Unlike vv. 6–11, where he states clearly the point that he wants the audience to draw from each passage, Paul leaves it to the audience to figure out the meaning of the parallels that he sets up in vv. 1–5. The informed audience would have known the exodus story well enough to recognize the interpretive key in the implicit analogy of v. 5: just as God was displeased with some of those who received divine blessings in the desert and allowed them to die there without reaching the promised land, so Christians who take God's gifts and presence for granted might find themselves, in the end, falling short of the heavenly reward (cf. 9:27).[27] This conjecture would have found confirmation in the allusions to episodes of divine judgment in vv. 7–10. Even the somewhat ambiguous quotation from Exod 32:6 in v. 7 would have made sense in this context, since the informed audi-

---

25. Fee (ibid., 448–49) and Thiselton (*First Corinthians*, 727–30) cite a number of extra-biblical Jewish sources that speak of a rock or well following the Israelites in the desert. As Paul no doubt was aware, a lack of familiarity with these traditions would not have hindered the audience from grasping his essential point. Richard Hays is exactly right at this point: "The identification of the rock with Christ is a parenthetical remark, an embellishment of the Israel/church trope. Consequently, rather than digressing to explain the grounds for his imaginative leap, he just leaps" (*Echoes of Scripture in the Letters of Paul* [New Haven: Yale University Press, 1989], 94).

26. Whether Paul also presupposed here a particular theological understanding of the elements of the Eucharist cannot be determined from the evidence. The fact that the passage has been used to support a variety of interpretations should caution us against reading too much into Paul's language.

27. C. K. Barrett (*A Commentary on the First Epistle to the Corinthians* [HNTC; New York: Harper & Row, 1968], 224) sees in these verses strong evidence that Paul was aware that many of the Corinthians were trusting in the efficacy of baptism and the Eucharist to insure their salvation regardless of their personal conduct (cf. Fee, *First Epistle,* 443; Witherington, *Conflict,* 220). If this is true, it offers a further refinement of the "provoking rhetorical urgency" that motivated Paul to argue from Scripture in 1 Cor 10:1–14. But Margaret Mitchell is probably correct in rejecting this view on the grounds that Paul nowhere says that the Corinthians have a problem in this area, and that the passage can be explained as a response to the divisions in the Corinthian church without resort to this hypothesis (*Rhetoric,* 251–53).

ence would have known from the exodus account that the verb "play" referred to practices associated with idolatrous worship and that a divine judgment fell upon the perpetrators—a fact not explicitly mentioned in v. 7.[28] The fact that the verse brings together "eating" and idolatry would have made the quotation seem all the more relevant to them, since it echoed their own debates over eating meat offered to "idols."[29] For the informed audience, this passage would have stood as a powerful reminder of the might and holiness of the God of Israel, who expects holy behavior from his people, including the Corinthians.[30] In this way, Paul implicitly brings the Corinthians into the presence of God, who challenges them through the authoritative Scriptures to follow Paul's injunctions or suffer the consequences. Unlike a direct command, this approach would have helped to motivate even those Corinthians who were suspicious of Paul's authority to accept his recommendations regarding their conduct. Thus, what appears to be an innocent discussion of a biblical story turns out to be a carefully crafted attempt to wield power over the minds and wills of the Corinthians.[31]

2. The "competent audience" is presumed to be familiar with the biblical stories and characters to which Paul refers without explanation in his letters. In this case, their level of knowledge and their response to Paul's use of Scripture would have been virtually identical to that of the informed audience, since Paul's argument in these verses presupposes a broad familiarity with the exodus story. The one place where the competent audience might have had trouble following Paul's argument is in v. 7. In his subsequent references to the exodus story (vv. 8–10), Paul explains clearly what the Israelites did wrong and how they were punished. His comments presuppose

---

28. Raymond Collins observes that the quotation from Exod 32:6 in v. 7, the only explicit quotation in the passage, serves as the *partitio* of Paul's argument: "Its first part with reference to eating and drinking sums up the narrative account and points to the eating and drinking of the Corinthians (vv. 2–4). Its second part with reference to child's play sums up the kind of immorality that devolves from idolatry, the kind of evil the Corinthians are urged to shun (vv. 8–10)" (*First Corinthians* [SP 7; Collegeville, Minn.: Liturgical Press, 1999], 367).

29. So Fee, *First Epistle,* 453–55; Grosheide, *First Epistle,* 218. Richard Hays sees the quotation as central to the entire passage: "The Exodus quotation anchors the discourse at the point of its central concern (idolatry) and does so in a way that permits the poetic expansion of Paul's germinal metaphorical intuition into a metaphorical conceit, spanning the experiences of Israel and church with multiple analogies" (*Echoes,* 92–93).

30. As Raymond Collins points out (*First Corinthians,* 364), Paul's allusions to various episodes of divine judgment in the exodus narrative served as examples (*paradeigmata*) within the context of Paul's rhetoric, as Paul himself makes clear in 10:11–13.

31. This recalls what Gillian Lane-Mercier said about the "inherently duplicitous" nature of the quotation act; see the discussion of her ideas in chapter 2.

only a general familiarity with the biblical story line. In v. 7, on the other hand, Paul presumes that his audience knows the context of a specific verse from the book of Exodus. Without this detailed knowledge they would have been unable to comprehend why Paul would use a word such as "idolatry" to characterize the actions of a group of people engaged in "play," nor would they have known about the divine judgment that followed. But the verse that Paul quotes here is not from an obscure passage of Scripture; it comes from a story that had become paradigmatic in Jewish circles by Paul's day. Apparently, Paul presumed that even the illiterate members of his audience knew the story of the golden calf well enough to recognize the source and meaning of the quotation. If he was correct, then the passage would have had the same motivating effect for the competent audience as for the informed audience.

3. When we consider the likely responses of the group whom we have labeled the "minimal audience," the situation is quite different. Those who were in fact "ignorant" (10:1) of the content of the Jewish Scriptures would have found it impossible to supply the background information that Paul presupposes throughout this passage. But this does not mean that Paul's argument was lost on them. Even if they knew nothing of the exodus story, the minimal audience could have recognized the references to baptism and the Eucharist in vv. 1–5. From Paul's allusive language they could have discerned at least the broad outlines of the exodus story, including the key point that God was displeased with "our forefathers" (understandable as a reference to Paul's Jewish ancestors) and therefore punished them. The precise nature of the parallels between this story and Christian baptism and Eucharist would have remained rather fuzzy, but the minimal audience could have grasped Paul's central point: they should not take these practices lightly or else they might suffer the same fate as those people in the desert.[32] But since they did not know the original story, Paul's allusive references to Scripture would not have spoken to them with the same power as to those who possessed the requisite knowledge. The same is true for vv. 7–11: those who were unfamiliar with the stories to which Paul refers would have missed

---

32. Raymond Collins is virtually alone in recognizing the way Paul frames his biblical exposition to suit the limited biblical knowledge of his audience. His reflection on Paul's strategy in 1 Cor 10 is exactly right: "Paul develops his exposition of the Scriptures in such a way that they are pertinent to the life of the Christians at Corinth. This is important since of themselves the Jewish Scriptures are for the most part alien to the largely Gentile Christian community at Corinth" (*First Corinthians*, 365).

the powerful voice of God speaking through the words of Scripture as Paul's words brought the biblical stories to mind.

But this does not mean that they would have remained unaffected. As long as the minimal audience acknowledged the authority of the Jewish Scriptures and respected Paul as a reliable interpreter of the biblical text, the fact that he could cite biblical examples in support of his position would have lent significant weight to his recommendations. This is especially true for vv. 8–10. Here Paul speaks in clear terms about the kinds of behavior that the Corinthians should avoid and the harsh punishments that await them if they engage in these behaviors. Although the minimal audience would not have known the specific biblical stories to which Paul alludes, his brief synopses contain enough information to instill fear in anyone who respects the source of the stories. The simple fact that their God had executed such terrible vengeance on a group of people who disobeyed in the past would have been enough to motivate the minimal audience to heed Paul's recommendations.

From this passage we can see that Paul knew how to craft even a heavily biblical argument so that audience members with varying levels of biblical literacy could grasp his essential point. Those who knew the stories to which Paul refers would have been most powerfully affected by his argument, since they would have heard the voice of the authoritative Scriptures (and the God who stood behind them) resounding in their heads in support of the voice of Paul. But even those who knew nothing of the biblical text could have been influenced by Paul's biblical references as long as they trusted Paul's handling of the authoritative Scriptures. By summarizing the biblical narratives and drawing explicit conclusions about their implications for the audience's conduct, Paul made the essential features of the biblical text available to individuals who were incapable of hearing its voice for themselves. By knitting his own voice so closely with the voice of Scripture, he crafted an argument that he hoped would motivate even those who questioned his authority to do as he said. Success in this strategy would have taken him far toward his goal of solidifying his control over the Corinthian congregation.

1 Corinthians 14:21

In 1 Cor 12–14 Paul turns to another issue that was dividing the Corinthian church: the proper exercise and relative importance of what he calls the *charismata*. Over the course of three chapters he employs a variety of rhetorical techniques to motivate the Corinthians to follow his recommendations, including reasoned instruction (12:4–11, 27–28, 14:6–12), analogies from ordinary experience (12:12–26, 14:7–8), personification (12:15–16, 21), rhetorical questions (12:17, 29–30, 14:7–8), personal examples (14:6, 11, 15, 18–19), poetry (13:1–13), hypothetical situations (13:1–3, 14:6, 23–25), authoritative pronouncements (14:5, 13, 20, 27–37), and ridicule (14:20, 36). Arguments from Scripture play only a minor role in this section, most likely because the precise problem finds few parallels outside a Christian setting.

Only once in these three chapters does Paul quote explicitly from the Jewish Scriptures.[33] In 1 Cor 14:21 Paul quotes a passage from Isa 28:11–12 that he proceeds to expound in vv. 22–25. The quotation-plus-exposition stands at the end of a lengthy section (14:1–20) in which Paul lays out a variety of arguments designed to limit the public exercise of "speaking in tongues" in the Corinthian congregation. From the amount of rhetorical energy that he expends on the problem, we can deduce three things: (1) Paul viewed the current Corinthian practice as highly problematic; (2) he expected the Corinthians (or a significant number of them) to disagree with his assessment of the situation; and (3) he did not believe that a simple appeal to authority would be effective in this situation. To overcome this "provoking rhetorical urgency," Paul put forward a variety of arguments that recalled the everyday experience of the Corinthians, primarily hypothetical situations and analogies. Beneath his many arguments lies a common theme: the public exercise of "tongues" should be limited because other people in the congregation cannot understand what the speaker is saying (vv. 2, 7–9, 11, 16, 23) and therefore cannot benefit from the experience (vv. 5, 6, 12–13, 17, 19). The problem for Paul is not "speaking in tongues" itself—he actually encourages the practice under appropriate circumstances (vv. 5, 13, 15, 18, 26–27)—but rather its unrestrained use in the gathered congregation.

---

33. The only other mention of Scripture appears in 14:34, where Paul (or a later redactor?) refers to an unidentified provision in the Torah that requires women to adopt a submissive role. The reference is so vague as to render all efforts at identification useless. Perhaps the Corinthians knew what passage he had in mind, though nothing in the passage suggests that he is referring to earlier teaching. Even if no one in the audience knew the specific reference, their respect for the Jewish Scriptures would have induced them to take Paul's pronouncement more seriously than if he had issued it on his own authority. The vagueness of the appeal might even have been part of an intentional strategy to suppress women in the congregation who were claiming to speak under the authority of divine inspiration (see Antoinette Clark Wire, *The Corinthian Women Prophets: A Reconstruction through Paul's Rhetoric* [Minneapolis: Fortress, 1990]).

By the time he reaches v. 20, however, Paul has had enough of these appeals to reason. He therefore moves to seal the argument with the rhetorical strategy that seems to come most naturally to him: the argument from authority. Though he addresses the Corinthians as "brothers" (v. 20), his filial language is little more than a thinly veiled attempt to mitigate the patronizing tone of the ensuing statement, which characterizes the Corinthians' position as the thinking of "children" and his own approach as the attitude of "the mature." This none-too-subtle reminder of his superior position is followed by a quotation from the authoritative Scriptures, whose force he underlines by identifying the verse (incorrectly) as a statement from "the law" (Torah).

How might the Corinthians have viewed this sudden intrusion of a verse of Scripture into an argument that to this point has relied on appeals to reason? Those who revered the Jewish Scriptures would have wanted to know how the verse applied to the issue under discussion. The language of the verse, with its references to "people of other tongues" and a people who "will not listen" to them, would have sounded pertinent to Paul's argument, since it echoes language that he himself had used in the preceding verses. But the meaning of the quotation would not have been obvious. Who is the "I" who speaks in this verse? Who are the people who "will not listen" to the "other tongues" mentioned in the quotation? How does the verse relate to the situation of the Corinthians? The comments that Paul appends to the citation (vv. 22–25) would have answered some of these questions, but the audience would have been left to "fill in the gaps" at other points.

1. The immediate reaction of the "informed audience" would have been to recall the original context of Isa 28:11–12. The first thing they would notice is that Paul has altered the wording of the quotation to make it coincide better with his argument.[34] This in itself would not have posed a problem for an ancient audience, since the practice of incorporating interpretive elements into the wording of a quotation was an accepted convention in antiquity.[35] But when they discovered how far the language and sense of Paul's quotation-plus-exposition had diverged from the original, even a sympathetic ancient audience might have been dismayed. Two points would

34. The exact nature of the changes that Paul has made in the wording of his quotation is difficult to determine because of the complex textual history of the Greek text of Isaiah at this point. Apart from the omission cited below, none of the other likely changes has a significant effect on the meaning of the quotation. See the discussion in Stanley, *Paul*, 197–205.

35. For more on the common ancient practice of incorporating interpretive cues into the wording of quotations, see Stanley, *Paul*, 267–337.

have been especially troubling. On the language side, the most obvious change is the omission of the central part of the verse, which contains the words that the prophet said would be spoken to "this people."[36] As the audience members could see when they reached v. 23, the most important part of the quotation for Paul's purposes was the negative reaction of "this people" when they encountered the incomprehensible speech of the "people of other tongues." If Paul had included the middle part of the verse, which reported the (entirely comprehensible) message that was spoken to "this people," it would have undercut his entire argument.

The other notable change concerns the sense of the verse. Unlike the MT, in which the prophet announces the coming judgment of "this people" (i.e., Judah), the Greek text heaps condemnation upon the "priest and prophet" who are first mentioned in v. 7.[37] This was problematic for Paul not only because it cast "prophets" in a negative light (cf. 1 Cor 14:1–5, 18–19), but also because designating those who speak in tongues as "priests and prophets" would have undermined one of Paul's central arguments in 1 Cor 14: the superiority of those who prophesy over those who speak in tongues. By extracting the verse from its original context, Paul effectively suppressed

36. The LXX text of Isa 28:11–12 actually begins in the middle of a sentence, but even when taken with the prior verse, its meaning is not entirely clear. The LXX text diverges from the MT throughout Isa 28:7–13. The following rather wooden translation shows what might have been available to Paul and the informed audience (underlines indicate the portion appropriated by Paul; italics mark the words he omitted in the middle of the verse): "[7] For these have been wronged by wine; they were led astray because of liquor. Priest and prophet have degenerated because of liquor; they have been swallowed up because of wine. They shake from drunkenness; they wander about. This is an omen. [8] A curse is attached to their [?] advice, for it is advice (that is) rooted in covetousness. [9] 'To whom did we announce evil things? To whom did we announce a report?' To [?] those who have been weaned from milk, those who have been torn away from the breast. [10] Receive trouble upon trouble, hope upon hope, a little more, a little more, [11] on account of (the) contempt of (your) [?] lips, on account of another language. For they speak to this people, *saying to them,* [12] '*This is the place of rest for the one who hungers, and this is the (place of) affliction,*' and they did not want to listen. [13] So the word of the Lord to them will be, 'Trouble upon trouble, hope upon hope, a little more, a little more,' that they may keep on going and fall backward. And they will be crushed and endangered, and they will perish."

37. See the translation in the preceding note. This point is consistently overlooked by the commentators, who look only at the Hebrew text despite ample evidence that Paul routinely worked with the Greek version of the Jewish Scriptures (see Stanley, *Paul,* 67–69). The only available referent for the third-person plural verb λαλήσουσι is the "priest and prophet" mentioned in v. 7 (similarly, the "we" in v. 9). The shift to first-person singular forms ("*I* will speak . . . they will not listen to *me*") probably had already occurred in Paul's *Vorlage*, but it would have looked like a Pauline change (along with the variation in the introductory words of the verse) to an audience that used a standard "LXX" edition of Isaiah. See the discussion in Stanley, *Paul,* 198–202.

this element of the text and so distorted its meaning.[38] In other words, Paul had to ignore both the original sense and the original language of Isa 28:11–12 in order to apply the passage to the Corinthians. This would not have escaped the attention of the informed audience. In this case, familiarity with the original context would have raised serious questions about Paul's handling of the biblical text (and his reputation as a reliable interpreter) instead of leading the audience to a better understanding of Paul's intentions.

2. Members of the "competent audience" would have experienced none of these problems, since they would have been unfamiliar with the original context of the quotation. Their understanding of the verse would have been mediated entirely through the interpretive comments that Paul offers in vv. 22–25. They had to figure out for themselves how Paul's comments relate to the quotation, since Paul never explains the connection. From these comments they would have seen that Paul intended to "depict" (i.e., call attention to) certain aspects of the quotation and not others.[39] The "depicted" portions are given an allegorical interpretation: the phrases "people of strange tongues" and "lips of others" refer to the Corinthians who speak in tongues in the congregational meetings, while the phrase "this people" refers to outsiders ("the unlearned and unbelievers"; v. 23b) who might enter the room as they were speaking and react negatively ("say that you are out of your minds"; v. 23) and therefore be unwilling to "listen" to the Christian message.[40] The identity of the "I" who speaks in the quotation is clarified by Paul's addition of the words "says the Lord" at the end of the verse, though

---

38. This recalls the comments of Meir Sternberg about the power that the "context-of-quotation" exerts over the excerpted text (see chapter 2), a power that leads inevitably to a change in the meaning of the text. As Sternberg puts it, "The very extraction of a part from a speech-event must, to a certain degree, modify, if not misrepresent, its role and import within the original whole, where it is qualified and supplemented, defined and substantiated, by a set of other components relating to the various parameters of context. And the resetting of the part within a different whole widens the distance still further by exposing it to the pressure of a new network of relations" ("Proteus in Quotation-Land: Mimesis and the Forms of Reported Discourse," *Poetics Today* 3 [1982]: 131).

39. For the importance of "depiction," see Herbert H. Clark and Richard R. Gerrig, "Quotations as Demonstrations" (*Language* 66 [1990]: 786–88), discussed in chapter 2.

40. The interpretive comments assume that the basic sense of the quotation is self-evident, so that all Paul needed to do was to explain how it applied to the Corinthians' situation. Whether this was a safe assumption for Paul's first-century audience is uncertain (see the discussions in Hays, *First Corinthians*, 239–40; Fee, *First Epistle*, 681–83). But as long as they acknowledged the authority of the Jewish Scriptures and trusted Paul as an interpreter, they did not need to understand exactly how Paul's comments related to the quotation, since the practical import for the Corinthians is clear enough from Paul's comments in vv. 22–25. The quotation simply added authority to Paul's points.

the resultant image of "speaking in tongues" as the voice of God speaking through the believer to others stands in tension with other verses in the passage that regard it as originating in the mind of the individual and being directed to God (14:2, 4, 9, 15, 18–19, 27–28). For the competent audience, the fact that these words are presented as the "word of God" on the subject would have reinforced Paul's other arguments on the subject.[41]

3. The reaction of the "minimal audience" would have been similar to that of the "competent audience" in this case. The language of the quotation is close enough to the language and ideas of the preceding verses that even a person who knew nothing about the Jewish Scriptures might have been able to figure out the meaning and significance of the quotation if given enough time. Paul's explanatory comments in vv. 22–25 are also clear enough that an uninformed audience could recognize the parallels between the situations he describes and the language of the quotation. As long as they accepted the authority of the Jewish Scriptures, the fact that they knew nothing about the book of Isaiah would not have interfered with the rhetorical effectiveness of Paul's quotation for the minimal audience.

Thus we see that in the present case, those hypothetical individuals in Paul's churches whom we have designated the "competent audience" and the "minimal audience" would have found it easier to follow and accept Paul's argument than those who were familiar with the original context (the "informed audience"). This sounds counterintuitive until we recall that there were few if any individuals in Paul's actual first-century audience who possessed the level of biblical literacy that we have assumed for the informed audience. If Paul had known that his letter would be read by an audience that would check his references and critique his handling of Scripture, he might have been more careful to clarify or change what he was doing.[42] Apparently, Paul counted on the fact that few people in his audience knew the biblical text well enough to challenge his interpretations. His purpose in

---

41. The superfluous addition of the words "says the Lord" at the end of the quotation would have served to underline the divine origins of the pronouncement, thus undercutting any potential objections by the Corinthians (i.e., "this word settles the matter").

42. Of course, we see Jewish interpreters taking similar liberties with the biblical text in the rabbinic literature and the Dead Sea Scrolls, but the parallel is only apparent. In the Jewish literature the authors were writing for a more literate audience that knew both the biblical text and the accepted modes of interpretation and therefore could be expected to appreciate the author's often playful use of Scripture. A high percentage of their quotations are what Gillian Lane-Mercier calls "parodic" uses of Scripture, in which the appeal to authority is less prominent.

quoting the words of Scripture was not to gain the Corinthians' assent to a particular interpretation of the biblical text, but rather to induce his audience to transfer to his own argument some of the respect that they accorded the Jewish Scriptures. The audience did not have to know the original text for this strategy to be successful; all that was needed was a general respect for the authority of Scripture and a recognition of Paul's status as a member of the literati and a reliable interpreter of Scripture. Even if we ignore his claims to apostolic authority, the fact that Paul was both literate and conversant with sacred texts guaranteed him a measure of respect among the less educated members of his congregations, and Paul did not hesitate to play on that respect in order to advance his arguments. Thus, even when he did not explicitly mention his own authority, the differential power relationship between Paul and his audience was encoded in all of his rhetorical appeals to Scripture.

CHAPTER 6
Second Corinthians

The Changed Situation in Corinth

By the time Paul began to write his "second" letter to the Corinthians, his relationship with the Christians in Corinth had changed markedly. Since we have only Paul's side of the story, we cannot be certain about what happened. It appears that someone in Corinth had led a challenge to Paul's authority and gained support from many of the Corinthians before the revolt was put down by a harsh letter from Paul (2 Cor 1:23–2:11, 7:8–12). Having dealt with the immediate problem, Paul wrote 2 Corinthians in an effort to rebuild his broken relationship with the church.

From the way Paul addresses the Corinthians in this letter, it seems that he has concluded that the problem has become so severe and the stakes so high that he will have to use all of his rhetorical skills to win the Corinthians back to his side. As in the first letter, Paul knew (or had reason to believe) that the Corinthians were deeply divided in their attitudes toward him. He commends "the majority" for remaining loyal to him in his time of trial (2 Cor 2:6–9), but his comments indicate that even those whom he regarded as "loyalists" were hurt by his letter (7:8–11), and some of them remained suspicious of his motives and actions (1:12, 16–18, 6:12–13, 7:2). Apparently, Paul feared that even his supporters had abandoned him until Titus returned with a positive report after his visit to Corinth (7:6–7, 13–16). Though his worst fears proved to be unfounded, Paul was faced with the difficult challenge of rebuilding his relationship with a church that questioned his authority and no longer trusted him. This, then, is the "provoking rhetorical urgency" that Paul seeks to overcome in 2 Corinthians.

In a situation in which his claims to apostolic authority were under suspicion, we might have expected Paul to appeal frequently to the authority of Scripture in order to motivate the Corinthians to accept his arguments (cf. Romans). Yet 2 Corinthians contains only six explicit quotations (4:6, 13,

6:2, 8:15, 9:9, 10:17 [?]),[1] none of which plays a significant role in his argumentation.[2] How are we to understand this fact? Although it certainly is possible that Paul could only think of a handful of biblical texts that would support his arguments in 2 Corinthians, another explanation lies ready at hand. The success of an appeal to Scripture depends in part on the audience's recognition of the quoting author as a skilled and reliable interpreter of the authoritative text. Is it possible that Paul had concluded that he could no longer count on that level of respect when writing 2 Corinthians? At several points in the letter he seems uncertain as to whether the Corinthians will follow his instructions (2:5–10, 8:6–15, 9:3–5), and he criticizes them soundly for accepting the authority of a group of newcomers whose apostolic credentials they regarded as superior to his own (11:4, 12, 19–23, 12:11).[3] Though Paul may have had other reasons for avoiding arguments from Scripture in 2 Corinthians, it seems reasonable to suspect that he had concluded that the Corinthians no longer trusted him enough to accept his interpretations as valid.

The Rhetoric of Quotations in 2 Corinthians

The following examples illustrate how Paul uses quotations to advance his argument in 2 Corinthians and how his quotations might have been understood by the various "audiences" described in chapter 4.

2 Corinthians 4:13

Second Corinthians 4:13 is one of the more obscure quotations in the Pauline corpus. The quotation (and the application that follows in vv. 13–

---

1. The quotations in 2 Cor 6:16–18 are not included in this count, since they appear (along with the whole of 2 Cor 6:14–7:1) to be a later interpolation. Second Corinthians 10:17 is listed with a question mark because though not marked as a quotation in the letter, it repeats a verse that Paul cited in his earlier letter (1 Cor 1:31) and might therefore have been recognized as a quotation by some in the audience. Second Corinthians 4:6 is included because Paul marks it as a quotation ("God who said . . ."), even though it is only a loose rendition of Gen 1:3.

2. The extended comparison of his own ministry with that of Moses in 2 Cor 3:6–18 occupies a fairly important place in Paul's argument, but the passage contains no explicit quotations, so it lies outside the scope of the present study. Its rhetorical effects could, however, be analyzed in the same manner as an explicit quotation because Paul clearly assumes that the Corinthians are familiar with the story. See the excursus at the end of the present chapter.

3. This, of course, assumes that chapters 10–13 are an integral part of 2 Corinthians and not a remnant of the "painful letter" that Paul wrote prior to 2 Corinthians (cf. 2:3–9, 7:8–12). The dating of these chapters is not crucial to the present argument, since there is ample evidence elsewhere in the book that Paul was worried about the Corinthians' attitude toward him.

15) plays a relatively minor role in a lengthy chain of arguments by which Paul seeks to defend his ministry against some of the questions that had been raised by the Corinthians (2:14–6:10). The function of the quotation is difficult to characterize. It does not serve as a "proof" for a specific argument; in fact, its link to the preceding verses is so loose that the audience would likely have been puzzled by its appearance. The interpretive comments that frame the verse imply that Paul viewed the quotation (or wanted the Corinthians to view it) as a biblical warrant for his own ministry of preaching Christ despite all manner of troubles and opposition (cf. 4:1, 8–11). The quotation consists of only three words in the Greek (ἐπίστευσα, διὸ ἐλάλησα), but Paul makes the most of every syllable. Just as the psalmist "believed" and therefore "spoke," says Paul, "so also we [i.e., Paul, using the editorial 'we'] believe and therefore keep on speaking" the message about Jesus' resurrection and the future resurrection of those who follow him (v. 14).[4] The shift from the aorist tense (in the quotation) to the present tense (in Paul's interpretation) is significant: he continues to have faith and to preach about Christ despite the troubles enumerated in vv. 8–11. Thus, in the end, the quotation does function somewhat like a "proof," since it serves to justify Paul's ministry, as do the other arguments in this portion of the letter.

So how might the Corinthians have responded to this quotation? Before we attempt to answer this question, we should recall that the method employed in this study assumes that the three model audiences (1) accept and respect the authority of the Jewish Scriptures; (2) take seriously Paul's claims to apostolic authority over his churches; (3) agree with Paul's ideas, or are at least willing to give them a fair hearing; and (4) are able to follow the main lines of Paul's arguments in his letters. In the case of 2 Corinthians, the actual audience may have included individuals who were so hostile to Paul that they were unwilling to accept any of his interpretations of Scripture. Thus, we need to be reminded once again that the "reactions" posited here refer only to audience members who approximated the

---

4. As many commentators have noted, Paul's introductory comment, "having the same spirit of faith," constitutes an implicit claim that his experience of "faith" parallels that of the psalmist. See the discussions by C. K. Barrett, *A Commentary on the Second Epistle to the Corinthians* (New York: Harper & Row, 1973); Victor Paul Furnish, *II Corinthians* (New York: Doubleday, 1984), 257-58; Jan Lambrecht, *Second Corinthians* (Collegeville, Minn.: Liturgical Press, 1999), 74; Philip E. Hughes, *Paul's Second Epistle to the Corinthians* (Grand Rapids: Eerdmans, 1962), 146.

assumptions of the model, not to those who rejected Paul's authority and/or arguments.

1. The "informed audience" would have most likely been taken aback by Paul's handling of this passage. Though he follows the wording of the original passage precisely, the sense in which he uses the verse is so far removed from the original context as to raise questions about Paul's reliability as an interpreter. In the standard "LXX" text, the verse that Paul quotes is the first verse in a new psalm (Ps 115:1) rather than the midpoint as in the Hebrew (Ps 116:10). But the issue remains the same: what the psalmist "spoke" was not "good news" as in Paul's case, but rather a word of complaint (or despair?) for which he was "humbled" by God.[5] The tone of complaint continues into the next verse, so Paul could not possibly have misunderstood the sense of the verse. The problem remains even if we presume that the informed audience could have recognized a link between the sufferings of Paul described in 2 Cor 4:8–12 and those of the psalmist.[6] Most likely, Paul simply ran across a set of words that sounded like a good "motto" for his ministry and then copied them down (or memorized them) for later use without regard for their original context.[7] Once they were placed into a new argumentative context, the words took on the meaning that Paul gave them.[8] This reappropriation of the language of the psalm would have been invisible to an audience unfamiliar with the original passage. But to an informed audience, the discrepancy between the original sense of the words and the way Paul used them in his argument would have been jarring. In a context

---

5. In the Hebrew text, the second line reports what the author said in his time of trouble ("I am greatly afflicted"); in the Greek text, the quotation is replaced by a statement of what transpired after the "speaking" ("and I was greatly humbled"). In both cases the words spoken by the psalmist are cast in a negative light.

6. Several commentators have noted the references to sufferings in both passages and suggested that Paul may have had the parallel in mind. See Philip E. Hughes, *Paul's Second Epistle to the Corinthians* (NICNT; Grand Rapids: Eerdmans, 1962), 146–47; Margaret Thrall, *A Critical and Exegetical Commentary on the Second Epistle to the Corinthians* (2 vols.; ICC; Edinburgh: T. & T. Clark, 1994–2000), 1.340–41.

7. As C. K. Barrett rightly observes, "Paul pays no heed to the context, but picks out the two significant words" (*Second Epistle*, 143).

8. This again recalls Meir Sternberg's comments about the dominant force that the context-of-quotation exerts over the meaning of a quotation (see chapter 2, notes 24–27). Though he focuses on Paul rather than the readers, Jan Lambrecht offers a similar observation: "Since in the psalm the 'speaking out' addresses God it is rather unlikely that Paul, who changes that speaking into preaching to people, intends to refer to the broader context of that psalm" (*Second Corinthians*, 74; cf. Barrett, *Second Epistle*, 143). For an argument to the contrary, see Frances Young and David F. Ford, *Meaning and Truth in 2 Corinthians* (BFT; Grand Rapids: Eerdmans, 1987), 63–69. (cf. Hughes, *Second Corinthians*, 146-47).

in which Paul's motives were already under a cloud, this kind of observation could have given ammunition to those who argued that Paul could not be trusted.

2. For the "competent audience," both the meaning of the quotation and its role in Paul's argument would have been fairly self-evident. The meaning could be determined from the framing comments: Paul declares that he has "the same spirit of faith" as someone in the Scriptures (i.e., the psalmist), which in turn leads him to "speak" as did the psalmist. From the verses preceding the quotation, the competent audience could have deduced that Paul's use of the words "faith" and "believe" in v. 13 was simply another way of describing the way he perseveres in his ministry despite obstacles.[9] From the ensuing verses they could have figured out that the "speaking" in v. 13 most likely referred to Paul's ministry of preaching about Jesus and the future resurrection. With the help of these interpretive cues, they could have seen that Paul was implicitly claiming that the example of the psalmist served as a model for his own behavior. Why Paul chose to use this particular example would have remained unclear, but the competent audience might have concluded that Paul's ability to apply a verse such as this to himself helped to validate his ministry.

3. The reaction of the "minimal audience" would have been the same as that of the competent audience. Since Paul's handling of the quotation presupposes no familiarity with the original text, their ignorance of the Jewish Scriptures would not have affected their ability to understand what Paul wanted to communicate. Paul does, of course, require the audience to deduce how the quotation fits into his broader argument, but his explanatory comments are clear enough that anyone who could follow his language could figure out what he meant by the verse. In this case it would have been those who knew the original text, not those who were ignorant of Scripture, who experienced the greater difficulty with Paul's quotation.

2 Corinthians 6:2

The quotation from Isa 49:8 in 2 Cor 6:2 appears near the end of the lengthy defense of Paul's ministry that occupies 2 Cor 2:14–6:10. Within this broader context the quotation serves as the final note of an argument that

9. This is likely even if the audience failed to understand the somewhat tortured imagery of vv. 11–12 that immediately preceded the quotation, since the idea runs throughout the passage.

began in 5:11. Throughout the passage Paul insists that he cannot be overly concerned about what the Corinthians think of him, since his ministry is motivated by higher concerns: to please God (5:9); to avoid the coming divine judgment (5:11); to share God's love with others (5:14); and above all to reconcile people to God (5:18–20). The argument is complex, however, as is the attitude that Paul adopts toward the Corinthians. Toward the beginning of the passage he appeals implicitly to the bond that unites him with the Corinthians as he commends himself to the judgment of their consciences (5:11), encourages them to take pride in his ministry (5:12), and tells them that he speaks in this way "for you" (5:13). But by the end of the argument he is depicting himself as God's ambassador to the Corinthians (5:20), one who "works together with" God (6:1), imploring them on God's behalf to "be reconciled to God" (5:20) and to take advantage of the present "day of salvation" (6:2) so as not to "receive the grace of God in vain" (6:1).[10] The quotation from Isa 49:8 stands at the pinnacle of this argument, accompanied by a simple *pesher*-type interpretation that stresses the urgent need for a response ("now . . . now . . ."). How might the Corinthians have understood the role of this quotation in Paul's developing argument?

1. For the "informed audience," Paul's quotation would have resounded with echoes of the great themes of Isa 49. There, the prophet is told by God that he has been called not only to restore Israel, but also to proclaim God's message of salvation to the nations (i.e., the "Gentiles"). With their close firsthand knowledge of Paul, the informed audience could hardly avoid hearing in Paul's quotation of Isa 49:8 an implicit justification for his own ministry of preaching salvation to the Gentiles.[11] The fact that Paul could

10. Alternately, one might argue that Paul has slipped into an evangelistic preaching mode here and lost sight of his audience, or that the appeal in 5:20–6:2 was meant to exemplify what he preaches as "Christ's ambassador" (5:20a) (i.e., the verses should be placed in quotation marks). But there is nothing in the passage that would suggest to the Corinthians that Paul's words were addressed to anyone but them. As Jan Lambrecht rightly observes, "The appeal to reconcile now when addressed to people who are already Christians could appear somewhat strange. The expression must be interpreted as a renewal and deepening of the reconciliation already received. However, the tense of the verb, an aorist, does not allow the sense of a repeated or continuing 'receiving.' Paul thus calls for a decision. He warns his readers; they should decide—to put it negatively—not to fail to live as 'reconciled' people. The tensions and difficulties in the Corinthian community necessitate this call" (*Second Corinthians,* 108 [cf. 100]). Francis T. Fallon takes this one step further: "To accept the true gospel means also to accept Paul as the authentic apostle of it, as an ambassador of Christ through whom God speaks, and thus to be reconciled to him" (*2 Corinthians* [NTM 11; Wilmington, Del.: Michael Glazier, 1980], 52).

11. The truly informed audience might also have heard echoes of Isa 49:7 in the catalogue of sufferings that Paul recounts in the succeeding verses (6:4–10). The LXX (diverging from the

adduce a biblical warrant for his ministry would certainly have helped to validate the other arguments that he has offered to the Corinthians in defense of his conduct.

On closer inspection, however, the informed audience might have found reason to question the validity of Paul's appeal to Isa 49:8. From Paul's interpretive comments in vv. 1–2 it seems clear that he meant for the Corinthians to take the second-person singular "you" in the quotation as a reference to themselves: the time of God's salvation is present for them (individually and collectively) if only they will accept Paul's call for "reconciliation" (5:20). The verse functions not as a "proof," but as an exemplary text, as Paul's *pesher* interpretation makes clear. The parallelism is fairly straightforward: just as God heard and helped his people of Israel in their "day of salvation," so also God is available "now" to do the same thing for the Corinthians if they are willing to respond. But such a reading of the passage would have raised problems for the informed audience, since the "you" in Isa 49:8 refers not to the people but to the prophet, as the ensuing verses make clear.[12] If one reads the "you" in 2 Cor 6:2 similarly as a reference to Paul rather than the Corinthians, the point of the verse is rendered obscure, if not lost altogether.[13] Thus in the end the informed audience would have found themselves both enlightened and confused when they referred back to the original context of Paul's quotation.

2. The "competent audience" would have missed the echoes of the prophet's call to ministry in Isa 49, but they would also have avoided the questions that might have been raised by Paul's application of Isa 49:8 to the Corinthians. Fortunately, no familiarity with the original text is required to understand Paul's rhetorical use of the verse, since he has included enough information in the surrounding verses to indicate how he meant the quotation to be understood. Both the introductory formula and the interpretive

---

MT at this point) could be rendered as follows: "Sanctify the one who counts his life as worthless, the one who is loathed by the Gentiles. . . ." Ross Wagner has argued rather convincingly that Paul saw in some of the prophecies of Isaiah a prefigure of his own apostolic ministry—see *Heralds*, 170–80, 356–59.

12. In both the LXX and the MT, the "you" is given a commission to restore the covenant and bring the people of Israel back to their land. Jan Lambrecht concurs: "Paul does not seem to take into account the rich theological ideas present in the Isaianic context, 49:1–13. . . . Without modifying the Septuagint text—but with the help of his own vv. 1 and 2b—he thoroughly interprets the citation within the new context" (*Second Corinthians*, 108, 111).

13. Perhaps one might understand Paul to be saying, "Just as God heard and helped me in my day of salvation, so he will help you if you respond today." But such a reading would be forced and unnatural in light of the clear reference to the Corinthians as "you" in 6:1.

comment identify the speaker in the passage as God, and the reference to the Corinthians as "you" in 6:1 would have inclined them toward identifying with the "you" in the quotation. Thus, when Paul appends the words, "Now is the time of God's favor, now is the day of salvation," members of the competent audience would have drawn the obvious conclusion that they were the ones to whom God's favor and salvation were "now" being offered. Paul's earlier injunction to the Corinthians to "be reconciled to God" (5:20) would have pointed them in the same direction. The fact that Paul could ground his appeal in the authoritative Scriptures would have given his words added weight. Unfortunately, Paul never states clearly what they should do to take advantage of this offer, so the quotation may have been less effective in reality than he wished. But the competent audience would have had no problem grasping the meaning of the quotation as it relates to Paul's argument.

3. Members of the "minimal audience" would have understood the quotation in the same manner as the competent audience, since Paul gives enough interpretive cues in the passage to indicate how he meant the verse to be understood.[14] If they had never encountered a text from the biblical prophets, the language of the verse (especially the past tenses of the verbs) might have sounded a bit odd to them, but this would not have seriously hindered their understanding. As long as they were familiar with Christian terms such as "God's favor" and "day of salvation," the interpretive framework in which Paul embeds the verse would have given them all the data they needed to grasp Paul's point.

In the end, no amount of familiarity with Isa 49 would have prepared the Corinthians to grasp the meaning that Paul has attached to his quotation from Isa 49:8 without his framing comments. By the time they encountered 2 Cor 6:2, Paul's argument (if they accepted it) would have conditioned them to hear the voice of God not only in the text of Scripture, but also in the interpretive comments that surround it, since they were spoken by "God's ambassador" (5:20).[15] Thus, Paul's insistence that he "works together

---

14. Since the hypothetical members of the "competent audience" were familiar with at least some verses of Scripture, they might have figured out that the passage came from somewhere in the prophetic books. This in turn might have given them a slightly deeper comprehension of the quotation than was available to the "minimal audience." But this limited knowledge would not have made a significant difference in the way they understood the verse.

15. James Scott also recognizes this dimension of Paul's quotation in 2 Cor. 6:2, though his observation focuses on Paul rather then the audience: "Evidently, Paul understands the authoritative interpretation of Scripture as one way in which God makes his appeal through the apostle (cf. 5:20)" (*2 Corinthians* [Peabody, Mass.: Hendrickson, 1998], 143).

with" God (6:1) is not a passing comment, but a vital part of his argumentation. The fact that he is "God's co-worker" (cf. 1 Cor 3:9) lends prima facie credence to his interpretations of Scripture, while the fact that he can quote Scripture in favor of his argument adds a note of authority to his argument. The argument is clearly circular, but for those who accepted the authority of the Jewish Scriptures, it could be compelling nonetheless.

2 Corinthians 9:9

In 2 Cor 8–9 Paul faces the delicate problem of encouraging the recalcitrant Corinthians to make good on their promised financial support for the offering that he intends to take to Jerusalem. By this point in the letter he apparently hoped that his arguments and explanations would have defused the Corinthians' negative feelings toward him.[16] However, he could not be certain how they would respond to his financial appeal. Paul's comments in 2 Cor 8–9 suggest that he was worried that the Corinthians would renege on their commitment to contribute to his offering (8:6, 11, 9:3–5), but there is no evidence that they had actually done so. He also seems to think that his reputation is at stake: if he were to arrive in Corinth and find the Corinthians unwilling to contribute, he would be shamed in front of the delegates from the other churches (8:24, 9:4–5). To avoid this potentially embarrassing situation, Paul decided to write to the Corinthians and encourage them to live up to their promise despite their mixed feelings toward him. This "provoking rhetorical urgency" required a carefully crafted rhetorical response.[17]

The delicacy of the situation that Paul faced is reflected in the diversity of the arguments that he marshals in support of his request. Arguments from authority are virtually absent from these chapters; on the contrary, he explicitly denies that he is "commanding" or "compelling" them to do anything (8:8, 9:7). What he seeks instead is a willful, generous action on their part (8:7, 11–12, 9:2, 9:5–7, 9:11). But he obviously did not trust their intentions; if he had, a simple reminder would have sufficed (cf. 1 Cor 16:1–3).

---

16. This, of course, assumes that chapters 1–7 and chapters 8–9 were written in their present order as part of a single letter—a point that some commentators dispute. The argument that follows here is not dependent on this assumption.

17. For a history of the discussion of whether 2 Cor 8 and 9 constitute one letter or two, see Hans Dieter Betz, *2 Corinthians 8 and 9: A Commentary on Two Administrative Letters of the Apostle Paul* (Hermeneia; Philadelphia: Fortress, 1985), 3–36. Betz's arguments in favor of two separate letters are effectively answered by Jan Lambrecht (*Second Corinthians,* 148–51).

Instead, he strung together a series of arguments designed to motivate and/or shame the Corinthians into supporting the offering.[18]

The quotation from Ps 112:9 (111:9 LXX) in 2 Cor 9:9 appears near the end of this series of arguments.[19] The passage in which it is embedded (9:6–15) seeks to motivate the Corinthians by highlighting the material and spiritual benefits that they will receive from participating in the offering. Like many good orators, Paul has saved his most powerful argument for last.[20] At the heart of Paul's argument in this passage is the unstated assumption that by giving to the church in Jerusalem, the Corinthians are really giving to God, who will reward them accordingly.[21] Again and again Paul brings the Corinthians face to face with God: God "loves a cheerful giver" (9:7); God "is able to make all grace abound" to them (9:8a); God will insure that they have all their needs met (9:8b, 10a) and even make them rich (9:11); God will enlarge their good deeds (9:8) and their righteousness (9:10); God will receive praise and thanksgiving when others see what they have done (9:11–13).[22] The message is clear: if the Corinthians want God's blessings, they must give to the offering. The power of the appeal is undeniable. The Corinthians could tolerate Paul's displeasure with their actions, and some of them might even have relished the thought of embarrassing him in front of

---

18. Among the arguments that Paul brings forward to encourage or embarrass the Corinthians into supporting the offering are (1) the example of the poor but generous Macedonians (8:1–7); (2) the flattering reference to the Corinthians "excelling" in all things (8:7); (3) the statement about "testing the sincerity" of their love (8:8); (4) the appeal to the example of Jesus (8:9); (5) the reminder of their earlier enthusiasm and commitment to the offering (8:10–12); (6) the description of the delegates who will accompany him to receive their gift (8:16–24); (7) the report of his bragging about the Corinthians' generosity (9:1–2); (8) the warning about possible embarrassment when he comes (9:3–4); (9) the promise of divine blessing (9:6–11); and (10) the acclaim that they will receive from others (9:12–15). Arguments that aim to counter potential objections include Paul's reference to the Corinthians' relative wealth (8:13–14) and his statement about the care with which he is handling the funds (8:19–21).

19. The only other explicit quotation in the passage appears in 2 Cor 8:15, where Paul quotes Exod 16:18 in an effort to undercut potential objections from the Corinthians about their own lack of resources.

20. For a rhetorical analysis of this passage using the ancient canons of rhetoric, see Betz, *2 Corinthians 8 and 9*, 100–128.

21. So also Betz, *2 Corinthians 8 and 9*, 109. Prior to this passage the name "God" appears only three times in Paul's argument concerning the collection, and always in a passing reference. In this closing argument, on the other hand, God appears eleven times (seven times by name, twice under the masculine pronoun, and twice in implicit references [9:6, 11]) and plays a key role in the argument.

22. As C. K. Barrett observes, "There is no hint here, as there is in Rom. xv. 30f., of the possibility of an unfavorable reception; Paul would not mention it here because it would discourage Corinthian generosity" (*Second Epistle*, 241).

his companions. But who would want to take the chance of losing God's favor? The argument from (divine) authority, though implicit, would have been impossible to miss.

So how does the biblical quotation fit into this argument? Why quote from Scripture at all here? The introductory formula ("as it is written") seems to indicate that the verse somehow reinforces the assertion in v. 8, but the link is by no means clear. Once again Paul has left it to his addressees to deduce how the quotation fits into his argument. But the verse leaves many questions unanswered. Who is the subject of the sentence? Is it "God" (the nearest antecedent in v. 8) or the "cheerful giver" of v. 7? Who are "the poor"? Are they the needy Christians in Jerusalem or the Corinthians who give from their resources to help them? The answers are by no means obvious, and different audiences would have answered these questions in different ways.

1. The "informed audience" would have found a clear answer to these questions in Ps 112 (Ps 111 LXX). The entire psalm is an encomium to the person "who fears the Lord, who delights greatly in his commandments" (v. 1). One of the many commendable features of such a person is that he or she gives freely to the poor (v. 9). Numerous blessings are pronounced on the person who acts in such a "righteous" manner, among them wealth and riches (v. 3), stability and security (vv. 6–8), admiration and honor (vv. 6, 9), and overflowing righteousness (vv. 3, 9). The ideas and language are so similar to those employed by Paul in 2 Cor 9:6–15 that the informed audience could hardly have missed the parallel: the first colon of the quotation refers to the person who contributes to Paul's offering for the Jerusalem church ("the poor"), and the second colon associates this action with other "good deeds" that elicit a divine blessing.[23] This implicit concatenation of the Jerusalem offering with a scriptural depiction of the deeds of a righteous person would have served as a powerful incentive for the informed audience to contribute to Paul's collection, since it casts Paul's request as a test of their relationship with God, and their response as an indication of whether they are truly "righteous."[24] If they understood the verse in this way, members of the informed audience would have had little choice but to lay aside their quarrels with Paul and fulfill their obligation to God.

---

23. The relevance of the second colon to Paul's argument is not immediately clear. This reading assumes that the audience would refer back to v. 8 for guidance, equating "righteousness" with "abounding in every good deed" and recalling the divine blessing that Paul promised in the same verse.

24. If they truly had "ears to hear," they might also have noticed the negative judgment that the psalmist pronounces on those who reject this course of action ("the sinner," v. 10).

2. For the "competent audience," the meaning of the quotation would have been found in its relation to Paul's developing argument, since there is nothing in 2 Cor 9:9 that mandates a reference to the original context. There are at least two ways in which the quotation could be understood, depending on what one takes to be the antecedent of the pronoun "he" at the beginning of the quotation. One approach would relate the pronoun to the "cheerful giver" of v. 7, yielding an interpretation similar to that posited for the informed audience. But the likelihood that the competent audience would take the verse in this way is low, since it requires a sudden shift in subject from the preceding verse.[25] A more natural reading would supply "God" as the subject of the verse, in line with the verses before and after the quotation.[26] The term "the poor" could then be taken in one of two ways: it could refer to the needy Christians in Jerusalem, who presumably would view Paul's collection as a gift from God, or to the Corinthians themselves, whom Paul depicts as being concerned about not having enough for themselves if they gave to the collection (8:12–13; cf. 8:2–3, 9:8, 11). The second reading is more natural in light of the preceding verse (v. 8), where Paul insists that God will graciously provide for the Corinthians' needs if they give generously to his collection.[27] The second colon of the quotation would then be understood as an implicit assurance that God could be trusted to do as Paul promised.[28] Although this reading is quite different from that of the informed audience, the rhetorical impact is the same: the Corinthians are brought face to face with the God of the Scriptures, who promises to take care of them if they give generously to Paul's fundraising project.

---

25. Members of the informed audience could overlook the awkward change of subject since they took their cues from the original context, not from Paul's grammar.

26. Hans Dieter Betz (*2 Corinthians 8 and 9,* 111–14) seems to regard this interpretation as self-evident; only in passing does he mention that the verbal parallel with v. 10 supports taking God as the subject. C. K. Barrett (*Second Epistle,* 238) does the same thing in reverse, assuming without argument that the verse refers to the individual who cares for the poor—that is, the Corinthians who contribute to Paul's collection. Victor Paul Furnish looks at four different ways of understanding the reference, but none of them includes God as the subject of the action (*II Corinthians,* 448–49). Jan Lambrecht comes to the same conclusion as Barrett and Furnish, but he admits that applying the verse to a human reads "somewhat strangely after v. 8" (*Second Corinthians,* 147).

27. This interpretation of the quotation finds confirmation in vv. 10–11, where Paul again speaks of God providing for the needs of the Corinthians if they give generously to his project.

28. The referent for the pronoun "his" must be the same as for "he" in the first line—that is, God. In this context the "enduring righteousness" of God becomes virtually a synonym for God's faithfulness or trustworthiness.

3. As with most other passages that require no knowledge of the original context, the "minimal audience" would have arrived at the same understanding of the quotation in 2 Cor 9:9 as the competent audience.[29] Both groups would have inferred the meaning of the quotation from the interpretive cues embedded in Paul's developing argument, not from the original context. In both cases the quotation would have been viewed as a biblical warrant for Paul's otherwise bald assertion in v. 8 that God would take care of the Corinthians if they contribute to his collection. Without this warrant, even a well-disposed audience might have questioned the validity of Paul's interpretation of the divine will, since it seems to run counter to much of human experience.[30] The fact that Paul could quote from the authoritative Scriptures in support of his argument would have served to mitigate some of these concerns, since to question Paul could now be viewed as questioning the very words of God.

This last point might help us to understand why Paul decided to include a biblical quotation at this point in his argument. The idea that God would bless the Corinthians for their generosity is the linchpin of Paul's final argument regarding the collection. For the argument to be effective, Paul needed to make sure that the Corinthians would not simply dismiss his assurances because of their distrust of Paul himself. The easiest way to do this was to show that his statements were grounded in the authoritative Jewish Scriptures. In the process, he recast the issue as a test of the Corinthians' relationship with God, effectively sidestepping his own troubled relationship with the Corinthians. The question was no longer "Will you give to my collection?" but rather "Do you want to make God happy and receive God's promised blessings?" By appealing simultaneously to the Corinthians' religious sentiments and their self-interest, Paul framed his appeal in a manner that few could resist.

29. Once again we should recall that the only difference between the "minimal audience" and the "competent audience" is their knowledge of the Jewish Scriptures. Both audiences are assumed to be capable of following Paul's nonbiblical argumentation. This cannot be assumed for the people of Paul's actual first-century audiences, many of whom probably found his arguments difficult and obscure. This would have further reduced their ability to understand his quotations.

30. Ernest Best in particular underlines the objections that could be raised against Paul's argument at this point (*Second Corinthians* [Interpretation; Louisville: John Knox, 1987], 85–86). As Best observes, "Paul is so desperately concerned about Jerusalem that he does not think it wrong to bring into play the self-interest of the Corinthians," even when he knows that his statement is subject to exceptions (86).

Excursus: Paul's Rhetorical Use of Scripture in 2 Corinthians 3:6–18

Though the present study focuses on Paul's rhetorical use of quotations, this is not the only way in which Paul uses Scripture to advance his arguments. In some cases he frames his argument around a passage of Scripture without quoting a specific verse. An excellent example of this practice can be seen in 2 Cor 3:6–18.

From the earliest verses of 2 Corinthians, Paul is engaged in a running defense of his actions and his ministry. In chapters 1–2 he defends himself against specific charges that some of the Corinthians had raised against him. In chapter 3 he turns to a more general defense of his ministry.

In 2 Cor 3:6–18 Paul makes the audacious claim that his own "ministry of the Spirit" is greater than the ministry of Moses, which he labels a "ministry of death" (3:7) and a "ministry of condemnation" (3:9). In the course of justifying this claim, he refers several times to the story of the (second) giving of the Torah to Moses at Mount Sinai (Exod 34), which he assumes his audience will know. At the heart of his argument is a series of contrasts that he sets up between his own ministry and that of Moses.[31] How might his Corinthian audience have responded to these biblical arguments?

1. The "informed audience" would have been familiar with the details of the exodus story and could therefore fill in the narrative framework behind Paul's repeated references to Exod 34. This background knowledge would have helped them to make sense of the few details that Paul mentions explicitly (i.e., "depicts") in the course of his exposition: the letters engraved on stone tablets (v. 7); the glorious presence of God accompanying the event (v. 7); the Israelites being unable to look on Moses' face (v. 7); Moses wearing a veil to hide his face from the Israelites (v. 12); and the glory "fading"

---

31. Paul's argument in this passage has received extensive attention in recent years. In addition to the commentaries, see Carol K. Stockhausen, *Moses' Veil and the Glory of the New Covenant: The Exegetical Substructure of II Cor. 3,1–4,6* (AnBib 116; Rome: Pontificio Instituto Biblico, 1989); Scott J. Hafemann, *Paul, Moses and the History of Israel: The Letter/Spirit Contrast and the Argument from Scripture in 2 Corinthians 3* (WUNT 81; Tübingen: Mohr-Siebeck, 1995); Linda J. Belleville, "Tradition or Creation? Paul's Use of the Exodus Tradition in 2 Corinthians 3.7–18," in *Paul and the Scriptures of Israel* (ed. Craig A. Evans and James A. Sanders; JSNTSup 83; Sheffield: Sheffield Academic Press, 1993), 165–86; Margaret E. Thrall, "Conversion to the Lord: The Interpretation of Exodus 34 in II Cor. 3:14b–18," in *Paolo, Ministro del Nuovo Testamento (2 Co 2,14–4,6)* (ed. Lorenzo de Lorenzi; Benedictina 9; Rome: Benedictina Editrice, 1987), 197–232; Richard B. Hays, *Echoes of Scripture in the Letters of Paul* (New Haven: Yale University Press, 1989), 122–53.

(or more properly, "being annulled") from Moses' face (vv. 7, 11, 13).[32] This last reference would have come as something of a surprise to the informed audience; there is nothing about it in Exod 34, yet it plays a key role in Paul's argument.[33] The same is true for Paul's references to Moses' ministry bringing "death" (v. 7) and "condemnation" (v. 9). Paul never explains what he means by this language, so the audience would have had to figure out his point for themselves. From what he says in his other letters, we might guess that the Corinthians had heard Paul use similar language to describe the Torah when he was with them and that they could figure out what he meant on this basis. But we should be careful about this assumption, since only once in his letter to the Corinthians does Paul refer to the Torah in negative terms (1 Cor 15:56). Most of his references are neutral or positive (1 Cor 9:8–9, 20, 14:21, 34).

If indeed they had no prior teaching to help them at this point, the natural response of the informed audience would have been to look back to Exod 34 for guidance. Here they would have found one explicit reference to divine punishment (34:7) and several other places where punishment was

---

32. Though Paul does not identify it as a quotation, the informed audience would undoubtedly have noticed the free rendering of Exod 34:34 in v. 16 and recognized that this near-quotation represented the climax of Paul's interpretation of Exod 34. As Richard Hays (*Echoes*, 146–47) observes, Paul has removed all context-specific language from the verse and reshaped its wording to coincide with his application in order to enhance the impression that Scripture (and thus God) stands behind his argument.

33. Although Paul may have been alluding to a nonbiblical tradition that he had taught the Corinthians during an earlier visit, his language in v. 13 sounds more informative than allusive. The source of Paul's idea that the glory of God's presence used to fade from Moses' face (used here to justify the veil) is unknown. C. K. Barrett notes that it does not coincide with any known Jewish tradition, and suggests that it may have been formulated by Paul himself for polemical purposes against a Judaizing threat (*Second Epistle*, 114–15). Philip Hughes, on the other hand, argues that commentators have misunderstood Paul's rather awkward Greek at this point: it is not the "fading" of the glory that Moses sought to hide from the Israelites, but the glory itself (*Second Epistle*, 108–10). Hughes fails to explain how this comports with the Greek, since τοῦ καταργουμένου most likely refers to the "glory" on Moses' face (cf. v. 7). Margaret Thrall is on firmer ground when she suggests that the participle in v. 13 could be taken as referring to the eventual abolition (or fulfillment) of the Mosaic covenant, but such a reading would not work as well for the feminine participle in v. 7, as she rightly observes (*Second Epistle*, 1.243–44, 256–61). Victor Paul Furnish reads v. 13 in the same manner as Thrall, but extends the idea to v. 7 as well. He translates both participles as "was being annulled," which he glosses as "doomed to extinction" (*II Corinthians*, 203, 207; cf. 227, 232). In support of this interpretation, Furnish observes that Paul consistently uses the verb καταργέω "with reference to something in some way invalidated or replaced" (203). Richard Hays (*Echoes*, 131–40) makes a similar argument. However we understand Paul's intention here, the point remains that the informed audience would have found none of this in the biblical text.

implicitly threatened (34:3, 9, 14, 16). From this they might have concluded that Paul was referring to the threat of divine punishment that hung over those who failed to abide by the Torah, a threat that presumably did not apply to them as "law-free" Gentiles. In this case knowledge of Scripture might have helped the informed audience to figure out what Paul was saying in a place where his language was rather obscure. But this same knowledge might have raised questions about Paul's argument when they saw how much weight he was placing on a point (the "fading" of the glory on Moses' face) that did not appear in the original passage.[34]

2. Members of the "competent audience" would have known little more than the broad outlines of the story in Exod 34, including the few details that Paul mentions in his argument. Whether they would have recognized the problem with Paul's reference to the "fading glory" of Moses' face depends on how well they knew the original story.[35] Those who knew the passage fairly well would have had the same questions as the informed audience; those who did not would simply have accepted Paul's statements as a reliable summary of the story. Unlike the informed audience, if they had no prior instruction about the Torah bringing "death" and "condemnation," members of the competent audience would have had to guess what Paul meant by these expressions, unless they knew the original text well enough to reflect on its content. But this would not have kept them from grasping the essential point of the passage, since Paul has framed the comparisons between himself and Moses clearly enough (and with enough repetition) to communicate his message to a person who knew very little about the Exod 34 narrative.

3. Members of the "minimal audience" would have found it more difficult to grasp what Paul was saying in this passage. If they had never heard of Moses, they might have wondered why Paul was so concerned to demonstrate the superiority of his ministry to that of Moses (perhaps another

---

34. This, of course, assumes that they would be willing to entertain Paul's candid assertion that his own ministry was superior to that of Moses—a position that might have been difficult for people steeped in the Jewish Scriptures to accept.

35. A number of commentators have argued that Paul constructed his argument in this passage to counter the teachings of other Christian leaders who had appealed to the story of Moses in support of their own ministries. If this were the case (a view rejected by many other commentators), we would have to presume that the competent audience knew more about the story of the giving of the Torah than Paul indicates here. But this would not substantially alter the argument spelled out above, since we know already from 1 Cor 10:1–14 that the competent audience was familiar with a number of individual episodes from the Exodus story (see chapter 5).

Christian preacher?). If, on the other hand, they knew that Moses was the revered lawgiver of the Jews (a piece of knowledge shared by many non-Jews in antiquity), they could have figured out that Paul was denigrating Judaism in favor his own message, even if they were unable to follow the intricacies of his biblical argumentation.[36] This same knowledge would have helped the minimal audience to follow the main lines of Paul's argument in v. 12–18, where the references to Exod 34 are mostly submerged. Even if they had never heard about Moses' veil, Paul's brief summary of the episode (v. 13) is sufficient to enable them to follow his analogy with the reading of Torah in the synagogue (vv. 14–15). Though there is still much here that would have escaped them, even the minimal audience could have learned enough from Paul's explicit statements to enable them to understand the essential point of his argument.

Thus, we see in 2 Cor 3:6–18 the same range of potential responses to Paul's rhetorical use of Scripture that we encountered in his explicit quotations. Since Paul had previously spent a long time with the Corinthians, we can presume that he had some idea of the biblical passages and stories that they knew. When, therefore, he presupposes that his audience knows a particular biblical story (as in 2 Cor 3:6–14), we can presume that there were individuals in the church who possessed that level of knowledge. But we should not conclude from this that they had read the written text for themselves, nor should we assume that everyone in the intended audience was familiar with the story. We must allow for diverse levels of understanding (and rhetorical effectiveness) even in cases where Paul had spent a significant amount of time in person with his churches.

---

36. The implicit anti-Judaism of the passage might actually have enhanced Paul's standing among those in the Corinthian church who shared the common anti-Jewish sentiments of the day. For more on pagan knowledge of Judaism and the prevalence of anti-Judaism in antiquity, see Jan Sevenster, *The Roots of Pagan Anti-Semitism in the Ancient World* (NovTSup 41; Leiden: Brill, 1975); Louis H. Feldman, *Jew and Gentile in the Ancient World* (Princeton, N.J.: Princeton University Press, 1993); J. L. Daniel, "Anti-Semitism in the Hellenistic-Roman Period," *JBL* 98 (1979): 45–65.

CHAPTER 7
Galatians

Paul and the Galatians

Like the Corinthian correspondence, Paul's letter to the Galatians is addressed to a group of Christians whom he had taught in person (Gal 4:13–15). Unlike the Corinthians, we have no way of knowing how much time Paul had spent with them or how well he knew them. Two problems contribute to this uncertainty.

The first problem is our ignorance concerning the identity of the people whom Paul calls "the churches of Galatia." If the term refers to the people of Lystra, Derbe, and Iconium, as the "south Galatia" theory holds—and if the story of Paul's travels in the book of Acts can be trusted—we can conclude that Paul knew the Galatians fairly well, since he had spent significant time with them during several visits to the region. But if the "north Galatia" theory is correct, we have no record of Paul's interaction with these churches apart from his own brief reference to his initial visit during a time of illness (Gal 4:13–15; cf. 3:1).

The second problem stems from the letter itself. At several points Paul refers to the troubles in Galatia in a manner that suggests that his knowledge of the situation there is limited. Apparently, he had received a report (by messenger? by letter?) about certain people who were "disturbing" (1:7; 5:12) the churches of Galatia by proclaiming what he calls a "different gospel" (1:6). Yet in the few verses in which he refers directly to the opposing party, his language is surprisingly obscure: "whoever he is," (5:9); "certain people," (1:7); "who bewitched you?" (3:1); "who hindered you?" (5:7).[1] A similar

1. J. Louis Martyn, who "mirror-reads" virtually every line of Galatians in an effort to formulate a description of those whom he calls "the Teachers," believes that Paul knew not only the content of their message but even their names, or at least the epithets that they used for themselves. For a summary of what Martyn believes he can infer about the "Teachers," see *Galatians: A New Translation With Introduction and Commentary* [New York: Doubleday, 1997], 117–26. In Martyn's view, the phrases that suggest Paul lacked knowledge about the "Teachers" must be taken as expressions of disdain (ibid., 121), since a literal reading would be fatal to his reconstruction of the situation in Galatia. Especially troublesome is the throwaway line in Gal 5:10

sketchiness is apparent in his references to the teachings of his opponents.[2] Paul is aware that the Galatians were being told that they needed to undergo circumcision (5:3, 6:12), observe certain calendrical rites (4:10; presumably, the Jewish festival seasons), and obey at least some of the requirements of the Jewish Torah (3:2, 5, 4:21, 5:4).[3] But if he knew more than this, he does not say so. All that can be said with certainty about Paul's knowledge of his "opponents" is that they had been and still were active in the churches of Galatia and that they were seeking to persuade Gentile Christians to undergo circumcision and observe at least some of the Jewish laws, presumably to insure their full participation in the Abrahamic covenant (though this is never stated).[4]

Why should this matter for a study of Paul's quotations? Because it alerts us to the possibility that Paul may have known significantly less about the Galatians' familiarity with the Jewish Scripture than he did with the Corinthians. If in fact he had spent little time with them, or if it had been a long time since his last visit, he could not have known precisely which passages of Scripture (if any) the Galatians had discussed in his absence.[5] The

("whoever he may be"), which Martyn completely ignores in his comments on Gal 5:2-12 (ibid., 467–79).

2. The term "opponents" is used throughout this chapter as a form of shorthand reflecting Paul's opinion of those who are seeking to influence the beliefs and conduct of the Galatians (hence the inclusion of quotation marks around the term). It should not be taken as implying any historical judgment about the intentions of those whom Paul sees as "troublemakers." In fact, there are reasons to suspect that they may have been teaching the Galatians without reference to any earlier teachings by Paul; see the evidence cited by Mark Nanos in *The Irony of Galatians* (Minneapolis: Fortress, 2002), 119–27. Fortunately, the present study is not affected by the ongoing debates over the nature of Paul's "opponents" except to the extent that they include assumptions about the biblical literacy of the Galatian Christians and their likely response to Paul's biblical argumentation.

3. Apparently, the opposing party did not expect the Galatians to obey all of the laws of Torah, since Paul can accuse them of not obeying the Torah themselves (6:13).

4. For more on Paul's limited familiarity with the situation in Galatia, see Christopher D. Stanley, "'Under a Curse': A Fresh Reading of Gal 3.10–14," *NTS* 36 (1990): 488–90. For a critique of "mirror-reading" approaches that claim to be able to uncover substantially more information from the letter about the identity and teachings of Paul's "opponents," see J. M. G. Barclay, "Mirror-Reading a Polemical Letter: Galatians as a Test Case," *JSNT* 31 (1987): 73–93; Ben C. Witherington III, *Grace in Galatia: A Commentary on Paul's Letter to the Galatians* (Grand Rapids: Eerdmans, 1998), 21–25; Nanos, *Irony*, 110–83. For a broader discussion of the problems associated with using "mirror-reading" to reconstruct Paul's "opponents," see Jerry L. Sumney, *Identifying Paul's Opponents: The Question of Method in 2 Corinthians* (JSNTSup 40; Sheffield: Sheffield Academic Press, 1990).

5. Of course, it is possible that the person(s) who informed Paul about the problems in Galatia might have given him information about the biblical arguments that the "trouble-

simple fact that Paul refers to a biblical passage in his letter cannot be taken as evidence that the audience knew the original text. Even when Paul frames his argument around a particular story (e.g., Abraham in Gal 3:6–18, 4:21–31), we should not presume that everyone in the congregation understood the reference, or that they would have understood it in the same way.[6] Clearly, the actual audience of Paul's quotations was more diverse than the "implied audience." As with Paul's letter to the Romans, we need to be alert to the possibility that this letter presents us with little more than his best guess as to what the Galatians knew about the Jewish Scriptures.

Biblical Literacy in Galatia

Most commentators would agree that quotations from the Jewish Scriptures play a key role in the argumentation of Paul's letter to the Galatians. From there, it is only a short step to the conclusion that the Galatians possessed a fairly broad knowledge of the Jewish Scriptures. But how accurate is this assessment? One of the little-noticed facts about Paul's rhetoric in Galatians is the limited extent of his arguments from Scripture. The letter contains, at most, ten explicit quotations in 146 verses of text, and all but one of these can be found in two fairly brief passages: Gal 3:6–16 and 4:27–30.[7] Each of these passages is in turn embedded in a broader biblical argument that contains additional references to biblical stories or characters (3:6–29, 4:21–31). Apart from these two passages (and a brief reference in 5:14), Paul conducts his argument with no clear reference to the Jewish Scriptures. Of course, these two passages play an important role in Paul's efforts to undercut his opponents' views, but so do passages such as 2:15–21, 3:1–5, 19–25, and 4:1–11, none of which contain quotations or references to

---

makers" were using in their efforts to convince the Galatians of the correctness of their views. This could explain, for example, why Paul speaks repeatedly about Abraham in his letters (3:6–9, 3:16–19, 3:29, 4:21–31). On the other hand, Paul's letters show clearly that he felt free to construct a biblical response to a situation where there was no hint of a prior biblical argument. Often a careful study of Paul's rhetoric will reveal that he is playing on the authority of the Jewish Scriptures without reference to any prior biblical argumentation by his "opponents."

6. J. Louis Martyn has recently underscored the divergent reactions to Paul's argumentation that might have taken place in the Galatian churches, as those who remained loyal to Paul argued in Paul's favor and those who were convinced by his "opponents" (including the "opponents" themselves) sought to counter Paul's arguments (*Galatians,* 28–29, 41–42).

7. Of the ten verses that are generally regarded as explicit quotations, three (3:6, 11, 12) are not clearly marked and might therefore have been unrecognizable to the audience. The only quotation that appears outside 3:6–16 and 4:27–30 is one from Lev 19:18 in 5:14.

Scripture. In other words, arguments from Scripture are only one of many rhetorical tools that Paul deploys in his effort to dissuade the Galatians from their present course of action.

So what can we learn from Paul's letter about the Galatians' familiarity with the Jewish Scriptures? Even if we assume that Paul is correct whenever he expects the Galatians to recognize a particular story or passage of Scripture, the results are still fairly meager.[8]

1. From the many unexplained references to Abraham and his family, we can deduce that Paul expected the Galatians to know at least the broad outlines of two story-cycles from the Abraham narrative: (a) the stories of the inauguration (Gen 12:1–3) and confirmation (Gen 13:14–17, 15:1–6) of God's covenant with Abraham, including God's promises to Abraham (Gal 3:8, 16, 18, 29), Abraham's faith in these promises (3:6, 9), and God's proclamation of Abraham's righteousness (3:6);[9] and (b) the stories of Sarah and Hagar and their respective sons, including Isaac's birth as the fulfillment of a divine promise (Gal 4:23, 28), Hagar's son "persecuting" Isaac (4:29), and Hagar and her son being cast out into the desert (4:30). Whether they were familiar with any other elements of the Abraham narrative cannot be determined from Paul's letter.[10]

---

8. As with the other letters, the approach used here yields only a minimal assessment of what the Galatians may have known about the Jewish Scriptures. But without further evidence, we have no basis for assuming that they knew more.

9. It probably is no accident that Paul never refers to the final (and most expansive) covenant narrative in Gen 17:1–27, since God in that passage commands Abraham to circumcise not only his descendants but also any foreigners (= "Gentiles") who are attached to his household (17:12–13; cf. 17:27). Martyn (*Galatians*, 339–40) sees a reference to Gen 17:8 in Gal 3:16, but the source of this brief allusion cannot be determined with confidence. Even if Martyn is correct, it is clear that Paul ignores key elements of the story in Gen 17 (see Martyn, *Galatians*, 302, 229, 448).

10. It is worth noting that a fairly coherent narrative can be constructed from the passages that Paul presumes the Galatians know, without the addition of further stories from Genesis. This is precisely the kind of skeletal summary that could be passed on in oral form and recalled later by an illiterate congregation. Of course, it is always possible that the Galatians had learned more from Paul's "opponents" in his absence, but their knowledge of Scripture would still have been limited (except for the few literate members) to what they could absorb and retain through oral instruction. A different view is offered by Hans Dieter Betz, who argues from the rhetorically and theologically sophisticated nature of Paul's argumentation that Paul "founded the Galatian churches not among the poor and the uneducated but among the Hellenized and Romanized city population" (*Galatians*, 2). But whether Paul's letter to the Galatians is any more "rhetorically and theologically sophisticated" than Paul's other letters is open to debate, and Betz offers no other evidence to support his position. In the end, his view is yet another example of the kind of "mirror-reading" that has led to so many different interpretations of Paul's letter to the Galatians in contemporary scholarship.

2. Paul also assumes that the Galatians know at least the rudiments of the story of the giving of Torah on Mount Sinai (Gal 3:17, 19, 4:25), including the fact that it occurred later than the time of Abraham (3:17) and that it was given through Moses (3:19).[11] No other details are mentioned.

Apart from these three story-cycles, Paul assumes no specific knowledge of the Jewish Scriptures on the part of the Galatians.[12] The remainder of his biblical arguments can be understood without reference to the original context of Scripture.[13] While we might suspect that the Galatians had learned something about the biblical laws pertaining to circumcision and holy days from Paul's opponents, we have no clear evidence to that effect. Both practices were well known to non-Jews as identity markers for Jews and Jewish converts, leaving no pressing need for Paul's opponents to justify either practice from Scripture. The meager biblical knowledge that Paul assumes in this letter is consistent with his description of the Galatians as former worshipers of pagan gods (4:8).[14]

---

11. Paul also refers to the activity of angels in the giving of the Torah (3:19), a detail not mentioned in the canonical text. Apparently, he expected the Galatians to understand this reference, since he offers no explanation. Here we see further evidence that the Galatians may have received their knowledge via oral tradition (including nonbiblical traditions), not through first-hand study of the written text.

12. J. Louis Martyn's "mirror-reading" approach to Paul's argumentation yields a substantially higher degree of biblical knowledge on the part of Paul's audience, since he presumes that Gal 3:6–20 and Gal 4:21–31 represent a point-by-point refutation of the biblical arguments used by Paul's "opponents." (See his comments on the two passages in *Galatians.*) If this is true, then Paul's attempt to counter their arguments must be judged a dismal failure, since anyone capable of consulting the original context of the verses that Paul quotes in Gal 3:10–14 could have seen that some of the passages are actually more consistent with the position of Paul's "opponents." (See the comments on Gal 3:6–14 below.) Martyn recognizes that the opposing party "will almost certainly meet scripture with scripture" in their effort to counter Paul's letter to the Galatians (*Galatians,* 315), but he seems to overlook the possibility that Paul's "opponents" could have undermined his arguments by highlighting his tendentious handling of their favorite verses of Scripture. Any decent rhetorician would have anticipated and defused this strategy if there were a realistic chance that it might be exercised. The fact that Paul offers no justification for his blatant "misreadings" of Scripture in Gal 3:6–14 and Gal 4:21–31 (as described below) suggests that he did not expect the Galatians to be able to check and approve the validity of his interpretations of Scripture.

13. See the discussions of individual verses below.

14. Ann Jervis makes a similar observation: "The Galatians were Gentiles and so would not have known much about the Jewish writings unless they had been taught them in the context of their new religion" (*Galatians* [Peabody, Mass.: Hendrickson, 1999], 122). On the other hand, Mark Nanos argues that the Galatians were by this time associated with the local Jewish synagogues as "righteous Gentiles," in which case they would have been exposed regularly to the reading and interpretation of the Jewish Scriptures in their original context—without Christian interpretive glosses (*Irony,* 6–9). If this is true—and there are many reasons to think that it is

The Rhetoric of Quotations in Galatians

Although there is much that we will never know about the situation in Galatia, we can learn a great deal from Paul's letter about the way he perceived the situation. In Paul's view, the Galatian churches were on the verge of abandoning the truth for a "different gospel" (1:6) and thus losing God's grace (5:4). In language that borders on the hyperbolic, Paul voices his exasperation with the Galatians (3:1, 4:20) and even questions his ability to reverse the inroads made by his "opponents" among them (4:11). Paul is aware that there are some who have resisted the teachings of the "Judaizers" (5:2, 6:12), but he senses that they, too, are teetering on the brink (4:17). The ongoing conflicts over this issue (5:15) have led to a state of "confusion" in the Galatian churches (1:7, 5:10). In Paul's mind, this "provoking rhetorical urgency" cried out for a forceful argument that would dissuade the Galatians from their current path.

In the first two chapters of this letter Paul employs a variety of rhetorical techniques to induce the Galatians to reconsider the teachings of his "opponents." Instead of attacking his "opponents" directly, however, he pursues a strategy of indirection, citing relevant data from his personal history and leaving it to the Galatians to figure out how these stories relate to their situation.[15] Along the way, he portrays himself as a divinely commissioned authority figure who deserves the Galatians' respect and obedience. By stressing the divine origins of his ministry and message (1:1, 11–12, 15–16) and showing disdain for anyone who would oppose him (2:6–14, 3:1–5),

---

not—the Galatians' knowledge of Scripture would have been greater than was suggested above. But we still have no way of knowing which passages of Scripture they would have recognized apart from the ones that Paul presumes in his letters, and it strains credulity to think that Paul was receiving regular reports about the verses that the Galatians were hearing in the synagogue. Nanos implies that the Galatians could have asked their literate Jewish friends about verses in Paul's letters that they failed to understand, but Paul's attitude toward his "opponents" shows clearly that he did not intend for the Galatians to consult with members of the local Jewish community about the meaning of his quotations. Thus, even if Nanos's thesis is correct, it is hard to see how his position would make any real difference for the questions under consideration here.

15. Though they may have wondered how the autobiographical data in chapter 1 related to their situation, they could not have missed the many implicit parallels in chapter 2: the reference to the noncircumcision of Titus (2:3); the depiction of the circumcision party as "false brothers" with evil motives (2:4); the Jerusalem leaders' endorsement of Paul's "law-free" gospel (2:6–9); the attack on Peter for obeying Torah at the expense of the "truth of the gospel" (and the unity of the church) (2:11–14); and the wording of Paul's "speech" to Peter (2:15–21; note ἰουδαΐζειν in v. 14 and the repeated contrast between "justification by faith in Christ" and "works of Torah" in vv. 15–21).

Paul seeks to shame and/or frighten the Galatians into turning away from the teaching of his "opponents" and returning to his earlier instruction.[16] Nowhere in these chapters does he discuss the merits of the opposing argument; the simple fact that it runs counter to his teaching of "justification by faith" (1:8–9, 2:15–17) is reason enough to reject it.

So why does Paul suddenly begin to offer reasoned arguments from Scripture, including explicit quotations, in 3:6? The simplest answer is that he knew that he would eventually have to offer a counterargument to the ideas put forward by his "opponents." Apparently, Paul had concluded that a stark assertion of his own authority (i.e., a direct command) would be ineffective, since many of the Galatians were solidly aligned with the circumcision party.[17] But he could trust that the Galatians would recognize the authority of the Jewish Scriptures, especially since the practices that they were being encouraged to adopt were rooted in the sacred texts of Judaism. Thus, Paul concluded that the most effective way to shake them up was to argue directly from the same authoritative Scriptures.[18]

Unlike the Corinthian correspondence, where he quotes from Scripture only sporadically to lend weight to a particular point in his argument (1 Cor 10:1–12 is the sole exception), Paul's letter to the Galatians includes three rather dense blocks of biblical argumentation (Gal 3:6–14, 3:15–25, 4:21–31) that play a key role in the development of his position.[19] To understand the

---

16. J. Louis Martyn suggest that the liturgical context in which Paul's letter would have been read to the Galatians might have had a similar effect. Referring specifically to the doxology in Gal 1:3–5, Martyn observes, "Paul brings the Galatians climactically into God's presence by inviting them to utter the word, 'Amen!' It is a signal of his conviction that his own words can and will become the active word of God, because God will be present as the letter is read to the Galatians in their services of worship. . . . With him, they stand in God's presence. Fundamentally, then, they are dealing with God, not merely Paul" (*Galatians*, 106).

17. The fact that Paul chose to begin his letter with a lengthy *apologia* for his ministry (1:1; 1:10–2:10) shows that he felt that his authority was under attack in Galatia, whether or not his "opponents" had actually challenged his relationship with the Galatian churches. See the discussion in Martyn, *Galatians*, 92–95.

18. This explanation avoids the usual expedient of "mirror-reading" Paul's argument to deduce a specific biblical argument that had been raised by his opponents. Paul may have known that his "opponents" were arguing from the Abraham story (see note 5) and crafted Gal 3:6–20 in response, but his biblical argumentation can be understood quite well without this assumption.

19. The frequency of explicit quotations is also significantly greater in Galatians than in the Corinthian correspondence. If we count only quotations that are clearly recognizable (see note 7), Paul quotes from Scripture (on average) once every twenty-one verses in Galatians (seven quotations in 146 verses), as compared with every thirty-six verses in 1 Corinthians (twelve quotations in 437 verses) and every forty-two verses in 2 Corinthians (six quotations in 256 verses).

way quotations function in Galatians, we must examine the entire argument of these passages rather than focusing on individual quotations as in Corinthians. A review of the first and last of these passages will give us a good idea of the way Paul uses biblical quotations in Galatians.[20]

Galatians 3:6–14

At first glance, it might appear that Paul has abandoned his earlier strategy of intimidating the Galatians with his God-given authority once he launches into the biblical arguments of Gal 3:6–29. But the first two chapters have not been forgotten; the voice that speaks in Gal 3 is still that of an authoritative apostle who received his message "by revelation from Jesus Christ" (1:12). Whether he intended it or not, Paul's forceful attempt to portray his mission and message as divinely ordained in Gal 1–2 served to pave the way for his presentation of himself as an authoritative interpreter of Scripture in Gal 3. Perhaps he was afraid that his "opponents" had so undermined his credibility with the Galatians that they would no longer accept his arguments from Scripture, or perhaps he knew that the Galatians did not possess the necessary expertise to judge between his biblical argumentation and that of his "opponents." Whatever his reasons, Paul's depiction of himself as the only reliable interpreter of God's will would have exercised a powerful influence on the Galatians' reactions to his arguments from Scripture, despite the more reasonable tone that he adopts from 3:6 onward.

The argument that Paul constructs in Gal 3:6–14 cannot be understood apart from the highly charged rhetoric of vv. 1–5, since the καθώς that introduces v. 6 and the final reference to the coming of the Spirit in v. 14 both tie vv. 6–14 back to v. 5.[21] When read together, both passages ultimately make

---

20. The biblical argument in Gal 3:15–29 is interesting for what it tells us about the level of biblical literacy that Paul presumed on the part of the Galatians, but it sheds little light on the rhetoric of explicit quotations in Galatians, since it contains only one brief excerpt (from Gen 13:15?) in 3:16.

21. The καθώς at the beginning of v. 6 is not an introduction to a quotation (καθώς is always followed by γέγραπται when used with quotations in Paul's letters). Instead, it introduces Abraham as an example for the Galatians to follow—that is, as one who exhibited the kind of "hearing of faith" that Paul implicitly recommends to the Galatians at the end of v. 5. Hans Dieter Betz (*Galatians*, 140) is one of the few commentators who take καθώς in v. 6 as an abbreviated form of Paul's standard introductory formula, καθώς γέγραπται, despite the fact that such an abbreviation appears nowhere else in Paul's letters. Ben Witherington has observed that the use of the positive or negative examples is a common feature of deliberative rhetoric (*Grace*, 216–17). See also Margaret Mitchell, *Paul and the Rhetoric of Reconciliation* (Louisville: Westminster John Knox, 1991), 42, and Kjell Arne Morland, *The Rhetoric of Curse in Galatians: Paul Confronts Another Gospel* (Atlanta: Scholars, 1995), 195–96.

the same point: the present activity of the Spirit in the Galatian churches (vv. 2–5; cf. v. 14) is proof that God has accepted them (made them "righteous"; vv. 6, 8) on the basis of their faith in the crucified Jesus (vv. 1–2; cf. vv. 7, 11, 13), so that obedience to the Jewish Torah (as recommended by the "Judaizers") is not only unnecessary but also useless, and possibly even dangerous (vv. 2–4; cf. vv. 10–12).[22] Yet the rhetorical strategies that Paul employs in the two passages could hardly be more different. In vv. 1–5 Paul casts himself as a "wise" father figure castigating his "foolish" Galatian children. Through a series of belittling epithets and rhetorical questions Paul challenges the Galatians to recognize the inconsistency between their current course of conduct and their prior experience. The confrontational tone of his language is clearly meant to shock the Galatians into questioning the teachings of the "Judaizers" and listening more attentively to the argument that he is about to present. In v. 6, however, Paul shifts from the persona of a chiding father to that of a skilled rabbi, an authoritative interpreter of Scripture who is capable of opening up to the Galatians the true meaning of the sacred text. Coinciding with the change of rhetorical persona, Paul shifts into a thoroughly rational mode of argument, appealing to the Galatians' minds rather than their emotions.

Yet the appeal to authority and to the Galatians' emotions has not been abandoned, only sublimated. By backing up virtually every one of his statements in vv. 6–14 with a quotation from the authoritative Scriptures, Paul seeks to show that the God of Israel stands firmly behind his position. In the process he issues an implicit challenge to the Galatians: "Will you hear and obey the words that God speaks to you through the Scriptures?" Whether or not they understood his biblical argumentation, the Galatians had to respect Paul's ability to craft such a complex argument from Scripture. Paul probably hoped that this reminder of his skill as an interpreter of the authoritative Scriptures would make the Galatians more willing to listen to his nonbiblical arguments in the rest of the letter.

How might the Galatians have responded to the complex biblical argumentation of Gal 3:6–14?

1. Members of the "informed audience," those hypothetical addressees who knew the original context of all of Paul's quotations, would have found Paul's biblical argumentation in Gal 3:6–14 both challenging and confusing.

---

22. For more on the unity of Paul's argument in Gal 3:1–14, see Stanley, "'Under a Curse,'" 492–95.

On the one hand, Paul's comments about Abraham in vv. 6–9 would have carried substantial weight with an audience that knew the Abraham narrative and shared Paul's Christian presuppositions.[23] Both of the quotations that Paul adduces (from Gen 15:6 in v. 6 and Gen 12:3 in v. 8) are central to the stories in which they appear, and both would have evoked memories of God's promises to Abraham (and through him to Israel) as well as Abraham's faithful response. In both cases the sense that Paul derives from the verse is consistent with the original context, though a careful observer would have observed that Paul has adapted the wording of the second quotation in order to make it better fit his argument.[24] Paul's incorporation of key words from the quotation into his interpretive comments ("believe" in v. 7, "justify" [cognate to "righteousness"] in v. 8, "blessed" in v. 9) would have strengthened the impression that his interpretation of the Abraham story was true to the text. From these verses the informed audience could have drawn the conclusion that the Scriptures (and the God of Israel) supported Paul's contention that faith alone was the basis for God's acceptance of the Gentiles. The relevance of the story to their own situation—left unstated by Paul—would have been apparent.

The same cannot be said for the four quotations in vv. 10–14, where the informed audience would have found ample reason to question the legitimacy of Paul's biblical argumentation. In the case of v. 10 (quoting Deut 27:26), the chief problem is the apparent conflict between the wording of the quotation and Paul's statement in the first part of the verse. Whereas the quotation pronounces a curse on the person who fails to abide by the requirements of Torah, Paul applies the curse to those who seek to *comply*

---

23. Hans Dieter Betz rightly observes that "[Paul's] contention that Gen 15:6 proves his understanding of 'justification by faith' as opposed to 'by works of the Torah' can convince only those who share his theological and methodological presuppositions" (*Galatians*, 141).

24. The replacement of πᾶσαι αἱ φυλαί with πάντα τὰ ἔθνη and the related omission of τῆς γῆς has no basis in the textual tradition of Gen 12:3. Though it is possible that Paul accidentally conflated the wording with the very similar language of Gen 18:18, it seems more likely that he substituted a close synonym to make the application of the verse to "Gentiles" (τὰ ἔθνη) more apparent. See the discussion in Christopher D. Stanley, *Paul and the Language of Scripture: Citation Technique in the Pauline Epistles and Contemporary Literature* (SNTSMS 74; Cambridge: Cambridge University Press, 1992), 237. Ann Jervis suggests that the change in wording might have been motivated by the impossibility of finding a passage earlier than Gen 15:6 when God had announced his intention to "justify the Gentiles by faith" (*Galatians*, 85, 88). But this is probably to read too much into the prefixes προ- on the two verbs in v. 8, since Paul does not ground his argument on the chronology of the Abraham narrative in Gal 3:6–9 as he does in Rom 4.

with the laws of Torah (ὅσοι . . . ἐξ ἔργων νόμου εἰσίν).[25] Paul's interpretation runs counter to the clear sense of Deut 27, which announces God's curse on individuals who violate various provisions of the Torah.[26] Taken in context, Deut 27:26 not only fails to support Paul's assertion in v. 10a, but could even be read as supporting the views of his "opponents" who insist that the Galatians should obey the Jewish Torah. This observation might have caused the informed audience to question the validity of Paul's handling of Scripture.[27]

A similar situation prevails in the case of the quotation in v. 11. When the informed audience turned to examine the original context of Hab 2:4, they would have found reason to be concerned about Paul's use of this passage. First they would have noticed that Paul had adapted the wording of the verse and altered its meaning in the process. By dropping the word μου from

---

25. Martin Luther saw the problem clearly: "Now these two sentences of Paul and Moses seem clean contrary. Paul saith: Whoever shall do the works of the law, is accursed. Moses saith: Whoever shall not do the works of the law is accursed. How shall the two sayings be reconciled together? Or else (which is more) how shall the one be proved by the other?" (*A Commentary on St. Paul's Epistle to the Galatians* [ed. Philip S. Watson; London: Clarke, 1953], 244). For an extended discussion of the problem and recent attempts to resolve it, see Stanley, "'Under a Curse,'" 481–86.

26. The contradiction could be avoided if the informed audience understood the "curse" in v. 10a as a threat rather than a present reality (see Stanley, "'Under a Curse,'" 497–501). But since most modern interpreters have overlooked this solution to the problem, we should not assume that it would have been evident to the Galatians. N. T. Wright believes that the continuity between Gal 3:10 and the context of Deut 27 becomes clear if one lays aside the individualistic interpretation common among scholars in favor of a widely held Jewish interpretation that sees Israel as a whole standing under God's "curse" due to the "publicly observable fact" that the Jews were still under foreign rule and thus living under the curse of "exile" pronounced in Deut 27–30 (*The Climax of the Covenant* [Minneapolis: Fortress, 1991], 140–41). Even if Wright is correct, it is hard to see how Paul could have expected his predominately Gentile Galatian audience to know and supply such an inner-Jewish idea in order to make sense of his arguments. Wright's interpretation has been criticized on both historical and exegetical grounds—see Seyoon Kim, *Paul and the New Perspective* (Grand Rapids: Eerdmans, 2002), 136–41, and the sources cited there.

27. Additional questions might have arisen from the fact that Paul quotes Deut 27:26 in a form that differs substantially from the standard LXX text. Though some of the deviations can probably be traced to the use of a different *Vorlage,* others are clearly Pauline adaptations, such as the insertion of the words "everything that is written in the book of the law" (cf. Deut 28:58) in place of "all the words of this law" in the middle of the verse. The cumulative effect of the variations and adaptations is to "dehistoricize" the text by eliminating all references to the covenant ceremony in Deuteronomy. But the language of the resultant quotation is not inconsistent with the original context of Deut 27, so the informed audience would not have found significant reason to be concerned. For a fuller discussion of how the wording of the quotation relates to Deut 27:26, see Stanley, *Paul,* 238–43.

the quotation and ignoring the first clause of the verse,[28] Paul has changed a statement about God's faithfulness into a proleptic reference to Christian faith in God. A close reading of Hab 2 might have raised questions about the legitimacy of such an interpretation. More importantly, a careful reader would have recognized that Hab 2:4 does not actually support the assertion Paul makes in v. 11a, since there is nothing in the verse or its original context that reflects negatively on the Torah. All that Paul's "opponents" needed to do was to point out, as they had probably already done in the past, that obedience to Torah was the best and only way for them to express their faith toward God.

As with the first two quotations, a careful reading of Lev 18:5 might have convinced the informed audience that the quotations in v. 12 supported the views of Paul's opponents rather than his own. Anyone who knew the context of Lev 18:5 could see that the verse actually insists on the importance of obeying God's laws as the pathway to "life." As in v. 11, the counterargument is fairly obvious: there is nothing in Lev 18 that pits "faith" against obedience to Torah; instead, God's people should obey the Torah as an expression of their faith in God. Despite his intentions, Paul's clumsy handling of Scripture in vv. 10–12 might actually have persuaded the informed audience to embrace the views of his "opponents."

The final quotation in this passage, the excerpt from Deut 21:23 in v. 13, would have added yet more fuel to the informed audience's growing suspicion of Paul's arguments from the Jewish Scriptures. A glance at the original passage would have shown that the verse Paul quotes actually refers to the ancient practice of hanging the dead body of a convicted criminal on a tree for public display, not the redeeming death of a crucified Messiah. Only by

28. Richard Hays's suggestion that Paul read as a reference to Jesus as the "righteous one" par excellence ignores the fact that such an interpretation would have been totally invisible to the audience in this context (*The Faith of Jesus Christ: An Investigation of the Narrative Substructure of Galatians 3:1–4:11* [Chico, Calif.: Scholars, 1983], 134–38, 177–81). The LXX of Hab 2:4 diverges sharply from the MT: "If he [?] should draw back, my soul will not be pleased with him; the righteous person will live by my faith(fulness)." The subject of the initial verb is not clear from the context, since there is no masculine antecedent, as would be required by the pronoun αὐτῷ at the end of the clause. The sense of the verse will not allow a continuation of the implied subject κύριος from v. 3b (cf. αὐτόν). The only evident way to make sense of the verse is to supply an indefinite human subject ("he"), as suggested in the translation above, though this leaves the verse disconnected from the broader context. Perhaps it was this very disconnection from the context that led Paul to disregard the context entirely when he adopted this verse as a motto for his gospel (cf. Rom 1:17). For more on the text of Hab 2:4, see Stanley, *Paul,* 83–84.

extracting the verse from its original context and revising its wording could Paul claim that it refers to the death of Jesus.[29] For the informed audience, the tendentiousness of such a reading would have been obvious.

Thus we see that an audience that was familiar with the original context of Paul's quotations in Gal 3:10–13 would have been led inexorably toward a point of view that was the opposite of what Paul intended. When they compared Paul's interpretive comments with the original context, the informed audience would have discovered that the passages not only failed to support Paul's arguments, but could in fact be read as upholding the views of his "opponents." The fact that Paul seems to have manipulated the wording of the text in several instances to create a closer fit with his argument might have added to their suspicions. Either Paul was a poor rhetor who failed to anticipate obvious objections to his arguments or he did not expect the Galatians to check his references in this manner.[30]

2. The experience of the "competent audience" would have been quite different. The only knowledge of Scripture that Paul clearly presupposes in Gal 3:6–14 is the story of Abraham, to which he refers repeatedly in vv. 6–9. As we observed earlier, Paul's handling of the biblical text in these verses is generally consistent with the original context. Like the "informed audience," the competent audience would have found in vv. 6–9 a convincing biblical argument in favor of Paul's position.[31]

When they came to the dense biblical argumentation of Gal 3:10–13, on the other hand, the competent audience would have turned to Paul's interpretive comments to guide them to the meaning of the quotations. Since no familiarity with the original context is assumed in any of these verses, the

---

29. Two revisions are obviously Pauline: the omission of ὑπὸ θεοῦ (clearly an embarrassment when applied to Jesus' death), and the replacement of κεκατηραμένος with ἐπικατάρατος from 3:10 (to eliminate the verbal implication that the "curse" was pronounced before the victim was "hung on a tree"). For more on the way Paul handles the wording of the quotation, see Stanley, *Paul,* 245–48.

30. Many commentators have suggested that the argument of Gal 3:10–13 was designed to offer a counter-reading of several verses that were already in use by Paul's "opponents." As Ann Jervis observes, "It is easy to see how at least three of the four Scriptural quotations (Deut 27:26; Lev 18:5; Deut 21:23) could have been put to good use by the rival evangelists" (*Galatians,* 90; cf. Martyn, *Galatians,* 307–21). If this was Paul's intention, his effort must be judged a failure, since the response posited here for the "informed audience" shows that it would have been fairly easy for Paul's "opponents" to refute his argument. For more on this point, see note 12.

31. Members of the competent audience might not have recognized v. 6 as a quotation since the marking is ambiguous (see note 21), but this would not have seriously interfered with their understanding of the passage.

competent audience would have been unaware of most of the problems that confronted the informed audience in this passage. The only verse that would have raised any serious problems for the competent audience is v. 10, where the conflict between Paul's statement and the verse that he cites to support it is clear even to a person with no knowledge of the original passage. The competent audience would have found this verse just as confusing as the informed audience, but since the competent audience could not consult the original passage for clarification, they would have had no choice but to leave the tension unresolved.

The quotation from Hab 2:4 in v. 11b would probably have passed unnoticed by the competent audience, since the statement is not explicitly marked as a quotation. The second part of the verse is clearly meant to ground the assertion in the first part, but Paul gives no sign that v. 11b is a quotation from Scripture rather than his own apostolic pronouncement on the subject. The relation of v. 11 to v. 10 is also unclear. But since members of the competent audience would have been unaware of the link with Hab 2:4, they would have had to base their understanding of the verses on the language of Paul's argument. Perhaps they would have taken the δέ at the beginning of v. 11 as an adversative and read the verse as a clarifying limitation of the quotation in v. 10.[32] However they understood the link between the verses, the competent audience would have found nothing here to hinder them from proceeding open-mindedly to the next stage of Paul's argument.[33]

Although the quotation from Lev 18:5 in v. 12b is also unmarked, the fact that the second clause stands in syntactical tension with the first part of

32. The fact that the quotation in v. 10 affirms the importance of "continuing in" and "doing" the deeds of Torah would have caused it to stand out as a foreign body in the argument of Galatians, leading the audience to expect some form of resolution in the following verse. The first part of v. 11 ("that no one is justified before God by Torah") appears, on the surface, to be a blatant contradiction of the quotation in v. 10. But since audiences normally assume that an author's argument is coherent unless proven otherwise, a handy solution would be to take v. 11a as a restriction of v. 10b, implying that no one actually lives up to the requirement of Deut 27:26. Of course, Paul does not actually say this, and many scholars have argued that the thought is foreign to Paul (see the discussion in Stanley, "'Under a Curse,'" 482–83). But it is easy to see how the language of the passage might lead one to that (possibly incorrect) conclusion. The problem arises from the terseness of Paul's language in vv. 10–12, which requires the addressees to figure out the inner links of the argument for themselves. This includes both the transitions between the verses and the relation between Paul's assertions and the verses he cites to support them.

33. The informed audience, by contrast, might have become more suspicious of Paul's argument by this point because of concern over the way he handled the quotations in vv. 10–11.

the verse (i.e., the pronouns have no antecedents) would have signified to the competent audience that a quotation was being offered. The meaning of the quotation might have seemed a bit obscure at first because of the dangling pronouns, but in the wake of v. 10 the competent audience could probably have figured out that "them" referred to the precepts of Torah and that v. 12a aimed to contrast the "doing" of Torah with the way of (Christian) faith. Since the competent audience would have known nothing about Paul's questionable application of the verse from Leviticus, their attention would have centered on the validity of Paul's assertion in the first part of the verse, not the quotation. The simple fact that Paul could quote a verse of Scripture to ground his point would have helped to commend his argument to members of the competent audience, but even they might have wondered whether the quotation actually supported his assertion in the first part of the verse.[34]

As with the other verses in this section, the competent audience would have had no reason to question Paul's handling of the quotation from Deut 21:23. Their only cue to the meaning of the verse would have come from Paul's framing comments, where the verse is applied to the death of Jesus on the cross. The logic of the primary argument would still have been obscure, since Paul simply assumes that the audience can figure out how Jesus being "cursed" on the cross could have redeemed others from the "curse of the law" (cf. v. 10).[35] But the meaning of the quotation and its application to Jesus would have been clear as long as the audience accepted the implied equation of crucifixion with being "hanged on a tree." Here again the fact that Paul could appeal to the authoritative Scriptures in support of his argument would have commended his position to the competent audience.

On the whole, then, the competent audience would have found little reason for concern and ample reason to be persuaded by Paul's arguments from Scripture in Gal 3:6–14. Of course, the argument that the quotations are

34. Like the informed audience, the competent audience might have asked whether the emphasis on "doing" the Torah necessarily implied a lack of concern for "faith." The inconsistency between "faith" and "doing" is simply taken for granted in these verses, not argued. In fact, Paul's opponents could have used the quotations in vv. 11–12 to argue for the opposite position (the priority of Torah over faith) by reversing the quotations and changing a few of the words in the framing verses. Doing so yields this (non-Pauline) argument: "It is obvious that no one is justified by God through faith alone, because (Scripture says,) 'The one who does these things will live by them.' But the righteousness that comes through Torah nonetheless requires faith, since (it says), 'The righteous person will live by faith.'"

35. Perhaps Paul had used similar language when he was with them (cf. 3:1), so that he had reason to think that they would be able to grasp his point.

intended to support is by no means clear, and the audience might not have been willing to grant the validity of all of Paul's assertions. But with the possible exception of v. 10, nothing in the biblical quotations would have detracted from the argument, and the fact that Paul could quote Scripture in his favor might have inclined the competent audience to give him the benefit of the doubt in his other arguments.

3. The reaction of the "minimal audience" would have been similar to that of the "competent audience" in this case, so only a few brief comments are needed. Since the quotations in vv. 10–13 do not assume familiarity with the original context of the verses, there is no reason to posit any difference between the two audiences' reactions to these verses. But since the minimal audience represents people with no prior knowledge of the Jewish Scriptures, this group could not have followed the repeated references to Abraham in vv. 6–9. The language of these verses is so allusive that a person who was unfamiliar with the story of Abraham would have found it difficult to make sense of the argument. Lacking knowledge of the original context, the minimal audience could not have known what Abraham had done to earn God's commendation, why his conduct was being held up as an example, what it meant to be called his "children," or why Paul spoke about the nations (or "Gentiles") being "blessed" through him. They could have inferred from Paul's comments that Abraham was a man who had demonstrated great faith in God and that his story offered a model of the way God makes Gentiles "righteous by faith" (v. 8), but the rest of the argument would have escaped them. As long as they acknowledged the authority of Scripture, however, they would have been inclined to respect a person who could construct such a carefully reasoned argument from Scripture. Fortunately for Paul, the argument in vv. 10–13 does not depend on a full understanding of vv. 6–9, so members of the minimal audience would not have been permanently disadvantaged by their inability to follow the prior argument.

Thus we see that the response of Paul's first-century Galatian addressees to his arguments in Gal 3:6–14 would have been heavily conditioned by their familiarity with the biblical text. Those with an extensive knowledge of Scripture would have found Paul's quotations troubling, to say the least, and some of them might have been led by their examination of his quotations to reject Paul's argument in favor of the views of his "opponents." Those with no prior knowledge of Scripture would have been confused by Paul's references to the Abraham story, but they would have found his interpretive comments clear enough to enable them to grasp the main points of the argument. The most positive response would have come from individuals who were familiar with the story of Abraham, where Paul's argument comports fairly well with the original context, but not the other passages that he cites, where the original context seems to undercut (or at least fail to support) Paul's argument. While we must be careful about generalizing from such limited evidence, the reactions proposed here for the three hypothetical audiences suggest that Paul was thinking of an audience that resembled the "competent audience" when he crafted the biblical argumentation of Gal 3:6–14.

Galatians 4:21–31

After a series of ad hominem arguments in Gal 4:8–20, Paul turns again to the authoritative Scriptures for support in 4:21–31. As in 3:6–20, Paul relies on the Torah itself to show those who "want to be under Torah" (v. 21a) that they are in fact following the wrong path.[36] His argument presupposes that the Galatians who had been influenced by the "Judaizers" will respect and accept a cogent argument from the sacred Scriptures of Judaism (v. 21b).[37] This strategy of erecting an argument on the presuppositions of one's opponent was commended as especially effective by the rhetoricians of antiquity.[38]

The argument of 4:21–31 presumes that the audience is familiar with the Genesis narrative about the births of Ishmael and Isaac and the ensuing tensions between their mothers, Hagar and Sarah, including the expulsion of Hagar and Ishmael into the desert (Gen 16:1–18:15, 21:1–21).[39] But the

---

36. It is unclear whether Paul is in fact addressing himself to this group or is using them as a rhetorical foil for his argument.

37. Cf. Witherington, *Grace*, 328: "Here Paul, in order to be persuasive, may be counting on the fact that he knows the Scriptures far better than they do, and that they will respect and perhaps even defer to his expertise on this matter."

38. The tactic would be all the more effective if C. K. Barrett is correct in suggesting that Paul is appropriating and reinterpreting a text (Gen 21:1–10) that had been used by his opponents to refute Paul's law-free Gospel ("The Allegory of Abraham, Sarah, and Hagar in the Argument of Galatians," in *Essays on Paul* [Philadelphia: Westminster, 1982], 154–70); cf. Frank J. Matera, *Galatians* (Sacra Pagina; Collegeville, Minn.: Liturgical Press, 1992), 9, 17, 174–75. But it is just as likely that Paul himself came up with the allegory. J. Louis Martyn reads the passage in the same way as Barrett, but he once again goes too far in presuming that every point in Paul's argument is intended to refute a similar point in the argument of his "opponents" (*Galatians*, 433).

39. This does not mean that Paul expected the Galatians to know all of the details of these stories, nor that they would have had to learn the stories through literary rather than oral channels. The precise content of what he expected them to know is outlined at the beginning of this chapter.

argument contains only one explicit quotation from the Genesis account (Gen 21:10 in v. 30), along with a quotation from a seemingly unrelated passage (Isa 54:1 in v. 26). In both cases the "meaning" of the quotation is heavily shaped by the rhetorical and literary context in which it appears. How might the Galatians have responded to these quotations?

1. Members of the "informed audience" would have known the literary context of all of Paul's references to the Abraham narrative as well as the original context of Isa 54:1. From their knowledge of the Genesis account they could have seen that Paul follows the biblical narrative quite closely, though those who agreed with his "opponents" might have questioned the way he structured his allegory.[40] Nothing in the original passage supports the association of Hagar with Mount Sinai and the earthly city of Jerusalem, nor of Sarah with "the Jerusalem that is above" (vv. 24–26). The appearance of the quotation from Isa 54:1 at this point in the argument might have appeared confusing at first, but a more careful review of both passages could have helped the informed audience to figure out the unstated link that Paul sees between them. Like Isaiah, Paul identifies Jerusalem as the "barren woman" who is now to become "mother" to a great multitude. Paul, however, relates this image not to the return of the exiles from Babylon (as in Isaiah), but to the extension of the Christian mission.[41] Such a "Christianizing" appropriation of the biblical image would have appealed to those who shared Paul's view of the Jewish Scriptures as pointing forward to Christ and the church. But once again Paul's "opponents" could have turned

---

40. We can assume that those who had adopted the "Judaizing" course would have been deeply offended by Paul's association of Mount Sinai and Jerusalem with the "slavery" aspects of the analogy. But the argument in this passage is directed primarily toward those who were wavering between the two sides, not toward those who had already made their decision (note "you who *want* to be under Torah" in v. 21; cf. "those people" in v. 17 vs. "my dear children" in v. 19 and "brothers" in vv. 28 and 31, plus the implied injunction in v. 30 to "throw out" those associated with the way of "slavery"). Clearly, this direct and potentially offensive challenge is a vital part of Paul's rhetorical strategy.

41. Though Paul never identifies the cause of the woman's "rejoicing," the pronoun "our" in v. 26 clearly applies to those who have accepted Paul's (law-free) gospel, so that the abundance of "children" in the quotation appear to refer to the success of Paul's mission (cf. Hays, *Echoes,* 119–20). Richard Hays suggests that Isa 51:1–3 was the mediating link that led Paul to insert Isa 54:1 into his allegory; according to Hayes, these earlier verses from Isaiah provide a "metaphorical linkage of Abraham and Sarah with an eschatologically restored Jerusalem that warrants Paul's use of Isa 54:1" (*Echoes,* 120). But the reference to Isa 51:1–3 is so brief and allusive (Sarah is mentioned only in passing) that it is unlikely that even the informed audience would have recognized the presence of such a link and found it helpful for interpreting Paul's allegory in Gal 4:21–31.

the quotation to their own advantage by saying that the passage spoke instead about the successful eschatological incorporation of Gentiles into a Torah-based faith in Christ under the leadership of the church in Jerusalem.[42] Thus, Paul's use of the verse from Isaiah would have been convincing only to those in the informed audience who shared his presuppositions.

The reaction of the informed audience to the quotation of Gen 21:10 in v. 30 would have mirrored their response to Paul's allegory in vv. 24–26, since vv. 29–30 continue the same analogical mode of reasoning. Paul effectively draws the audience into the argument by forcing them to figure out the meaning and application of the quotation in v. 30,[43] though their conclusions are virtually predetermined by the preceding verses, including Paul's modification of the wording of the quotation.[44] If they accepted the Hagar-Sarah allegory, members of the informed audience would by this point have come to see themselves as "Isaac" (v. 29) and Paul's opponents (those who uphold the ways of Torah) as Ishmael, "the slave woman's son," who "persecuted" (or perhaps "pursued"; cf. 4:17, 5:7) the divinely generated ("Spirit-born") son (those who follow Paul's law-free gospel). From this standpoint, the meaning of the quotation would have been fairly obvious: the Galatians are to "throw out" the "Judaizers" from their midst, just as Abraham (the great man of faith!) ejected Hagar and Ishmael from his household.[45] For those who were willing to accept the terms of Paul's allegory, the injunction in v. 30 would have sounded like a natural application of the biblical story to their own situation, though in reality it represents no more than a deduction

42. Surprisingly, J. Louis Martyn asserts that Isa 54:1 would have been of no use to Paul's "opponents" and therefore takes it as a Pauline contribution to the argument (*Galatians*, 441).

43. Hans Dieter Betz quotes several ancient rhetoricians who recommend allowing the audience to infer some of the links in the argument for themselves so that they are forced to grapple with the evidence and thereby come to share the speaker's viewpoint (*Galatians*, 240).

44. Paul has dropped the two demonstrative pronouns from the middle of the verse and replaced "my son Isaac" with "the son of the free woman" at the end of the verse (see Stanley, *Paul*, 248–51). As Richard Hays notes, "This adjustment of the quotation highlights the slave/free contrast and thus emphasizes its application to the decision confronting Paul's readers, which Paul has already categorized as a choice between slavery and freedom (cf. Gal 4:1–11)" (*Echoes*, 112).

45. Richard Hays captures this point well: "This [v. 30] is the climax of Paul's argument, drawing together in a single fertile sentence the motifs of slavery, freedom, sonship, and inheritance, and calling on the reader to act on the demand. In quoting Gen 21:10 (LXX), Paul effaces all hints that these are the words of Sarah. They become the words of *Graphe* (Scripture), whose second person imperative ('Cast out') is now directed to the reader of the letter" (*Echoes*, 117). J. Louis Martyn comments similarly that both here and in Gal 3:8 "Paul portrays Scripture itself as an actor with a speaking part in the divine-human drama" (*Galatians*, 445).

from the rather arbitrary premise of the analogy. The fact that Paul has followed the biblical storyline fairly closely in developing his allegory would have reinforced the impression that his quotation of Gen 21:10 represented a responsible application of Scripture. By figuratively stepping aside and allowing the words of Scripture to speak in his place, Paul sought to sidestep the objections that he knew would be raised if he issued such a command on his own authority.[46] It is no longer Paul but "Scripture" that tells the Galatians what to do (v. 30a)—and behind the voice of Scripture lies the voice of God. For the informed audience, this would have been enough to promote serious consideration of Paul's injunction, regardless of what they thought about Paul himself.[47]

2. The response of the "competent audience" would have both resembled and diverged from that of the informed audience. Since members of the competent audience could be expected to know at least the broad framework of the story of Hagar and Sarah and their sons, they would have understood the references to the Genesis account in much the same way as the informed audience did. They, too, would have been faced with the decision of whether to accept the terms of Paul's allegory, and those who did so would have felt the full force of the final injunction to "throw out" the "Judaizers" from their midst. They would have differed, however, in their understanding of the quotation from Isa 54:1 in v. 26. With no knowledge of the original context, the competent audience would have been left to figure out the meaning of this verse on their own. From the reference to "our mother" in v. 26, they could have inferred that the "barren woman" who now has a multitude of children is the same as "the Jerusalem that is above," and that those who are "born of the Spirit" (v. 29) (i.e., those who have faith in Christ) are in some sense her "children" (cf. "children of promise" in v. 28). Perhaps they would have concluded, with the informed audience, that the reason for the woman's "rejoicing" was the success of the (law-free) Christian mission. But the expression "the Jerusalem that is above" would have remained obscure,

---

46. Paul uses a similar construction in 1 Cor 5:13, though in that case the rhetorical impact would have been muted by the fact that the quotation is unmarked and would therefore have been invisible to most of the people in Paul's audience.

47. Cf. the words of James D. G. Dunn on this passage: "Given the reversal of categories in v. 29, the harsh word of Sarah . . . becomes a word of powerful application to the present situation—whose power depends not on the propriety of its use here so much as on its emotional impact at the end of the typological allegory. . . . Certainly for those who had allowed themselves to be caught up in Paul's exposition, even as an illustration, this final Scripture would speak with tremendous force" (*The Epistle to the Galatians* [Peabody, Mass.: Hendrickson, 1993], 258).

since they would have had no reason to associate the verse with the return of the exiles as in Isa 54. In an effort to make sense of the reference, they might have remembered that Sarah is depicted as a "barren woman" in the Genesis account, thus strengthening the link between the allegory and the quotation.[48] The resultant artistry of the passage might have impressed the competent audience enough to motivate its members to accept both the allegory and the closing injunction as valid applications of the authoritative Scriptures that commanded their obedience.

3. Since members of the "minimal audience" would have been unfamiliar with the story of Sarah and Hagar, we might suspect that they would be as confused by this passage as they were by 3:6–9. But in the present passage Paul has included enough explanatory comments to insure that those who knew little or nothing about the patriarchal narratives could follow the main lines of his argument.[49] With a few minor exceptions (e.g., the sudden intrusion of proper names in vv. 22, 24, 28), Paul narrates the story as though his audience is hearing it for the first time. This is particularly apparent in vv. 22–23 and v. 29, where he summarizes the key points that the audience needs to know in order to make sense of his allegory and obey his final injunction. Although the minimal audience would not have recognized the characters to whom Paul refers in his exposition, this would not have been fatal to their understanding, since he substitutes generic terms such as "the slave woman" and "the free woman" at key points to give the story a more generic tone. In short, the minimal audience could have grasped the point of the allegory from the materials that Paul has supplied, though they would have missed some of the deeper resonances that come from knowing the original story.

The same is true for the two quotations. Like the competent audience, members of the minimal audience would have found the interpretive key to the first quotation in the parallel between the "barren woman" in v. 27 and the reference to "our mother" (i.e., "the Jerusalem that is above") in v. 26. From here, their reasoning would have been similar to that outlined for the competent audience, except that they would not have known to associate the

48. Of course, members of the informed audience could have recognized this as well, but their focus on the original context of the passage might have short-circuited their recognition of this secondary application of the quotation, as it has done for many modern interpreters.

49. Paul thus follows a different strategy in these verses than in 3:6–9 and 3:16, where his comments are so allusive that a person with no knowledge of the Abrahamic narrative could not possibly have understood the allusions.

"barren woman" in v. 27 with the experience of Sarah in the Genesis narrative. Without this association, the significance of the woman in the story being "barren" would have escaped them entirely.[50] As for the second quotation in v. 30, their reaction would have depended on how well they were able to follow the allegory to this point. Unlike the other two audiences, members of the minimal audience would have had no reason to question Paul's allegorical interpretation of the Abraham story, since they possessed no outside knowledge on which to base a critique. If they were able to ignore the points that they failed to understand (e.g., the proper names) and concentrate on Paul's summary of the storyline in vv. 22–23 and 29, then the final injunction to "throw out" those depicted symbolically as "the slave woman and her son" (i.e., the "Judaizers") would have come to them as the voice of God, since it represents a direct quotation from the holy Scriptures. Thus, Paul's strategy of veiling his own prescriptions in the words of Scripture might have been effective even for an audience that knew nothing of the Jewish Scriptures.

From these investigations we can conclude that the audience that Paul had in mind when he dictated his letter to the Galatians (the "implied audience") was not deeply grounded in the Jewish Scriptures, since anyone who knew (or could check) the original context of Paul's quotations would have noted grave problems with the arguments that he erects on these verses. Nor was he writing for an audience that was ignorant of the Jewish Scriptures, since these people would have had trouble following many of his biblical references. As with the Corinthian correspondence, it appears that Paul framed his quotations and the related arguments for an audience that possessed a modest knowledge of the Jewish Scriptures, primarily the stories about Abraham and the giving of the Torah at Mount Sinai. Whether they had obtained this knowledge from Paul's earlier teaching or from his "opponents" is impossible to say. Nor do we have any way of knowing how well Paul's view of the capabilities of his audience corresponded to reality. But the level of biblical literacy that Paul presupposes in his letters is not unrealistic for a predominately illiterate Gentile audience that has received instruction through oral channels in a Christian house-church. Thus we have reason to believe that Paul made a serious attempt in his letter to the Galatians to tailor his biblical rhetoric to the needs and capabilities of his audience.

---

50. The idea of associating the reference with Sarah would not have occurred to them, not only because she is never named in the passage, but also because she is depicted as having a son, not being "barren."

CHAPTER 8

Romans

PAUL AND THE ROMANS

The nature of Paul's relationship with the church at Rome remains unclear despite significant recent attention from scholars in what has become known as "the Romans Debate."[1] The primary disagreement is between those who believe that Paul was addressing one or more specific problems in the church at Rome about which he had reliable knowledge (normally centering on relations between Jews and Gentiles) and those who view the letter as a more general treatise prompted by broader concerns.[2] Both sides agree, however, that Paul had never visited the city (Rom 1:11–15, 15:22–24), so any information that he possessed about the Romans would have come to him secondhand, perhaps through Priscilla and Aquila or some of the other people named in Rom 16:1–16.

What information might Paul have learned from his friends and acquaintances regarding the church in Rome? The maximalist answer—the view of those who see the letter as a response to Jew-Gentile tensions in Rome—suggests that he possessed at least a broad outline of the history of Christianity in Rome, including its origins in the synagogue, the expulsion of at least some of the Jewish Christians from Rome under Claudius, the extension of the gospel to the Gentiles, and the strains that subsequently arose between the Jewish and Gentile branches of the church.[3] The minimal-

1. The key articles through 1990 are collected in Karl F. Donfried, ed., *The Romans Debate* (rev. ed.; Peabody, Mass.: Hendrickson, 1991). Additional surveys of the major alternatives can be found in A. J. M. Wedderburn, *The Reasons for Romans* (Edinburgh: T. & T. Clark, 1988) and the introductory chapter in Neil Elliott, *The Rhetoric of Romans: Argumentative Constraint and Strategy and Paul's Dialogue with Judaism* (JSNTSup 45; Sheffield: Sheffield Academic Press, 1990).

2. In the Donfried collection, the articles by Wiefel, Karris, and Watson represent the former position, while those by Manson, Bornkamm, and Jervell reflect the latter view.

3. The outline here follows the influential article by Wolfgang Wiefel, "The Jewish Community in Ancient Rome and the Origins of Roman Christianity," in Donfried, ed., *Romans Debate,* 85–101. Most recent commentators follow a similar model; see Joseph A. Fitzmyer, *Romans* (AB 33; New York: Doubleday, 1993), 25–36; James D. G. Dunn, *Romans* (2 vols., WBC

ist view, on the other hand, credits Paul with very little knowledge of the situation in Rome, or else argues that the letter provides too little information to form an opinion.

The fact that Paul quotes so often from the Jewish Scriptures in Romans, far more than in any of his other letters, is sometimes cited as evidence for a maximalist reading of the letter. Supporters of this view point out that Paul seems to assume that his Roman audience will know the original context of many of his quotations and be able to supply the links needed to make sense of his argument. From this they conclude that Paul must have known that the church in Rome was composed primarily of Jews and/or Gentiles sympathetic to Judaism who had learned the Jewish Scriptures from regular participation in the synagogue.

This sounds like a reasonable conclusion. But what evidence do we have to support it? Although we know that the church in Rome included a substantial Gentile component (Rom 1:13, 11:13, 11:17–24), we should be careful about assuming that the Gentile Christians in Rome had been associated with the Jewish synagogue prior to their conversion. As Neil Elliott points out, "There is no explicit evidence in Romans that Paul addresses Christians enthralled by the synagogue, or cowed by the impressive salvation-historical claims of Israel. . . . Far from being overwhelmed by Jewish claims of privilege, they run the risk, in Paul's estimation, of holding God's mercy in contempt by boasting of having 'replaced' Israel (cf. 11.17–24)."[4] William Campbell offers a similar observation: "It is not too much Judaism that Paul fears," he says, "but too little an appreciation of the Jewish roots of the church."[5] Such an attitude is hardly typical of a group of Gentiles who had once been attached to the synagogue. But it is exactly what one would expect from a predominantly Gentile congregation that had been converted directly out of a Roman culture in which anti-Jewish sentiments ran wide and deep.[6]

38A, 38B; Dallas: Word, 1988), 1.xlv–liv. For a critical review of this theory, see Johann D. Kim, *God, Israel, and the Gentiles: Rhetoric and Situation in Romans 9–11* (SBLDS 176; Atlanta: Scholars Press, 2000), 50–56; Mark D. Nanos, *The Mystery of Romans: The Jewish Context of Paul's Letter* (Minneapolis: Fortress, 1996), 372–87.

4. Elliott, *Rhetoric*, 38. Cf. Nanos, *The Mystery of Romans,* 22: "Paul does not seem to be confronting an inflated view of the Torah in Rome among the Christian gentiles ('judaizing') as is often assumed. Instead, he confronts the failure of the Christian gentiles in Rome to respect the role of Torah in the life of Israel as God's special gift."

5. William S. Campbell, "Revisiting Romans," *Scripture Bulletin* 12 (1981): 8.

6. On anti-Jewish ideas in Rome, see (among many others) Menahem Stern, ed., *Greek and Latin Authors on Jews and Judaism* (3 vols.; Jerusalem: Israel Academy of Science and Humanities,

Even if we understand Suetonius's statement about troubles arising in the Roman synagogues at the instigation of "Chrestus" as a reference to conflicts over the Christian gospel, we have no way of knowing how many Jews and Jewish sympathizers may have joined the nascent Christian movement at that time, nor how many were still around at the time Paul wrote his letter.[7]

When we turn to the letter itself, we find no clear evidence that Paul knew anything about the origins and history of the church in Rome. Paul indicates that he has heard about the Romans' faith (1:8), that he prays for them regularly (1:9–10), and that he has long desired to visit them (1:10, 13; 15:23), but none of these statements requires more than a cursory familiarity with the Roman church. More to the point, the letter contains not one direct reference to the Romans' lives before Christ (whether Jewish or Gentile), such as we find in passages like Gal 4:8–9, 1 Thess 1:9, and 1 Cor 6:9–11. The closest he comes is in Rom 6:19, where the words "impurity" (ἀκαθαρσία; cf. 1:24) and "lawlessness" (ἀνομία; cf. 4:7) could be read as implying a strictly "pagan" background for the recipients of the letter.[8] On the other hand, Paul clearly assumes that the Roman Christians will understand his many allusions to Jewish beliefs (the righteousness of God, the final judgment, the idea of atonement) and practices (circumcision, sacrifice, obedience to Torah); in fact, his letter would make little sense to a person who knew nothing of these matters. But the level of knowledge that Paul

---

1974–84); Louis H. Feldman, *Jew and Gentile in the Ancient World* (Princeton, N.J.: Princeton University Press, 1993); John G. Gager, *The Origins of Anti-Semitism* (Oxford: Oxford University Press, 1983); and the summary in Nanos, *Mystery*, 64–68.

7. On the meaning of Suetonius's words in *Claudius* 25.4, see the sources cited in the following essays in Donfried, ed., *Romans Debate:* Karl Donfried, "A Short Note on Romans 16," 46–49; Wolfgang Wiefel, "Jewish Community," 92–93; F. F. Bruce, "The Romans Debate—Continued," 178–80. If Wiefel's historical reconstruction is correct, many of the Gentiles in the Roman house-churches would have converted to Christianity at a time when Judaism was being suppressed, not directly out of the synagogue ("Jewish Community," 93-96; cf. Bruce, "Romans Debate," 180-81). Mark Nanos offers an alternative scenario for influence from the Jewish community: the Gentile Christians in Rome had begun to associate with the local Jewish synagogues after they became followers of Jesus (*Mystery*, 30-40). If Nanos is correct, the Romans would have known more about the Jewish Scriptures than we can discern from Paul's letters, since they would have heard the Scriptures read and expounded every week in the synagogue. But it is hard to see how Paul could have known precisely what the Romans were being taught and what they had retained at the time when he was composing his letter. Nanos's supposition that Paul expected them to ask their Jewish friends about his biblical quotations founders on the fact that there is much in the letter that would have been offensive to Jewish sensibilities (2:17–29, 3:9–30, 4:11, 16, 17, 5:20, 7:6, etc.).

8. The words are used explicitly of Gentiles in Rom 1:24; 2 Cor 6:14; Eph 4:19 (cf. 1 Cor 9:21).

presupposes does not exceed what the Romans could have gathered from common cultural experience with Jews and Judaism or the Jewish framework of Christian catechesis. Thus, if we leave aside the biblical quotations (in order to avoid a circular argument), we find little evidence that Paul possessed much reliable information about the backgrounds of the Roman Christians.

Biblical Literacy in Rome

What, then, are we to make of the quotations? It seems reasonable to think that when Paul quoted from the Jewish Scriptures in his letter to the Romans, he expected them to understand him. But how much biblical literacy was required to understand Paul's quotations? As we have seen in prior chapters, there is no reason to think that Paul expected his audience to know the original context of all of his quotations. The precise nature of his expectations must be investigated on a case-by-case basis.

When we ask precisely what Paul expected his Roman audience to know from the Jewish Scriptures, the results are more diverse than with the other letters:

1. As in his letters to the Corinthians, Paul assumes that the Romans are familiar with the story of Adam's sin and the "death" that resulted from it (5:12–19), though he refers to no other aspects of the creation account.

2. As in Galatians, he assumes that the Romans know key elements of the Abraham story, including the inauguration of the covenant with Abraham and his descendants, the importance of Abraham's faith, God's recognition of Abraham's righteousness, the requirement that Abraham circumcise his descendants, and God's promise to bless "the nations" through Abraham (ch. 4). He also assumes that they have heard the story of the birth of Isaac as a child of promise (4:18–21, 9:7–9) and possibly the related story of Hagar and Ishmael.

3. Unlike his other letters, Paul expects the Romans to understand the significance of a passing reference to "the patriarchs" (9:5, 11:28, 15:8), and he explicitly mentions the story of Esau and Jacob, including their birth (as twins) to Isaac and Rebekah and the eventual reversal of their birthrights (9:10–13). How much more of the patriarchal narrative he expected them to know is unclear.

4. As in his other letters, Paul assumes that the Romans know something about the exodus story, though the only episodes that he mentions are the contest between Moses and Pharaoh (9:14–17) and the giving of the Torah

through Moses (5:13–14). He also assumes that they are familiar with the story of Elijah's battle with Jezebel (11:2–4), a story mentioned nowhere else in his letters.

5. In several cases Paul cites without explanation the names of the supposed authors of specific biblical passages, including Moses (10:5, 19), David (4:6, 11:9), and Isaiah (9:27, 29, 10:16, 20, 15:12). He also expects the Romans to understand what he means when he refers to "the prophets" (1:2), "the prophetic writings" (16:25–26), and "the law and the prophets" (3:21).[9]

6. In a number of passages Paul assumes that the Romans are familiar with specific laws from the Jewish Torah, including its injunctions against idolatry (1:21–23), promiscuity (1:24), homosexuality (1:26–27), stealing (2:21), adultery (2:22, 7:1–3), coveting (7:7), eating unclean food (14:14), and the Decalogue in general (13:8–10).

What are to we to make of this evidence? Clearly, Paul assumes a much broader knowledge of Scripture in his letter to the Romans, whom he did not know, than in his letters to his own churches. The difference is not only quantitative (i.e., expecting them to know more stories and laws), but also qualitative (expecting them to recognize more subtle references to the names of biblical "authors" and portions of Scripture). Yet even here the difference is not as great as it appears, since he still frames the majority of his quotations in such a way that a person with little or no specific knowledge of the Jewish Scriptures could grasp his essential point.[10] To put it differently, the level of biblical literacy that Paul assumes in Romans is broader (i.e., it encompasses more stories and laws) than in his other letters, but not notice-

---

9. His identification of Jesus as a "descendant of David" (1:3), on the other hand, requires no specific knowledge of the prophetic corpus, since the phrase was a stock element of early Christian preaching. Cf. C.E.B. Cranfield, *A Critical and Exegetical Commentary on the Epistle to the Romans* (2 vols.; Edinburgh: T & T Clark, 1975), 1.58–59; Brendan Byrne, *Romans* (Collegeville, Minn.: Liturgical Press, 1996), 44.

10. See the discussions of individual passages below. Mark Nanos recognizes the cultural barriers that would have limited the Romans' awareness of the Jewish Scriptures: "We must come to grips with the fact that outside the synagogue environment the early Christians would have had little opportunity to learn the 'Scriptures': gentiles in particular would have had no previous exposure to the religious life of the people of god and the ways of righteousness associated with Judaism's monotheistic practices. . . . How could he [Paul] expect his audience, primarily gentile in composition, to understand his letter replete with direct and indirect uses of the Scriptures and Judaic concepts of righteousness?" (*Mystery*, 73) But the conclusion that Nanos draws from this observation—that the Roman Christians must have learned the Scriptures through participation in the Jewish synagogue—does not necessarily follow, since it rests on the assumption that Paul expected the Romans to know (or look up) the original context of his quotations and approve his handling of the text rather than deriving their meaning from the comments provided in the letter.

ably deeper (i.e., he does not require them to supply the original context of quotations outside of the narrative passages that he explicitly mentions).

This survey of Paul's assumptions raises one final question: how could Paul know which passages of Scripture the Roman Christians would recognize? When writing to the churches of Corinth and (possibly) Galatia, Paul could have assumed (rightly or wrongly) that his audience remembered the verses that he had taught them while he was with them. But he had no prior experience with the Christians at Rome. How did he know what to expect? We might imagine that one of the co-workers mentioned in Rom 16 had told him about some of the passages that the Romans had been discussing, or that he had received word that they were using a particular "testimony book" with which he was familiar.[11] But this is a modern way of looking at the problem, an anachronistic solution that ignores the realities of communication and literacy levels in the ancient world. If Paul had had occasion to talk with someone who knew the Roman churches firsthand, it is hard to imagine that he would have peppered the person with questions about which biblical passages the Romans had been studying. Paul also gives no sign that he expected the Romans to recognize the passages that he cites from prior use of a "testimony book."[12] In fact, it is difficult to envision any culturally appropriate mechanism by which Paul could have learned precisely which passages of Scripture the Romans would recognize. Instead of viewing Paul's letter as a window to the Romans' knowledge of Scripture, we should accept the fact that the letter gives us little more than his best guess as to what they might have known.[13] His guesses may have been intelligent ones (e.g., they

11. For a helpful survey of the debate over the use of "testimony books" in early Christianity, see the materials cited in Christopher D. Stanley, *Paul and the Language of Scripture: Citation Technique in the Pauline Epistles and Contemporary Literature* (SNTSMS 74; Cambridge: Cambridge University Press, 1992), 71–72, and the recent study by Martin C. Albl, *And Scripture Cannot Be Broken: The Form and Function of the Early Christian Testimonia Collections* (NovTSup 96; Leiden: Brill, 1999), 7–69. Most recent proponents of the hypothesis prefer to speak of local collections of oral or written traditions rather than common texts that were widely disseminated.

12. The possibility that Paul drew his quotations from a "testimony book" that he shared with the Romans is also undercut by the fact that almost none of the verses that Paul cites in Romans appears on any of the "testimony" lists that have been proposed by various scholars.

13. Stanley Stowers makes a similar point: "The encoded audience is a feature of the text itself. I can know with certainty that the audience in the text is gentiles at Rome who know something about the Jewish scripture and Jesus Christ, but I can only speculate about who actually read the letter, their assumptions, knowledge, and reactions to the letter. This is true even if Paul knew the empirical audience well—and we do not know this to be true—and even if he had consciously or unconsciously identified the reader in the text with the empirical readers" (*A Rereading of Romans: Justice, Jews, and Gentiles* [New Haven: Yale University Press, 1994], 22).

might reflect his experience with other churches in the Mediterranean region), but we should not simply presume that he guessed correctly.

The Rhetoric of Quotations in Romans

The epistle to the Romans contains significantly more quotations from the Jewish Scriptures than any of Paul's other letters.[14] Included in the letter are forty-two quotations that are marked by introductory formulae (1:17, 2:24, 3:4, 10–18, 4:3, 7–8, 17, 18, 7:7, 8:36, 9:9, 12, 13, 15, 17, 25–26, 27–28, 29, 33, 10:5, 6–8, 11, 15, 16, 19, 20, 21, 11:3, 4, 8, 9–10, 26–27, 12:19, 13:9a, 9b, 14:11, 15:3, 9, 10, 11, 12, 21),[15] three that could be recognized by other means (4:22, 9:7, 10:18),[16] and nine that are unmarked and therefore would have been unrecognizable to the Romans unless they happened to know the original passage (2:6, 3:20, 9:20, 10:13, 11:2, 34, 35, 12:17, 20).[17]

Clearly, biblical quotations occupy an important place in Paul's letter to the Romans. Yet their importance to the argumentation of the letter can be overstated. As in Galatians, explicit quotations from Scripture are not dispersed evenly across the letter; fully three-quarters of them are concentrated in three passages: 4:1–25, 9:6–11:36, and 15:1–12.[18] At several points in the letter Paul develops a lengthy argument with little or no explicit reference to the Jewish Scriptures (e.g., 1:18–2:29, 5:1–8:30, 12:1–14:23). The handful of

---

14. As a rough guide, Paul adduces an explicit quotation (on average) every ten verses in Romans, as compared with every twenty-one verses in Galatians, every thirty-six verses in 1 Corinthians, and every forty-two verses in 2 Corinthians.

15. Romans 3:10–18 is counted here as one quotation because it appears under a single introductory formula, so that an uninformed audience would have assumed that it came from a single source.

16. The presence of a quotation in Rom 4:22 (Gen 15:6) is evident not only because the same verse is quoted in v. 3, but also because v. 23 repeats and comments on a portion of the verse. In Rom 9:7 (Gen 21:12), the sudden intrusion of the second-person pronoun σοι would have signified that Paul was citing an outside source. A similar grammatical tension marks Rom 10:18 (quoting Ps 18:5 LXX), where the antecedent of the third-person pronouns cannot be the same as the subject of the verb ἤκουσαν in the introductory formula.

17. The verbatim quotation of Prov 25:21–22 in Rom 12:20 is included here because it is not marked in a way that would be clearly recognizable to an uninformed reader. The intrusion of ἀλλά at the beginning of the verse and the shift to imperative forms suggest a return to direct speech (cf. δότε in v. 19a), while the same factors make it impossible to take v. 20 as a continuation of the quotation in v. 19b. Romans 12:16 (Prov 3:7) and 12:17 (Prov 3:4) are best regarded as allusions rather than unmarked quotations, since the wording in both cases diverges significantly from the original passage, and the language is clearly proverbial. Neither is marked as a quotation in the body of the letter.

18. The exceptions are 1:17, 2:24, 3:4, 10–18, 7:7, 8:36, 12:19, 13:9a, 9b, 14:11, 15:21.

quotations that do appear in these passages play a subsidiary role in his argumentation, usually reinforcing a point that Paul has already made in his own words.

So why does Paul rely so heavily on arguments from Scripture in the three passages where the bulk of his quotations are found? The answer is less clear for Romans than for similar concentrations in Galatians, since no one has suggested that Paul felt the need to offer a biblical counterargument to undercut a troublesome interpretation of Scripture that had gained currency with his intended audience. The uncertainty is compounded by the ongoing debate over the nature of the "provoking rhetorical urgency" that motivated Paul to write the letter to the Romans.[19] Probably the most important clue to Paul's rhetorical purpose is to be found in the fact that all three passages (4:1–25, 9:6–11:36, and 15:1–12) center on a common theme: the plan of God to create a chosen people that would include both Jews and Gentiles. This close conjunction of thematic content and rhetorical strategy becomes especially significant when we observe that these are the only passages in the letter where the issue is explicitly addressed[20] and that quotations appear only sporadically elsewhere in the letter.[21]

Apparently, Paul felt compelled to justify his views about Jews and Gentiles from Scripture when writing to the Romans. But why? Three possibilities come to mind, depending on how one defines the "provoking rhetorical urgency" of the letter.

First, if the letter represents a veiled attempt to resolve tensions that Paul knew were dividing the Jewish and Gentile Christians in Rome (whether individuals or entire congregations), he might have felt that the authoritative Jewish Scriptures offered the only common ground from which he could argue effectively with both sides. His own claims to apostolic authority

---

19. The nature of the "provoking rhetorical urgency" is unclear because of the aforementioned disagreements about Paul's reason(s) for writing the letter. All interpreters seem to agree that Paul was concerned about gaining the Romans' support for his upcoming mission to Spain, and most would agree that he wanted to challenge what he perceived as an attitude of superiority on the part of Gentile Christians in Rome toward their Jewish colleagues (11:18). Beyond these points, however, the reconstructions vary widely.

20. Romans 1:16–17 is the exception that proves the rule: though it lies outside the three passages cited above, it underlines the same point with a quotation from Scripture (cf. 15:14–21). It is perhaps worth noting that Paul also appeals to Scripture in several passages in which he stresses the equality of Jew and Gentile under God's judgment (2:24, 3:4, 10–18; cf. 2:6), though the pattern is less consistent here.

21. If we exclude the three passages cited above, the rate of quotation in Romans drops to a level comparable to that of the other letters: once every twenty-eight verses (see note 14).

would have carried little weight at Rome because he had no prior relationship with the church. But he could presume that both sides would listen to an argument that was grounded in Scripture.

Second, if the letter was written to commend Paul's ministry (i.e., his "gospel") to the Romans in order to gain their support for his mission to Spain, his negative experiences with "Judaizers" elsewhere might have led him to think that he should defuse any potential problems in this area with a series of preemptive arguments from the authoritative Scriptures. The fact that he could handle Scripture with such efficacy would have enhanced his stature among the Romans while simultaneously undercutting any accusations that he had abandoned the Jewish Torah (cf. 3:8).

Third, if the letter represents Paul's anticipated defense of his ministry before the apostles (or his Jewish opponents) in Jerusalem, he would have known that the chief bone of contention between them was his claim that God was now accepting Gentiles on equal terms with Jews. As a devout Jew, Paul had no doubt struggled to formulate a biblical argument to undergird his altered opinions about God's way of dealing with Jews and Gentiles, and he could have guessed that others from Jewish backgrounds, including Christian leaders in Jerusalem, had grappled with the same problem. In this view, Paul's use of biblical quotations says more about his perception of his anticipated audience in Jerusalem than about his actual audience in Rome.[22]

Whatever his reasoning, it seems evident that there is a close link between Paul's strategy of biblical argumentation in Romans and his contention that God accepts Jews and Gentiles on equal terms on the basis of their faith. Was this an effective strategy for Paul to use with the Romans? The answer depends in part on how we understand the level of biblical literacy in Rome. If we think that Paul is reasonably accurate in what he presumes the Romans know, we will probably conclude that he was well advised to quote from the authoritative Scriptures when dealing with this contentious issue. If, on the other hand, we believe that he has assumed too much biblical knowledge on the part of his audience, we will probably offer a less charitable evaluation of his rhetorical effectiveness. The best way to resolve this issue is through an examination of a few sample passages.

---

22. The same result is obtained if we read Paul's biblical argumentation as being directed primarily toward a hypothetical Jewish interlocutor who was familiar with the Jewish Scriptures and only secondarily toward the mostly Gentile Christians in Rome, as Stanley Stowers has argued (see note 34).

Romans 2:24

The quotation from Isa 52:5 in Rom 2:24 is a typical example of the way Paul uses biblical citations to advance his argument outside the three sections where the bulk of his quotations are found. The verse appears in the middle of a rhetorically stylized passage (2:17–29) in which Paul accuses a hypothetical Jewish opponent of a host of sinful actions. The passage represents a turning point in the argument of 1:18–3:20, where Paul labors mightily to show that all humans, Jew and Gentile alike, are "under sin" (3:9) and thus liable to God's judgment. Establishing the sinfulness of Gentiles presented no special problem; Jewish polemical literature contained a wealth of charges that Paul could appropriate for his own purposes in 1:18–32. But demonstrating the universal sinfulness of the Jews, God's chosen people, was more problematic, since anyone could see that there were many devout Jews in the Greco-Roman world who were serious about fulfilling their covenantal obligations. Faced with such a difficult rhetorical problem, Paul followed his common practice of laying out a series of arguments of varying weight in the hope that one or more of them would strike home with the audience (Cf. 1 Cor 11:1–16, 15:1–58; 2 Cor 8:1–9:15; Gal 3:1–4:7). The result is Rom 2:1–3:20.

Since Paul did not know the Romans personally, he could not be sure how they would respond to a frontal attack on Jewish privilege. Apparently, he had heard that some of them were already suspicious of him on this score.[23] He could not afford to alienate a portion of his audience this early in the letter, since that would have undermined his plan to ask for their support for his upcoming mission to Spain. Thus, he chose to frame his argument initially in generic terms (2:1–16), addressing himself to an unidentified "you" (cf. "O human" vv. 1, 3) rather than challenging Jewish reliance on Torah directly. Once he had enticed his audience to assent to a series of general principles concerning who is and is not liable to God's judgment, he

---

23. Behind Rom 3:8 most likely stands the charge that Paul has been promoting libertinism by abandoning the Jewish Torah as a standard for Christian behavior. As Ernst Käsemann observes, "Libertinism really could develop out of Paul's view of justification, and his adversaries claim that it is an unavoidable result" (*Commentary on Romans* [trans. and ed. Geoffrey W. Bromiley; Grand Rapids: Eerdmans, 1980], 84). To avoid encouraging this interpretation of his message (and thus antagonizing his audience), Paul constructed a somewhat forced distinction between "deeds of Torah" (3:20, 28, 4:2, 6, 9:11, 32, 11:6), which he criticizes, and the Torah itself, which he generally affirms (2:12–27, 3:19, 31, 7:7–16, 22, 8:4, 7, 13:8, 10). The artificiality of the distinction becomes evident in verses such as 2:6–7, 10, 13–15, 26–27, where "doing Torah" is actually commended as the path to divine blessings.

could offer evidence that Jews, like Gentiles, practice the kinds of conduct that elicit God's condemnation (2:17–29).[24]

This brings us to the passage that frames the quotation in 2:24. If the Romans had followed Paul to this point, they could hardly avoid seeing in the conduct of the apostrophized "Jew" (2:17–24) a concretization of the negative behaviors described (and condemned) in 2:1–16.[25] Like all ad hominem arguments, the argument would have been effective only if the audience was willing to accept the implied demand to generalize from the negative conduct of the literary individual to the character of the historical group.[26] Clearly, any Jew (or Jewish Christian?) who heard Paul's argument would have objected to his language as either a gross and offensive caricature of Judaism or an irrelevant sideswipe at a few "bad apples." Paul's letter, however, was not directed to Jews, but to a group of Gentile Christians living in a city in which anti-Jewish prejudice was rife.[27] For these people, the objec-

---

24. Brendan Byrne makes a similar point in *Romans* 80, 96; cf. Dunn, *Romans*, 1.78–80, 89–91. That Paul followed such a rhetorical strategy is apparent from the parallel depictions of good and bad behaviors in the two passages: "doing good" is defined in both cases as obeying the requirements of Torah (even for Gentiles!) (2:7, 9, 13–15; cf. 2:26–27), while "doing evil" is defined as violating Torah (2:8–9, 12; cf. 2:21–23, 25, 27). More significantly, both passages make the individual's inner attitude the ultimate criterion for divine approval: those who are motivated by a sincere desire to obey God (even Gentiles!) are commended (2:14–15; cf. 2:29), while those who proudly (and hypocritically) pass judgment on the conduct of others (even Jews!) are condemned (2:1–3; cf. 2:17–24).

25. As the commentators routinely point out, Paul follows the pattern of diatribal speech in these verses, including its use of rhetorical questions and stock accusations against its opponents. Stanley Stowers (*Rereading*, 145–53) makes a strong case that Paul has been influenced more specifically by a common form of philosophical diatribe, the censure of the pretentious teacher. But Stowers's more precise identification of the addressee as a Jewish competitor of Paul—that is, a teacher who seeks to enlighten Gentiles as to the way to be "righteous" before the Jewish God—relies too much on a literal "mirror-reading" of Paul's rather stereotyped and exaggerated language.

26. The validity of Paul's argument here has vexed many interpreters, with conservative scholars generally seeking to defend Paul, and more critical scholars calling attention to the weakness of Paul's argument at this point. Thomas Schreiner (*Romans* [BECNT 6; Grand Rapids: Baker, 1998]) attempts to stake out a middle ground. While acknowledging that Paul's specific criticisms would have applied only to "a few extremists within the Jewish community" (133), he still thinks that Paul's argument is effective once one understands his purpose: "Paul uses particularly blatant and shocking examples (like any good preacher) to illustrate the principle that Jews violated the law that they possessed" (134). But the problem remains: by what logic could Paul have expected the Romans to be able to generalize from his attacks on the reprehensible behavior of a few hypocritical Jews to the conclusion that all Israel was "under sin" (Rom 3:9)? In the final analysis, the link defies logic, as do all ad hominem arguments.

27. Stanley Stowers has rightly pointed out that whatever we conclude about the actual composition of the Christian community in Rome, the "implied audience" of the letter is Gentile Christians from beginning to end (cf. Rom 11:13). On anti-Judaism in Rome, see the sources cited in note 6.

tionable nature of the argument would have been less apparent. In fact, the argument of vv. 17–24 would have been most effective with individuals who already harbored negative opinions of Jews, since they would have been more than ready to accept Paul's ad hominem attack as a valid depiction of Judaism. Evidently this was what Paul wanted, since the argument seems to require such an unfounded generalization in order to work.

What role, then, does the quotation play in the argument? Clearly, Paul could have moved directly from the rhetorical questions of vv. 21–23 to the more general assertions of vv. 25–29, yet he chose to interject a verse of Scripture at this point in the argument. Why? One possible clue can be found in the observation that this is the only place in Paul's letters where the phrase "just as it is written" appears at the end of the quotation rather than the beginning. Without this introductory formula, the audience would have heard the words of v. 24 (at least initially) as an extension of the accusations in vv. 21–23. The sudden shift from rhetorical questions to direct accusations in v. 24 would have focused attention on v. 24, giving the audience the impression that it was in fact the culmination of the argument.[28] This impression would have been confirmed by the appearance of the phrase "just as it is written" at the end of the verse, since by this phrase Paul places the final accusation in the very mouth of God.

How might Paul's Roman audience have responded to this carefully crafted constellation of rhetorical devices?

1. The "informed audience" would have turned immediately to the original context of the quotation for help in making sense of the text. In this case they would have found themselves more confused than helped. In the Greek text of Isa 52:5, the "blaspheming" of God's name is tied to the exiles' expressions of astonishment (θαυμάζετε) and mourning (ὀλολύζετε) over the way Yahweh has handed them over to the "Assyrians" (actually, the Babylonians). Though the text is unclear, it implies that the exiles' negative response to their situation has caused their captors to mock the name of their God. In order to clear the divine name, Yahweh announces the coming of a day of deliverance when the people of Judah will return to Zion, where they will praise and worship their God (vv. 6–12).

A reader familiar with this passage would have found it difficult to grasp Paul's use of Isa 52:5 in Rom 2:24. In Isa 52, it is not the people's hypocriti-

---

28. The point is virtually the same if v. 23 is understood as a summary statement rather than a question (so Cranfield, *Romans,* 1.170; Fitzmyer, *Romans,* 318), except that the "culmination" would now begin in v. 23—as signaled by the shift from the articular participle to the relative pronoun—rather than v. 24.

cal violations of Torah (as in Paul) that prompt "the nations" (Gentiles) to blaspheme the name of their God, but their bewilderment at the circumstances of their exile. More importantly, the "solution" that Yahweh promises in Isa 52 is not rejection and judgment (as in Paul), but deliverance and blessing. Whereas Paul's aim in Rom 2–3 was to show that the Jews of his day were as deserving of divine judgment as the Gentiles, an audience familiar with Isa 52 would have heard Yahweh speaking of his covenant loyalty to his people and his merciful attitude toward them.[29] This recognition could have led the informed audience to question the entire premise of Paul's argument concerning the Jews. Apparently, Paul did not anticipate that the Romans would be able to consult the original context of Isa 52.[30]

2. Since Paul gives no indication that he expected the Romans to supply any background material from Isa 52, members of the "competent audience" would have derived their understanding of the quotation from the broader rhetorical context of Rom 2. Their interpretation would have been colored by the fact that the verse follows immediately after a series of stinging indictments against "the hypocritical Jew" in 2:17–23. In this context the shift from the singular "you" of vv. 21–23 to the plural form in the quotation would have signified to the competent audience that the individual addressed in vv. 17–23 was intended to represent an entire class of people: hypocritical Jews who boast about their covenant with God while failing to follow its

---

29. As Brendan Byrne points out, "According to both the Hebrew original and the LXX it was Israel's *misfortune* that led to the reviling of God's name by the nations. Paul, however, interprets the LXX phrase 'on account of you' as 'because of your fault,' thereby converting what was originally an oracle of compassion towards Israel into one of judgment" (*Romans*, 101). Richard Hays describes Paul's use of Isa 52:5 here as "a stunning misreading of the text" in which "Paul transforms Isaiah's oracle of promise into a word of reproach" (*Echoes of Scripture in the Letters of Paul* [New Haven: Yale University Press, 1989], 45). Similar evaluations are offered by Fitzmyer (*Romans*, 318–19) and Käsemann (*Romans*, 71).

30. Thomas Schreiner (*Romans*, 134–35) argues that Paul's interpretation of Isa 52 is in fact consistent with the original sense of the passage, since many Jews in Paul's day would have interpreted Roman domination as a sign that they were still being punished for their sins (and thus still in "exile") like the Israelites in the original passage. (Cf. J. Ross Wagner, *Heralds of the Gospel: Paul and Isaiah "In Concert" in the Letter to the Romans* [Leiden: Brill, 2002], 176–78). But Paul gives no indication that he was thinking in these terms, and even if he was, this does not explain how the quotation relates to Paul's accusations in vv. 21–23, which bear no evident relation to the situation of Israel in Isa 52. More importantly, it is hard to see how Paul could have expected a Gentile Roman audience to supply this kind of interpretive grid for the passage. The same is true for the suggestion by Heinrich Schlier (*Der Römerbrief* [HTKNT 6; Freiburg: Herder, 1977], 87) that Paul is reading Isa 52:5 through the lens of Ezek 36:20. How could Paul have expected the Romans to know this in the absence of any explicit reference?

terms.[31] The close verbal link with the preceding verse—causing God's name to be "blasphemed" is clearly a form of "dishonoring God"—would have tied the quotation even more firmly to its immediate context, reinforcing the impression that the verse offered a divine indictment of precisely the kind of people whom Paul was attacking.[32] Since Paul had already declared in 2:1–12 that individuals who practice the kinds of conduct described in vv. 17–23 (pride, hypocrisy, violation of Torah) were liable to God's judgment, the competent audience would naturally conclude that the quotation in v. 24 implied a similar threat of condemnation. Thus, although the quotation and the passage as a whole do not support Paul's eventual assertion that Jews as a class stand alongside Gentiles as the objects of God's threatened judgment (3:8, 19–20), the competent audience would have seen in the quotation a strong support for Paul's more limited indictment in 2:17–23 of Jews who hypocritically neglect their covenantal obligations.[33]

3. Since the "minimal audience" would have had no contact with the original context of Paul's quotation, their understanding of the verse, like that of the "competent audience," would have been determined entirely by its place in Paul's argument. In this case there is nothing to distinguish the interpretations of the two audiences—the minimal audience would also

31. Brendan Byrne probably narrows the passage too much when he identifies Paul's implied target as "a Jewish teacher who seeks to instruct Gentiles in basic moral precepts of the law" (*Romans*, 96). But he is surely correct that "Paul is not asserting that all Jews failed in the areas suggested or that the vices were characteristic of the nation as a whole" (98). Nothing in the language that Paul uses in vv. 21–23 would have suggested to Paul's audience that the quotation in v. 24 was intended to refer to the conduct of all "Jews"; after the momentary shift to the plural "you" in the quotation, Paul reverts in v. 25 to the singular form that he has been using since v. 17. The same is true for vv. 25–29, where it is Jews (and Gentiles) who fail to follow Torah who come in for criticism, not "the Jews" as a group. Commentators have routinely struggled with this aspect of Paul's argument, with many asserting that Paul appears to presume a radical interpretation of the Torah such as one finds in Matt 5:21-48; as Cranfield puts it, "Where the seriousness of the law's requirements is understood, there it is recognized that all are transgressors" (*Romans*, 169; cf. C.K. Barrett, *The Epistle to the Romans* [New York: Harper and Row, 1957], 56-57). But as Stanley Stowers has pointed out, Paul's real target in these verses is a particular type of person well known in Hellenistic moral literature: the pretentious person (ὁ ἀλάζων) (*Rereading*, 145–49).

32. This may have been what Paul had in mind when he moved the words τὸ ὄνομα τοῦ θεοῦ to the beginning of the verse, where they stand immediately after the words τὸν θεὸν ἀτιμάζεις. See the discussion in Stanley, *Paul*, 84–85.

33. Brendan Byrne says it well: "God's view, revealed in scripture, clinches the matter for the religious conscience; against this verdict no merely human awareness of contrary evidence can prevail. . . . Paul could hardly have made his case more sharply or offensively than this" (*Romans*, 98–99).

have viewed the quotation as a divine indictment of the kinds of people whom Paul has already challenged in vv. 17–23. In both cases the divine voice adds a note of credibility and authority to Paul's own rhetorical attack, laying the foundation for his subsequent distinction between "true" and "false" Jews in vv. 25–29. This enhancement of his *ethos* is particularly important in a letter directed to a congregation that has no reason to automatically accept Paul's assertions of apostolic authority. The simple fact that Paul could quote verses from the authoritative Scriptures in support of his argument would have enhanced his stature among the Romans and thus increased their openness to his argument.

Romans 4:3

In Rom 4 Paul offers an extended commentary on the story of Abraham, including references and allusions to several different episodes from Gen 12–21. Clearly his account is selective, incorporating only those parts of the narrative that could be said to support his contention that God accepts as "righteous" anyone who shows faith in God's promises, whether Jew or Gentile (4:11–12, 16–17). Throughout the chapter he assumes that the Romans know the story of Abraham; again and again he alludes to details of the narrative in the expectation that the Romans will be able to fill in the gaps.[34]

The quotation from Gen 15:6 in Rom 4:3 plays a key role in Paul's argument. Although it is technically not a proposition or thesis statement, the entire chapter is devoted to its exposition. As with the rabbinic midrashim, the verse serves as the lemma to which the interpreter returns repeatedly for inspiration, like a musician playing variations on a theme.[35] The quotation is restated in v. 5, echoed in v. 9, expounded in vv. 10–12, abbreviated in v. 13, exemplified in vv. 18–21, requoted in v. 22, and applied in vv. 23–24. Clearly, Gen 15:6 is the backbone of Paul's argument in Rom 4.

---

34. It is more proper to say that Paul assumes such knowledge on the part of the hypothetical Jewish interlocutor with whom he has been in dialogue since Rom 2:17 (via an extended "speech-in-character"), as argued by Stowers (*Rereading*, 16–21, 37–38, 227–34, 242–43) and supported by Byrne (*Romans*, 96, 104, 108–10, 141, 145, 147). But for this rhetorical exercise to work, Paul had to frame his argument in such a way that the implied Gentile Christian audience would be capable not only of "overhearing" his response to his Jewish opponent, but also of understanding and accepting it. Thus, Paul also assumes (at least indirectly) that the Romans know something about the Abraham story.

35. James Dunn calls Rom 4 "one of the finest examples of Jewish midrash available to us from this era" (*Romans,* 1.197).

How might the Christians in Rome have responded to Paul's use of Gen 15:6 in the context of his developing argument? The answer depends in part on how much they knew about the Abraham story.

1. The "informed audience" would have been familiar not only with those aspects of the Abraham narrative that Paul mentions in Rom 4, but also with the portions that he omits. Thus, they would have been in a position to evaluate and criticize the whole of Paul's interpretation of the Abraham narrative. What might they have concluded about his approach to Scripture? A comparison of Rom 4 with Gen 15 would have shown them that Paul had adhered fairly closely to the biblical storyline.[36] Among the points that the informed audience could have checked and approved are Paul's insistence on the importance of Abraham's "faith" as the basis for God's acknowledgment of his "righteousness" (4:9, 11, 13, 22); his linking of Abraham's "faith" with the divine promise of a son (4:18–21); his reference to the promise of "the land" to Abraham's descendants (4:13); and his recognition that the events of Gen 15 took place before God issued the command for Abraham to be circumcised (4:10–11). Other points from the Abraham story that the audience could have verified include God's promise to bless "the nations" through Abraham (4:17; cf. Gen 12:3); Abraham's age when God promised to give him a child through Sarah (4:19; cf. Gen 17:1); and the "deadness" of Sarah's womb at the time of the promise (4:19; cf. Gen 16:1, 18:11). The fact that Paul had hewed so closely to the storyline in places where it could be checked against the original text would have lent prima facie credibility to those parts of his argument that could not be verified (i.e., his claim that God accepts Gentiles on the same terms as Jews). In other words, Paul's handling of the Abraham story would probably have enhanced his reputation with the informed audience.

On the other hand, a more skeptical member of the informed audience might have found reason to be critical of Paul's interpretation of Gen 15:6 (and the entire Abraham narrative) in Rom 4. The principal problem is that Paul actually builds his argument on silence: the passage says nothing about whether Abraham's "deeds" (whether before or after his encounter with God) played any role in Yahweh's acknowledgment of his "righteousness" (cf. Rom 4:3–4).[37] A person who opposed Paul's message might well argue that

---

36. It is worth recalling that Paul treated the Abraham narrative the same way in Gal 3:6–9. See the discussion in chapter 7.

37. Paul's argument in Gal 3:10–12 is marked by the same problem (see chapter 7). Nonetheless, F. F. Bruce is probably correct in defending Paul's reading of the story at this point:

it was the fact that Abraham put his "faith" into action (as narrated in Gen 12–14) that led God to promise him a son and declare him "righteous" (cf. Jas 2:20–24).[38] The same could be said about Abraham's subsequent actions, including his willingness to offer Isaac on the altar (cf. Heb 11:17–19; Jas 2:20–24). As for the broader narrative, a critical reader of the Genesis story could point to several places where it appears that Paul has either left out key ideas or read his own ideas into the text—for example, when he ignores the covenantal context of circumcision (Gen 17) or injects his own critical judgments about Torah into the argument (Rom 4:13–15).[39] In other words, an

"Paul's argument is not merely textual and verbal, dependent on a selection of Genesis xv.6 in preference to other texts from those chapters in Genesis which might have pointed in the other direction. For Abraham's good works, his obedience to the divine commandments, were the fruit of his unquestioning faith in God; had he not first believed the promises of God he would never have conducted his life from then on in the light of what he knew of God's will" (*The Epistle of Paul to the Romans: An Introduction and Commentary* [TNTC; Grand Rapids: Eerdmans, 1963], 110).

38. C. E. B. Cranfield (*Romans,* 1.229) cites a number of Jewish texts, from 1 Macc 2:52 to *Mekilta* 35b and 40b, to demonstrate that ancient Jews viewed Abraham's faith as a meritorious act, not something that existed apart from his actions (cf. Barrett, *Romans,* 87-88). According to Cranfield, "In appealing to Gen 15.6 in support of his contention that Abraham was not justified on the ground of works and has no right to glory before God, Paul was deliberately appealing to a verse which his fellow Jews generally assumed to be clear support for the diametrically opposite view. . . . It was clearly essential to the credibility of his argument that he should not by-pass a text which would seem to many of his fellow Jews the conclusive disproof of the point he was trying to establish" (229–30). See also the materials presented in Dunn, *Romans,* 1.200–202, 226–28; Byrne, *Romans,* 142; Schreiner, *Romans,* 215–16; Schlier, *Römerbrief,* 123–24; Luke Timothy Johnson, *Reading Romans: A Literary and Theological Commentary* (New York: Crossroad, 1997), 64–66. A similar idea can be seen in Ps 106:31, where the psalmist describes the actions of Phinehas in language that echoes Gen 15:6 but draws exactly the opposite conclusion from Rom 4, as noted by John Murray (*The Epistle to the Romans* [2 vols., NICNT; Grand Rapids: Eerdmans, 1959], 1.131). Murray fails to recognize the challenge that the parallel poses for Paul's argument, but his observation is correct nonetheless: "Paul could not have appealed to Psalm 106:31 in this connection without violating his whole argument. For if he had appealed to Psalm 106:31 in the matter of *justification,* . . . then the case of Phinehas would have provided an inherent contradiction and would have demonstrated *justification* by a righteous and zealous act" (131). Fitzmyer notes that the apparent conflict between these two verses was "hotly disputed in Reformation times" (*Romans,* 374).

39. John Murray argues that "there is no incompatibility" between Paul's description of circumcision as a "seal of the righteousness of faith" in Rom 4:11 and its role as a "sign" of the covenant between God and Abraham in Gen 17:11, since "the promises of Genesis 15:4, 5, to which the faith of Abraham, mentioned in Genesis 15:6, was directed and for the fulfillment of which Abraham trusted in the Lord, were essentially the same promises as were embedded in and confirmed by the covenant of Genesis 17:2–14" (*Romans,* 1.138). Paul would probably have agreed with this statement, but a skeptical reader could have pointed out that the link between circumcision and the covenant (including its eventual expression in the Torah) is explicit in the

audience familiar with the original context of Gen 15:6 and the Abraham story in general could have found ample reason either to accept or to reject Paul's ideas after analyzing the way he handled the Jewish Scriptures.

While Paul no doubt hoped that the Romans would find his argument in Rom 4 convincing, his experience with the Galatians would have taught him that the Abraham story could be turned in more than one direction. Since he used the story anyway, he must have assumed either that the Romans would be charitable toward his proposed interpretation or that they would not know the story well enough to raise questions about his handling of the text. In either case, the ready availability of an alternative reading suggests that Paul did not expect the Romans to conduct a careful verse-by-verse analysis of his argument on the basis of their own independent readings of Gen 12–21.

2. The situation of the "competent audience" is less clear in this case than in others, since it is hard to determine how much of the Abraham narrative Paul expected the Romans to know (the key criterion for defining the "competent audience"). It is also unclear whether the level of familiarity that he assumes could have been derived from oral sources or whether his argument assumes knowledge of the written text. A maximalist view of the competent audience yields the same results as for the "informed audience": Paul's treatment of the Abraham story could be viewed as either helping or hurting his argument, depending on whether the audience was disposed to be charitable or critical toward the ideas that he sought to advance with his interpretation of the Genesis narrative. The less biblical literacy that one grants to the competent audience, on the other hand, the more it appears that the argument from Gen 15:6 (and the Abraham story in general) would have served to enhance the audience's receptivity to Paul's argument in Romans. The reason for this judgment is that an audience with less knowledge of the original text would have been more impressed by Paul's facility with the Jewish Scriptures and less prepared to criticize his efforts. By referring again and again to Gen 15:6 in Rom 4, Paul reinforced the impression that he was an expert interpreter who knew exactly what the text meant. This

---

text, while its relation to Abraham's "faith" is, at best, implied (as rightly noted by Terence Donaldson, *Paul and the Gentiles: Remapping the Apostle's Convictional World* [Minneapolis: Fortress, 1997], 122-28). Joseph Fitzmyer sees the issue more clearly: "Significantly, Paul avoids mention of the covenant or pact, and 'the sign of the covenant' becomes for him 'the seal of uprightness.' He seems to have identified the covenant too much with the law and insinuates that God's true covenant was made with people of faith" (*Romans,* 381).

in turn could have led members of the competent audience to be more receptive to the position that Paul advances in Rom 4 (i.e., that God accepts both Jews and Gentiles on the basis of faith alone), since they would have perceived that the authority of Scripture stood behind Paul's words. Thus, even if Paul was wrong in expecting the Romans to know very much about the Abraham narrative, the argument of Rom 4 might nonetheless have served to enhance their acceptance of his argument.

3. The same is true for the "minimal audience." For the person who knew nothing about the Jewish Scriptures (or who knew little more than the name of Abraham through common cultural lore about the Jews), Paul's argument in Rom 4 could have seemed overwhelming, especially his repeated references to Gen 15:6. But Paul includes enough snippets of information about Abraham in his argument to enable even the minimal audience to grasp at least the broad outlines of the story. From Paul's passing comments, members of this group could have gathered that Abraham was an important man about whom stories were told in the Jewish Scriptures; that he was a Jew (from the reference to his circumcision); that he had a barren wife named Sarah; that he succeeded in having children, probably through Sarah; that God had made a series of promises to him; and that he had demonstrated great faith and was therefore declared "righteous" by God. Although this bare outline would have been insufficient for them to comprehend the full story, it was enough to allow them to follow the main lines of Paul's argument. Since they would have had no way to check Paul's handling of the biblical text, they would have had to trust that Paul was giving them a reliable interpretation of the Jewish Scriptures unless someone informed them to the contrary. And since they regarded the words of Scripture as authoritative, the fact that Paul could adduce Scripture so effectively in support of his position would have inclined them toward accepting Paul's view that God accepts Jews and Gentiles alike on the basis of faith.

It seems safe to assume that Paul was aware that arguments from Scripture would exercise this kind of power over the minds of the Christians at Rome. This in turn helps us to understand why Paul was willing to quote Scripture so freely in a letter to a group of Christians whom he had never met. From a rhetorical standpoint, it was not particularly vital that the Romans understand and approve his handling of the many verses that he cites in his letter. As long as they accepted the authority of the Jewish Scriptures and viewed Paul as a reliable interpreter of the sacred text, the inclusion of arguments from Scripture would have enhanced their acceptance of Paul's positions.[40] And in case anyone needed evidence that Paul was in fact a skilled interpreter, the demonstration of his skills in the letter itself would have been enough to gain him the respect of a predominantly illiterate audience.

Romans 9:25–26

The rhetorical artistry of Rom 9–11 has elicited a variety of suggestions about precisely what Paul was seeking to accomplish in these chapters. Several points seem clear. Paul's argument centers on important questions with which he himself has wrestled regarding the divergent responses of Jews and Gentiles to his missionary preaching. In his mind, nothing less than the faithfulness of God, and perhaps God's goodness and power as well, are at stake in the Jews' rejection of his message. Thus, any explanation of their response had to make sense of God's conduct as well. Eventually Paul's questioning led him to formulate his famous "two-stage" model of salvation history, which says that God has temporarily "hardened" the Jews so that the message of salvation can go to the Gentiles, after which God will at last "unharden" the Jews so that "all Israel will be saved" (11:1–36).

But this does not explain why Paul included these chapters in his letter to the Christians in Rome. At the rhetorical level, these chapters must pertain in some way to Paul's perception of the needs of his Roman audience or he would not have included them. But the sheer generality of the letter makes it difficult to ascertain what Paul had in mind. From Paul's consistent third-person references to "Israel" (and his explicit statement in 11:13) we can see that the implied audience of Rom 9–11 is a group of Gentile Christians. Though we should be careful about "mirror-reading" from Paul's rhetoric to the actual situation in Rome, it appears that Paul is aware (or at least believes) that the Gentile element of the Roman church has come to see itself as the true "people of God" to the exclusion of the Jews (11:18–21, 25).[41] This belief

---

40. Joseph Fitzmyer stands virtually alone in calling attention to this aspect of Paul's appeal to the Abraham story: "In writing to a Christian community that he himself has neither visited nor founded, he appeals to something that he knows his readers will not only understand but even accept, the testimony of Scripture" (*Romans,* 370).

41. Alternately, one could argue that this "problem" existed only in Paul's mind; that is, that he included these chapters to address an attitude that he thought might arise in the minds of Gentile Christians as a result of his "universalist" rhetoric in chapters 1–8 (see Byrne, *Romans,* 282–84). If so, Paul did not need to know anything about the actual attitudes of Gentile Christians in Rome. The possibility that Rom 11:13–24 represents yet another "speech-in-

was enough to constitute a "provoking rhetorical urgency" in Paul's mind, since it contradicted his own deep commitment to the people of Israel (9:1–5, 10:1, 11:1), a commitment that he believed he shared with God (9:6, 11:2, 23). Whether the "arrogance" that Paul rebukes in the implied audience is rooted in reality (i.e., based on what he has heard from Rome) or simply a feature of his diatribal style, the result is the same: he writes to provoke a change of belief and attitude on the part of the implied audience.[42]

The combined quotation from Hos 2:23 (2:25 LXX) and 1:10 (2:1 LXX) in Rom 9:25–26 occupies a key place in the development of Paul's argument. In the first eighteen verses of the chapter, Paul adduces a series of biblical examples to demonstrate that God has the freedom to choose whomever God desires as "objects of mercy" and to reject (or even "harden") others. At first he focuses only on distinctions that God has made within Israel (vv. 6–13), but then he widens the scope of his argument to include a Gentile (Pharaoh) as well (vv. 14–18). The purpose of this argument is not spelled out, though the answer is implied in 9:1–6, where Paul professes his undying grief for his fellow Jews and insists that God's word has not failed. Clearly, he is referring to the fact that most Jews have rejected his preaching about Christ, though it is not at all clear why he leaves it to the audience to fill in this key piece of the argument.[43] His decision to conduct the argument at the level of broad principles has the clear rhetorical benefit of distracting the audience from questions that might have arisen over missionary strategy and who was to blame for the failure of the mission to the Jews.

---

character" to an imaginary audience seems not to have occurred to Stanley Stowers, despite his insistence that "the audience in the letter is a rhetorical construction, a textual strategy meant to persuade and affect" (*Rereading*, 290). If such a reading could be sustained, it would seriously undermine Stowers's argument (grounded in these verses) that the entire letter was directed to Gentile Christians in Rome (287–89).

42. While it is often asserted that Paul is arguing here against "arrogant" attitudes that the Gentile Christians of Rome had adopted toward Jewish *Christianity* (e.g., Bruce, *Romans*, 182–83; Schreiner, *Romans*, 471), this must be read into the passage. In the few places where Paul refers to Jewish Christians in these chapters (Rom 9:24, 27–28, 10:12, 11:5), the focus is on their role as the "faithful remnant" of God's people, not their contemporary relations with Gentile Christians.

43. If the omission is regarded as intentional, a variety of rhetorical purposes could be posited, though the evidence for any of them is scanty. Perhaps Paul felt that a direct admission of failure would make him look ineffective at a time when he intended to seek the Romans' support for his mission to Spain. Perhaps he was so concerned with defending himself against accusations of having abandoned the Jews (9:1–3) that he failed to notice that he had been unclear. Perhaps it was not his own missionary failure but that of the Romans that concerned him, and he wanted to avoid offending them with a direct challenge. The argument of 9:6–19 reads the same in any case.

In v. 19, Paul raises the obvious diatribal response to his argument in vv. 6–18: "Why, then, does God still affix blame? Who has resisted his will?" Instead of responding directly to the question, Paul presents an ad hominem response consisting of a series of rhetorical questions (vv. 20–24) supported by three biblical quotations (vv. 25–29). The only new argument that he offers appears in vv. 22–23, where he speaks for the first time about a divine plan that is being worked out in human history. The argument is elliptical, but Paul seems to be dividing history into two periods: a time in the past when God chose to bear patiently with those whom he calls "objects of wrath" who merited "destruction," and the present day when God has "called" a group of people whom Paul labels "objects of mercy." Who are the people to whom Paul is referring here? The identity of the "objects of mercy" is clarified in v. 24, where Paul identifies them as a group of Jews and Gentiles (presumable a reference to the Christian church—note the pronoun "us"). But the same cannot be said for the "objects of wrath."[44] By his failure to identify this group, Paul leaves room (whether intentionally or not) for the audience to supply their own interpretation.

What, then, does the quotation in vv. 25–26 add to the argument? The answer depends on the level of biblical literacy that we assume for Paul's audience.

1. The "informed audience" would have recognized that Paul has blended together two poignant verses from the book of Hosea (2:25 and 2:1 [LXX]) that speak similarly of God's abiding love for Israel.[45] According to Hosea, the judgment that is about to be released against Israel does not mean that God has rejected Israel forever. The time will come when God will again

---

44. Rightly noted by Schlier (*Römerbrief*, 302), Wagner (*Heralds*, 75), and Byrne (*Romans*, 302). After cautioning against moving too quickly to equate these terms with "real-world" groups, Byrne finally succumbs to that temptation when he concludes that v. 24 makes it "inescapably clear that the 'vessels of wrath, ripe for destruction' are in fact that large part of Israel that has not responded positively to the Christian gospel" (302). This conclusion is by no means "inescapably clear," as will be shown below. For a helpful discussion of the many ambiguities that confront a reader trying to make sense of Paul's language in vv. 22–24 (and the various ways in which his statements might be understood), see John G. Lodge, *Romans 9–11: A Reader-Response Analysis* (Atlanta: Scholars, 1996), 85–93.

45. This audience also would have seen that Paul has substantially modified the wording of the first verse to create a more effective verbal link between the quotation and the framing comments (see the analysis in Stanley, *Paul*, 109–13). These modifications include reversing the order of the clauses, replacing the verb ἐρῶ with καλέσω, and making several minor grammatical changes that were needed to fit the verse into Paul's sentence structure. None of the adaptations has any notable effect on the meaning of the verse, but taken together they strengthen the verbal link between the quotation and the surrounding verses, thus reinforcing the impression that the verse supports Paul's argument. The purpose of the changes is entirely rhetorical.

speak a word of acceptance to Israel and restore them to their former status as God's people. Since Paul does not explain how the quotation relates to his rather elliptical statement in vv. 22–24, members of the informed audience would have referred to the original Hosean contexts in order to gain insight into Paul's quotation. There they would have found that the "people" about whom Hosea was speaking in the verses quoted by Paul was the nation of Israel. On this basis they probably would have concluded that the "people" about whom Paul was speaking in 9:25–26 are likewise the people of Israel—that is, the Jews.[46] In the context of 9:22–24, the quotation might have come across to them as an assertion that the prophecy of Hosea had at last come true: the time when God would again show "mercy" to Israel was now being fulfilled as Jews responded favorably (along with Gentiles) to God's "call" to embrace the Christian gospel.[47] This understanding of the quotation would have led them to conclude retrospectively that the term "objects of wrath" in v. 22 referred to Jews who had been unfaithful to God and thus placed themselves under the same threat of punishment that the prophet Hosea had issued to their ancestors.[48] This reading of vv. 22–26 would have found confirmation in the two quotations from the prophet Isaiah in vv. 27– 29, both of which speak of a small portion of Israel (a "remnant," according to Isa 10:22) who will be "saved" from the coming judgment.[49]

---

46. In his eagerness to uncover the reasoning behind Paul's "strong misreading" of Hos 1:10b and 2:23 as referring to the inclusion of the Gentiles, Ross Wagner never pauses to ask whether a literate audience who was familiar with the original context could have figured out that this was what Paul meant (*Heralds*, 79–89). It would have been much more natural for them to relate the verses to Israel, and Paul says nothing that would have "corrected" that interpretation.

47. In other words, an audience that took its bearings from the context of Hosea need never come to the conclusion that the phrase "not my people" in vv. 24–25 refers to "Gentiles"—a point missed by virtually all commentators. Douglas Moo thinks that "the explicit reference to Israel in the introduction to the Isaiah quotations in v. 27 suggests that Paul views the Hosea quotations as related to the calling of the Gentiles" (*The Epistle to the Romans* [NICNT; Grand Rapids: Eerdmans, 1996], 613). But this is true only if one takes the δέ in v. 27 as disjunctive; a conjunctive reading would find in v. 27 a clarification of the identity of the addressees in vv. 25–26. John Lodge (*Romans 9–11*, 94–96) rightly notes the ambiguity of Paul's language here, pointing out that it could be taken as referring to Jews, Gentiles, or some combination of the two.

48. Schreiner (*Romans*, 521), Dunn (*Romans*, 2.567–68), and Schlier (*Römerbrief*, 301) read the text in this way.

49. As Richard Hays observes, "It makes better sense to read the Isaiah prophecy as a word of condemnation: the quotation from Hosea proves that he calls Jews (*Echoes*, 68; cf. Stowers, *Rereading*, 301–3; Wagner, *Heralds*, 92–116). But John Lodge is also correct when he points out that the language of vv. 27–29 could be taken as either promise or threat, depending on how the reader has constructed the previous verses (*Romans 9–11*, 94–98).

Thus we see that in this case members of the informed audience would have found their understanding of the combined quotation in Rom 9:25–26 enhanced by their ability to refer to the original context of the verses in Hosea.[50] The fact that Paul's argument seemed to coincide so well with a natural reading of the original text would no doubt have inclined the informed audience to view Paul's position in a more favorable light.

2. Since the quotation in Rom 9:25–26 can be understood perfectly well without reference to its original context, the "competent audience" would have derived its understanding of the quotation entirely from the cues provided in the Pauline context. For these addressees, the key would have been found in the obvious verbal and conceptual links between the framing comments in vv. 23–24 and the quotation in vv. 25–26. In both places God is depicted as "calling" a group of people, and in both instances the outcome is similar: "mercy" (v. 23) is shown to those who were "not my people" (v. 25), so that they experience the "riches of God's glory" (v. 23) by being called "children of the living God" (v. 26). In v. 24 Paul states clearly that this group includes both Jews and Gentiles. From all that Paul has said thus far in Romans, the competent audience would have known that he was referring to the Christian church, the mixed nature of which he proceeds to amplify and explain in the remainder of chapters 9–11. From here they could infer that the group described as "not my people" in vv. 25–26 was the same as those labeled "objects of wrath" in v. 22, and that both phrases were simply poetic terms for the mass of Jews and Gentiles whom Paul has already declared to be equally "under sin" (3:9–20) and equally able to be made "righteous" through faith in Christ (3:22–24, 28–30, 4:11–12).[51] This way of making

---

50. Whether this was in fact the meaning that Paul intended is doubtful, since the perspective of the "competent audience" fits better with Paul's summary statements in vv. 30–33 (see below). Of course, the "informed audience" might also have been led to modify its original judgments about the meaning of the quotation when they encountered these subsequent verses.

51. C. K. Barrett (*Romans,* 190–91) is one of the few commentators who understand the text in this way, though Richard Hays (*Echoes,* 67) offers a similar suggestion. Most commentators take the quotation in vv. 25–26 as referring to the Gentiles, who once were excluded ("not my people") but have now been included in God's plan ("my people"/"children of the living God"). In this reading, the quotation pertains primarily to the phrase at the end of v. 24 ("but also from among the Gentiles"). This view of the passage is certainly plausible, but one has to wonder whether it would have occurred to the original audience of the text, since the argument of chapter 9 to this point would have conditioned them to understand vv. 22–23 (including the phrase "objects of wrath" in v. 22) as relating in some way to God's dealings with the Jews (cf. 9:1–6), and there has been no mention of "the Gentiles" since chapter 4. Under these circumstances, the fact that the word "called" occupies a central position in v. 24 and in the quotation (where Paul has moved it to the primary position) would probably have been decisive, leading the audience to infer the same object (i.e., "Jews and Gentiles") for both occurrences of the verb.

sense of the passage would have found support in vv. 27–30, where Paul speaks first about a "remnant" of Israel who will be saved from the coming judgment, then about "the Gentiles" who have now obtained righteousness.

Thus, the competent audience could have arrived at a satisfying and holistic understanding of Paul's argument in the passage (including the biblical quotations) without knowing anything about the original context of the verses cited. The close verbal and conceptual links between the quotation and the Pauline argument would have served to reinforce the impression that the authoritative Scriptures (and thus God) stood behind the position that Paul was advocating in Rom 9–11.

3. By the time they reached the quotations from Hosea in Rom 9:25–26, members of the "minimal audience" would likely have lost the thread of Paul's argument. The problem would have been especially acute in vv. 6–18, where the bulk of the argument would have made no sense to a person who was unfamiliar with the biblical storyline.[52] The shift to a more direct mode of argumentation in vv. 19–24 would therefore have come as a welcome relief to these addressees. But without an understanding of Paul's argument in vv. 6–18, they could not have anticipated the objection that Paul raises in v. 19, which in turn would have limited their ability to appreciate the "answer" that he offers in vv. 20–29. On the other hand, Paul does not assume that his audience is familiar with the original context of the quotations in vv. 25–29, so the more thoughtful members of the minimal audience might have been able to arrive at an understanding of vv. 22–29 that approximated that of the "competent audience." But even if their level of understanding remained more limited, the minimal audience would have been impressed by Paul's ability to marshal arguments from the authoritative Scriptures in support of his position. This alone could have been enough to motivate them to accept those parts of Paul's argument that they were able to understand.

Romans 10:19–21

Since Rom 9–11 contains the densest concentration of biblical quotations in the Pauline corpus, a further example from this section should prove helpful for understanding the diverse ways in which Paul's audiences might have reacted to the intensive biblical argumentation that characterizes these chapters.

---

52. The only statements in these verses that would have been comprehensible to a person unfamiliar with the biblical storyline appear in vv. 6, 16, and 18.

The three quotations in Rom 10:19–21 occupy a transitional place in the argument of Rom 9–11. On the one hand, they look backward, linking the argument of 10:1–12, where Paul speaks of the universal availability of salvation, with that of chapter 9, where he underlines the divergent responses of Jews and Gentiles to the Christian message. On the other hand, the quotations point forward, since they depict a rather stark disjunction between the responses of Jews and Gentiles, raising the question of how to explain Israel's lack of response to the Christian gospel.

On a more proximate level, the three quotations form the second half of a two-part subargument (10:14–21) in which Paul explores the implications of the position that he spelled out in 10:5–13. Having argued that salvation is now available to all, Jew and Gentile alike, through faith in Christ, Paul is immediately faced with the question of why not everyone has accepted this message. In vv. 14–15 he implies that the failure can be attributed in part to a lack of preachers to proclaim the message.[53] Whether he intended to suggest that the churches should send out more missionaries or that ordinary Christians should be more vocal about their faith is unclear. In vv. 16–21 he shifts his attention to the responsibility of those who have received the message. Clearly, not everyone who has heard the message of salvation has accepted it (v. 16). But why not? Paul never answers the question. He simply offers a few elliptical observations that emphasize their culpability and leaves the solution to the audience (vv. 16–18).[54]

---

53. Virtually all commentators read vv. 14–15 as though Paul were making a theological assertion about the importance of preaching in God's plan of salvation. Joseph Fitzmyer's statement is typical: "Paul is summarizing the conditions for salvation: salvation stems from calling upon the Lord, which implies faith. Faith implies knowing about the gospel, which has to be preached by someone, someone who is authorized or sent with a commission to do so" (*Romans*, 596). This is true as far as it goes, but it begs the question of why Paul used such a rhetorically stylized mode of expression to make his point. In a formal sense, the questions are addressed to an audience who from Paul's perspective either does not recognize or is unconcerned about the vital necessity of sending out preachers to carry the "good news" ("the word of faith that we preach," v. 8) to Jews and Gentile alike (v. 12) so that all may have the opportunity to "believe" and be "saved" (v. 9). Even if the addressee is purely hypothetical, Paul's questions seem designed to motivate the Romans to lend more support to Christian missionary efforts (including his own, 15:23–24).

54. The significance of the quotation in v. 16b is unclear. Is Paul saying that the lack of response noted in v. 16a is a direct fulfillment of prophecy (so Cranfield, *Romans,* 2.535; Byrne, *Romans,* 324; Dunn, *Romans,* 2.622–23), or the recurrence of a pattern observed long ago by the followers of Second Isaiah (so Fitzmyer, *Romans,* 598; Bruce, *Romans,* 208–9), or perhaps even a reference to the Jews' failure to understand Second Isaiah's predictions of a suffering Messiah

As Paul makes clear in vv. 19–21, the issue that really concerns him is the divergent responses of Jews and Gentiles to the Christian gospel, especially the broad rejection of the message by his fellow Jews (cf. 10:1). The rhetorical situation that Paul faced at this point in his argument was delicate: he wanted the Romans to understand why he preached a "law-free" gospel for Jews and Gentiles alike, which meant emphasizing the universality of the Christian message. But he did not want to reinforce the supersessionist tendencies that he thought he had detected (or could anticipate) among the Gentile Christians at Rome toward the Jewish people as a whole (cf. 11:17–21). He therefore had to maintain a careful balance between statements critical of Israel and statements that revealed his own (and God's) abiding concern for the Jewish people.

The three quotations that Paul offers in rapid sequence in Rom 10:19–21 offer a brief introductory glimpse into his eventual solution to this problem. The full import of these verses, however, does not become clear until chapter 11, where Paul finally spells out his understanding of the divine plan that lay hidden behind the present negative reactions of his fellow Jews. How might the Romans have responded to the three quotations that Paul offers at this point in his argument?

1. Although Paul offers only the briefest interpretive comments to explain how he meant for the verses to be understood, the "informed audience" would have been able to refer to the original context for additional information about the meaning of the quotations. This was especially important for v. 19, where the relation between the quotation and Paul's

(so Johnson, *Reading Romans,* 161–62, Wagner, *Heralds*, 180)? No clarification is to be found in v. 17, where Paul's comments about the conjunction of "hearing" and "faith" in the quotation imply that he meant for the verse to be understood as supporting vv. 14–15 rather than v. 16a. A similar problem surrounds the quotation in v. 18. Who is the antecedent of the third-person plural pronouns? The closest referent is the Christian preachers mentioned in v. 15. But in this case the quotation must be taken either as an intentional hyperbole (so most commentators) or a prophecy of future missionary success (so Byrne, *Romans*, 327), since "any literal application of the text to the extent of the gospel's proclamation in Paul's day involves on immense exaggeration" (ibid., 327). If, on the other hand, Paul meant to imply (in accordance with Ps 19) that the beauty of nature ought to be enough to point people everywhere to God (cf. Rom 1:19–20), he does not indicate this to his audience, most of whom would have had no knowledge of the original context of the quotation. Richard Hays offers a useful corrective to such speculations: "In cases such as these, there is no indication that Paul has wrestled seriously with the texts from which the citations are drawn. He has simply appropriated their language to lend rhetorical force to his own discourse, with minimal attention to the integrity of the semiotic universe of the precursor" (*Echoes,* 175). Cf. Dunn, *Romans,* 2.624; Moo, *Romans,* 666–67.

introductory comment is by no means obvious. From the wording of the question that Paul uses to introduce the quotation (μὴ Ἰσραὴλ οὐκ ἔγνω;), one would expect to find a verse that could be understood as pointing toward some form of "knowledge" on the part of Israel. Instead, we find a quotation that speaks of Israel being made "jealous" by another nation. In Deut 32, the identity of this nation is not specified, but the verse appears in the middle of a long section that describes the many disasters that God will send upon wayward Israel.[55] Seeing this, the informed audience might have been inclined to read the quotation in v. 19 as an oracle of judgment against Israel.[56] But they would have been left to puzzle over the link between this idea and Paul's introductory comment about Israel "not knowing," since Paul nowhere explains what he means, and the broader context of Rom 10 offers no obvious assistance. Perhaps they might have guessed that the idea of judgment implies a morally culpable level of "knowledge," or that the kind of "envy" and "anger" described here required some degree of "knowledge" about the "nation" mentioned in this verse. But with Paul offering no

55. Ross Wagner (*Heralds*, 190–205) believes that Paul was drawing on the message of hope and restoration that comes at the end of Deut 32 rather than the language of judgment that fills the previous verses. But this future "restoration" is clearly adumbrated only in the last verse of the passage (Deut 32:43) and a passing reference in v. 36. The language of vv. 28-38 contains numerous echoes of the prophets' pronouncements against Israel, and should therefore be taken as referring to Israel, not to Israel's enemies as Wagner claims. The verse that Paul chose to quote in Rom 10:19 appears in the middle of a "judgment" passage that runs for at least 24 verses in our modern versions (Deut 32:15-38). For the "informed audience", the language of divine judgment against Israel would have dominated the horizon, regardless of Paul's intentions.

56. According to Fitzmyer, Paul's use of Scripture here implies an analogy: "Paul thus compares the present status of Israel with what its condition was at the time of its wandering in the desert. If it was humiliated then for its infidelity, how much greater should its humiliation be now; Gentiles, the 'nonpeople' and 'a foolish nation,' understand the gospel message, yet Israel is uncomprehending" (*Romans*, 599). Cranfield makes a similar point (*Romans*, 2.539). But this interpretation is problematic on two counts: it ignores the future orientation of Deut 32:21, which is clearly present in the Greek version that Paul quotes, and it assumes that the Romans could figure out the implicit reference to "Gentiles," even though there is no mention of them in the immediate context of Rom 10 (so also on 10:20). Even if Fitzmyer and Cranfield are correct, only those addressees who knew the original context of the quotation could have inferred such a meaning for the quotation, and even they would have had to reflect on the passage to grasp Paul's point. Neither commentator remarks on the difficulty that this quotation would have posed for Paul's Roman audience. Schreiner (*Romans*, 573) takes the future tense of the verse more seriously, arguing that Paul read the verse as a prophecy of what was happening in his own day in response to his preaching about Christ (cf. Dunn, *Romans*, 2.631; Moo, *Romans*, 668). But the Romans still would have had to know the original context in order to understand the verse in this way.

further guidance, they would have had no choice but to shelve their conjectures for the moment and look for clarification in the ensuing verses.[57]

To their dismay, they would have found little help in v. 20. Here, as in v. 19, Paul quotes an enigmatic verse from the Jewish Scriptures and offers no explanation as to how it relates to his argument. Once again the informed audience would have turned to the original context for clarification, and once again they would have been disappointed. As in Deut 32:21 (quoted in v. 19), the text of Isa 65:1 is ambiguous about the identity of the "nation" to whom God is said to have been revealed as well as the nature of the divine "revelation."[58] Since the prophecy of Isa 65 turns quickly to a message of judgment against wayward Israel, members of the informed audience would most likely have inferred that Paul meant for his quotation to refer to Israel as well, though its sense (and how it was supposed to relate to v. 19) would have remained unclear.[59] They might have inferred that Paul was saying that Israel has "known" about the message of salvation (v. 19a) because God (through the authoritative Scriptures) speaks of a time when God was "revealed" to Israel despite their lack of interest in God (v. 20). But the precise nature and timing of this "revelation" would still be obscure. In light of the multiple references to "preaching" in Rom 10:14–15, the most natural

57. Even if they were able to hear a verbal parallel between οὐκ ἔθνει in 10:19 and οὐ λαόν in 9:25–26, there is nothing in the earlier passage that would help them to understand the "jealousy" motif or the reference to Israel's "knowledge" in v. 19. There is also nothing in either passage that points the audience unambiguously toward relating either verse to "Gentiles." See the discussion of 9:25–26.

58. Although it may seem obvious that the "nation" in Isa 65:1 is wayward Israel, Isa 65:1–7 could be read as a description of a "pagan" nation as well. (Fitzmyer notes that the matter is "disputed among OT commentators" [*Romans*, 600].) Since Paul does not clarify how he means for the verse to be applied, some of the members of the "informed audience" might have concluded that Paul was reading Isa 65:1 as a reference to God's acceptance of the "Gentiles" (cf. Wagner, *Heralds*, 205–16). Not until v. 9 does it become clear that the oracle is addressed to Israel. The description of the "revelation" is also ambiguous: though the language of v. 1 sounds a positive tone, vv. 6–8 speak of the coming "revelation" of God's judgment (cf. v. 12). Dunn (*Romans*, 2.631) brushes these ambiguities aside too quickly when he relates the passage to Jewish expectation of the end-time conversion of the Gentiles and then adds his opinion that "Paul's reading is hardly forced and would not be dismissed as an unjustified interpretation of Isaiah by even his more critical readers." The implicit assumption that Paul's letters were routinely scrutinized by "critical readers" who compared his interpretations with the original text of Scripture is, of course, highly anachronistic.

59. Thus, a familiarity with Isa 65 would have inclined the informed audience to read the δέ at the beginning of v. 20 as a conjunctive rather than a disjunctive particle.

conjecture would have been that this "revelation" took place in the course of Christian missionary preaching to Jews.[60]

Turning finally to v. 21, the informed audience would have noticed that Paul had skipped over the latter part of Isa 65:1 (because it sounded redundant?) and then resumed the quotation from Isa 65 that he began in v. 20.[61] Unlike vv. 19–20, where the phrasing of the quotations was ambiguous, the meaning of this one would have been fairly obvious, since Paul relates the verse explicitly to Israel (v. 21a).[62] Here at last the informed audience would have found confirmation for its conjectures regarding the meanings of the quotations in v. 19 and v. 20. In all three passages they would have heard the voice of God speaking a word of judgment against Israel due to Israel's refusal to hear and obey the divine revelation, which for them probably meant the Christian gospel.[63] The threefold repetition of the pronouncement would have added to the gravity of the passage for the informed audience, reinforcing the aura of doom. Of course, the rhetorical effect would have been stronger if Paul had indicated his intentions more clearly than he does. But in the end, the informed audience would probably have concluded that the three quotations provided substantial support for the argument of Rom 9–11.[64]

---

60. To see this verse as referring to God's self-revelation to *Gentiles* (via Christian missionary preaching) would require the informed audience to ignore the clear references to Israel in Isa 65. Even the double presence of the word ἔθνει in the quotation in v. 19 would not necessarily point them in this direction, since the two colons would make little sense if the first ἔθνει were to be rendered as "Gentiles." In this case, the presumption that one should interpret the quotation in light of its original context would have distracted the informed audience from wrestling with the Pauline rhetorical context, where they could have found more guidance regarding the way Paul intended the verse to be understood (see below).

61. Ross Wagner (*Heralds*, 209) suggests that Paul might have omitted v. 1b ("I said, 'Here I am,' to the nation that did not call on my name") because of a potential conflict with his statements in Rom 10:12–13 that linked "salvation" with "calling on the name" of God.

62. Thus the informed audience would have been led by their interpretation of the prior verses to take the δέ at the beginning of v. 21 as a conjunctive rather than a disjunctive particle, as in v. 20.

63. As James Dunn comments, "Here again Israel ought to have recognized the perfect match between such a Scripture and the situation now resulting from the Gentile mission of the believers in Jesus the Messiah. Those who rejoice in the Scriptures cannot put forward the excuse that they never knew what is so plainly prophesied therein" (*Romans*, 2.632).

64. On the other hand, Paul seems to have anticipated that his concluding emphasis on Israel's failure to respond to God's self-revelation might have led some in the audience to question his handling of the biblical text. To foreclose this possibility, Paul turns in the next verse to address the obvious question: does Israel's current "hardness" toward God's revelatory word (i.e., the Christian gospel) signify that God has rejected them as his people? Had he not addressed this question, the rhetorical effectiveness of his biblical quotations in vv. 19–21 might have been seriously compromised.

2. The fact that they could not consult the original context of the verses would have led the "competent audience" to a very different understanding of Paul's quotations in Rom 10:19–21. Upon reaching v. 19, they would have experienced the same uncertainty as the "informed audience" regarding the link between the quotation and the introductory comment. But since they did not have the text of Deut 32 to guide them toward a solution, they would have had to look to the Pauline context for assistance. Though they could have inferred from the introductory comment that the "you" who was being addressed in the quotation was "Israel" and the speaker was God (despite the mention of "Moses" in v. 19a), they would have found little guidance in the broader context regarding the identity of the "nation" by whom God would "make them jealous" or how the quotation was intended to relate to the question of Israel's "knowledge." But they could not have overlooked Paul's consistent pattern of dividing humanity into two classes, "Israel" (i.e., "Jews") and "Gentiles," including several times in Rom 9–11 (9:24, 30–31, 10:12). Thus, it would have been natural for them to assume that the same distinction was at work here and to take "those who are not a nation" as a veiled reference to "the Gentiles," who (as the quotation said) did not constitute a single "nation."[65] On the other hand, the sheer generality of the third-person plural pronouns in the preceding verses (10:14–18) might have reminded them of the similarly general references in 9:22–26, which they most likely understood as referring to a mixed group of Jews and Gentiles—i.e., the Christian church.[66] On this basis they might have guessed that the quotation was saying that God would somehow use the church (made up of people from more than one ἔθνος) to make Israel "jealous." This interpretation had the additional benefit of suggesting a possible meaning for Paul's framing comment about Israel's "knowledge," since the presence of Jews in the church implied that at least some of "Israel" had indeed "known" (or "understood") the Christian gospel.[67] But the very ambiguity of the verse would have left the competent audience looking for additional clarification regarding how the quotation should be understood.

---

65. Most commentators assume that this reading of the verse is obvious. But the fact that "Gentiles" have not been mentioned since 9:30 means that the Roman audience had to recall Paul's earlier comments in order to make sense of the implied reference.

66. See the discussion of Rom 9:24–26. The close verbal parallel with the quotations in 9:25–26 is often cited as another indication that the verse refers to "Gentiles" (so Cranfield, *Romans,* 1.539; Bruce, *Romans,* 210), but this ignores the ambiguity of the references in the former passage as well (see the discussion above).

67. On the other hand, the application of the adjective ἀσύνετος to the church is rather awkward unless taken in an ironic sense.

When they came to v. 20, members of the competent audience would have found not clarity but more ambiguity. Though they could have inferred that the speaker in the verse was God (despite the introductory comment that implies that the "I" refers to "Isaiah"), they were left to guess about the identity of those who "did not seek" and "did not ask for" God. On the one hand, the loose verbal parallelism with the prior verse might have suggested that they should identify this group with the οὐκ ἔθνος of v. 19. The two quotations would then be understood as saying that God was revealed to a group other than Israel (whether "Gentiles" or the Christian church) when they were not seeking God, and that God now planned to use this group in some way to provoke "Israel" (i.e., the Jews) to jealousy.[68] On the other hand, they might have taken v. 20 as a continuation of Paul's response to the question that he raised in v. 19a regarding Israel's "knowledge." In this case, "Israel" was a more likely candidate for the unnamed recipient of the divine "revelation" in v. 20, since the verse could then be taken as evidence that Israel had in fact "known" about God's purposes through an (unidentified) earlier self-disclosure. This reading would be rejected, however, by anyone who recalled Paul's argument in 9:30–10:3, where he spoke of Gentiles "obtaining" what they did not "pursue," while crediting Israel with being "zealous for God" but not "attaining" what they sought. Though the meaning of the verse would have remained unclear, the competent audience would most likely have concluded that it referred to the spread of the Christian gospel to the Gentiles and/or the mixed congregation that comprised the Christian church. This interpretation would have found added support from the fact that it was consistent with this audience's tentative understanding of v. 19.

Upon reaching v. 21, the competent audience would have felt that they were finally standing on solid ground. Here Paul states clearly that the quotation concerns "Israel," and the "I" is easily understood as the voice of God lamenting over Israel's lack of response to the divine initiative. The nature of this initiative is not spelled out, but the argument would have conditioned the addressees to take the verse as a reference to the proclamation of the message about Christ (cf. 10:8–9, 12–17). Unfortunately, the apparent clarity of v. 21 sheds little light on the meaning of the ambiguous quotations in vv. 19–20, since v. 21 implies nothing about the identity of the "other nation" in v. 19 or the ones to whom God was "revealed" in v. 20. The most that can

---

68. This reading might have suggested a disjunctive reading for the δέ at the beginning of the verse, as might the use of the verb ἀποτολμᾷ to describe Isaiah's speech (i.e., Isaiah is "bold" to contradict Moses). But a conjunctive reading would not be out of place, since the two verses could then be taken together as a response to the question in v. 19a.

be said is that it seems to confirm the supposition that "Israel" is indeed the group that God intends to "make jealous" in v. 19.

On the other hand, the negative depiction of "Israel" in v. 21 adds a new element to the argument of Rom 9–11, since this is the first time that Paul has explicitly accused "Israel" (i.e., the Jews) of being "disobedient" and willfully rejecting the divine initiative. Until now he has been more charitable in his remarks, charging them only with pursuing "righteousness" by the wrong route (9:31–32, 10:2–3) and failing to recognize God's new way of salvation (9:32–33). By relying on the words of Scripture to make this new point, Paul has insured that his accusation will be taken seriously, while simultaneously shielding himself from any criticism that might have been aroused by such a statement.

For the competent audience, then, the three quotations would have advanced Paul's argument by summing up his earlier comments about "Israel" and the "Gentiles," while simultaneously foreshadowing the solution that he plans to offer in chapter 11 (cf. 10:19 with 11:14). But if Paul thought that his quotations provided an effective answer to the important question that he raised in v. 19a, his efforts must be judged less than successful, since the significance of some of his references in vv. 19–20 remains ambiguous due to the brevity of his explanatory comments. In the end, the rhetorical effectiveness of these quotations for the competent audience would have been severely limited by Paul's cryptic style.[69]

3. Since Paul assumes no familiarity with the original context of the three quotations in Rom 10:19–21, there is no obvious reason to distinguish the reactions of the "minimal audience" from those of the "competent audience." Though Rom 10 contains nearly as many biblical quotations as Rom 9, the argument of Rom 10 is more accessible to an audience with no knowledge of the Jewish Scriptures, since none of the quotations in Rom 10 require the audience to supply background material from the biblical text as in Rom 9. Quotations also play a more subordinate (mostly confirmatory) role in Rom 10, whereas they formed the backbone of the argument in Rom 9.

But when we attempt to look at this passage through the eyes of the minimal audience, a different sort of problem emerges. As they tried to make sense of Paul's argument in vv. 16–21, the minimal audience would have encountered many of the same uncertainties and ambiguities as the "competent audience." But instead of charging Paul with a lack of clarity and con-

69. Of course, this judgment only applies to the argument as it exists to this point. Paul goes on to explain his argument more fully in chapter 11.

tinuing to grapple with the passage, the minimal audience might well have attributed their inability to understand the quotations to their own ignorance of the biblical text. This judgment might have caused them to skip over this part of Paul's argument entirely without making a serious effort to grasp what he was saying. As a result, their understanding of the argument in Rom 9–11 would have become even more fragmented, since Paul actually expands the scope of his argument in these verses.

Thus, while the minimal audience might have been impressed by Paul's skill in arguing from the sacred text, their ability to follow and embrace his argument would have been hindered rather than helped by the obscure manner in which he frames his argument from Scripture in these verses. If Paul was in fact aiming to persuade an audience that resembled the minimal audience, then his use of biblical quotations in this passage must be judged a rhetorical failure.

The Role of Quotations in Romans

From this brief sampling of verses we can see that Paul used Scripture in a variety of ways in his letter to the Romans. The sheer breadth of his references to the Jewish Scriptures cries out for explanation. Since he was writing to a group of Christians whom he did not know personally, Paul had no way of knowing exactly which verses from the Jewish Scriptures they would recognize. The safest route was to avoid biblical quotations altogether, or at least to include enough interpretive comments to insure that the Romans could follow his argument without resorting to the original text. That is exactly what Paul does in the bulk of the letter.

But there are a number of places where Paul elects to pursue the rhetorically risky strategy of assuming that the Romans will recognize a particular passage or episode from the Jewish Scriptures. Why does he do this? Was he not concerned that such a strategy could undercut the effectiveness of his rhetoric if the Romans failed to understand his references? Perhaps he never thought of the problem. Or perhaps he was so accustomed to quoting from Scripture in support of his arguments that he could hardly do otherwise. But neither of these explanations finds much support in Paul's letters. In Romans, as elsewhere, Paul shows that he is quite capable of addressing important issues in a thoughtful manner with little or no immediate reference to the Jewish Scriptures (e.g., 1:18–2:29, 5:1–8:30, 12:1–14:23). When he includes a quotation from Scripture in his argument, we should assume that it was a conscious (or at least semiconscious) choice.

In the case of Romans, the bulk of Paul's explicit quotations appears in passages where he is seeking to advance his thesis that God has acted in Christ to open up a new way for Jews and Gentiles alike to be "righteous" and therefore counted among God's chosen people—that is, the way of "faith." Of course, this is not really a "new" way for Jews, since faith in God had always been one of the requirements of the covenant. This is precisely what Paul seeks to show in many of his quotations from the Jewish Scriptures. However, he still had to explain why a "new way" was needed at all. On the one hand, Paul knew that the Scriptures declared that God had chosen the Jews as his covenant people out of all the nations of the earth. On the other hand, he was convinced that God was using his own missionary preaching to bring Gentiles to God and thus to incorporate them into God's "chosen people" alongside the Jews. Since he was committed to the authority of Scripture, he could not simply reject what the Scriptures said about God's unique election of the Jews; he had to find a way to justify his Gentile mission from the Scriptures of Judaism.

But why bring this up in Romans? Apparently, Paul had reason to think that there were people in Rome who had a different view of the situation, though the precise nature of the problem is obscured by his rhetoric. Perhaps there were Christians in Rome who were arguing against the Gentile mission on the basis of Scripture. Perhaps there were disagreements about whether Jewish and Gentile Christians should meet together or as separate bodies. Or perhaps Paul simply decided on his own that it would be wise to anticipate and defuse an argument that he had encountered from "Judaizers" in his own churches.

Whatever his motivation, Paul apparently thought that the rhetorical value of arguing from Scripture was so great that he was willing to accept the risk of undermining his own argument by misjudging the Romans' familiarity with specific biblical texts. Unlike his own churches, Paul could not assume that the Romans would accept his message on the basis of his own apostolic authority. But he must have felt confident that they would respect the authority of Scripture. Thus, even if he was wrong about what the Romans actually knew from the Jewish Scriptures, he could anticipate that his use of biblical argumentation would lend credibility to his positions and enhance his reputation with the Romans in advance of his impending visit. In the end, that was all he really needed.

CHAPTER 9

Conclusions

EVALUATING PAUL'S BIBLICAL RHETORIC

As a Jewish rabbi, Paul spent many years studying his ancestral Scriptures. As a follower of Jesus of Nazareth, he labored to interpret his newfound faith in the light of those same Scriptures. As a Christian missionary, he sometimes found it useful to appeal to specific verses of Scripture to motivate his churches to follow or to avoid a particular course of action. It is this last mode of interaction with the biblical text that we have been exploring in the present study.

In chapter 4 we identified two interrelated questions that lay at the heart of this study: (1) how do Paul's quotations serve to advance the developing arguments of his letters? and (2) how well does Paul's strategy of biblical argumentation cohere with what we can surmise about the capabilities and inclinations of his audiences? The time has come to summarize what we have learned in these two areas.

THE RHETORIC OF PAUL'S QUOTATIONS

The rhetorical model of Eugene White outlined in chapter 1 gives us a helpful framework for integrating what we have learned about the role of biblical quotations within the broader rhetorical context of Paul's letters.

1. To use White's terms, Paul faced a different "provoking rhetorical urgency" when writing to each of his churches. The identification of each situation as a "rhetorical urgency" that called for a written response reflects Paul's perception of the situation of the audience, a perception that may or may not have been shared by those to whom the letters were addressed. In each case Paul crafted a response that he believed would persuade the audience to see things as he did and follow his recommendations to eliminate the "rhetorical urgency." In the process, Paul assumed a stance of social and ideological dominance/power over his intended audience, a dominance for which he claimed divine support.

2. In a few of these letters (Galatians, 1 and 2 Corinthians, and Romans) Paul used explicit quotations from the Jewish Scriptures as part of his rhetorical arsenal. In each of the churches addressed in these letters, Paul's integrity and/or apostolic authority had been called into question. In this context, Paul's repeated appeals to the authoritative Scriptures served to reinforce his standing with the audience by highlighting the common bond that united speaker and audience, Jew and Gentile alike, around the God of Israel. He may also have hoped that his knowledge and skill in handling the community's holy text would enhance his stature with the audience and thus secure a favorable hearing for his message.

3. Though he wrote to predominantly Gentile congregations, Paul did not make a practice of discussing the literary background of his quotations. Instead, he seems to have made a serious effort to embed his quotations within a network of interpretive remarks that would enable his audiences to grasp his rhetorical point without having to know the original context of the quotation. While there are certainly instances where a familiarity with the original context would have deepened the rhetorical impact of a quotation, there are far more places where a reader who knew the source text would have found reason to question Paul's handling of the biblical text, and possibly his entire argument. In other words, Paul seems to have directed his quotations toward an implied audience that resembled the "competent audience" more closely than the "informed audience" or the "minimal audience."

4. In some cases, Paul framed his quotations in such a way that the audience had to supply the background and context of the quotation in order to make sense of his argument. Most of the time the quotation points back to a narrative passage, primarily the stories of Abraham and the exodus. Apparently Paul felt confident that his audiences, including the Romans, knew these stories well enough that he could appeal to them in support of his argument without having to retell the whole story. This requirement that the audience "fill in the gaps" in his argumentation would have encouraged the audience to participate in the construction of his message.[1] To do so, the audience had to recall not only the particular passages to which Paul refers, but also the major elements of the belief-system that they had inherited from

1. Wolfgang Iser (*The Act of Reading: A Theory of Aesthetic Response* [Baltimore: Johns Hopkins University Press, 1978]) argues that this process of "filling in the gaps" is central to all experiences of reading, so that every encounter with a text is an interactive process that produces both intellectual and affective responses in the reader.

Judaism and its Scriptures. This implicit appeal to a common belief-system served to reinforce the ideological and social bond that united Paul and his audience and allowed him to build on these shared beliefs and values when framing his response to the "provoking rhetorical urgency."[2] This same act of recollection may also have helped the recipients to follow the remainder of Paul's argumentation, since he clearly presupposes a common belief-system even when it is not cited.

5. Like other Jews, Paul maintained a deep respect for the Scriptures of Israel and believed that a quotation from the holy text should close off all debate on a subject.[3] His many appeals to the Jewish Scriptures reveal his conviction that the words of Israel's God carry a force that transcends all human argumentation. By recalling the words of Scripture, Paul aimed to lead his audience into a firsthand encounter with the God of Israel, whose presence was believed to accompany the recitation of Scripture. By aligning his own voice with the voice of God, he also implicitly reinforced his claims to a God-given authority over the recipients of his letters. Apparently he assumed that this experience of the divine voice would overcome any resistance that they might have felt toward his arguments and motivate them to follow his instructions.

6. Quotations from Scripture play a variety of roles in Paul's argumentation. Most common is the appeal to authority, where Paul appeals to a verse of Scripture in an effort to add further weight to his own argument. But Paul also adduces the words of Scripture for other reasons: to illustrate or exemplify a point; to provide the premise for an argument; to draw a lesson from a biblical character or event; to say something in a particularly apt manner, etc.[4] His usual practice was to embed a quotation within a series of

---

2. According to Eugene White, this two-way process of "identification" between speaker and audience is crucial to the success of any rhetorical endeavor (see chapter 2, note 35).

3. As Chaïm Perelman observes concerning arguments from authority, "The greater the authority, the more unquestionable does [the speaker's] pronouncement become. The extreme case is the divine authority which overcomes all the obstacles that reason might raise" (Chaïm Perelman and L. Olbrechts-Tyteca, *The New Rhetoric: A Treatise on Argumentation* [trans. John Wilkinson and Purcell Weaver; Notre Dame, Ind.: University of Notre Dame Press, 1969], 308). Eugene White would probably class Paul's belief in the authority of Scripture under the heading of "*Zeitgeist* influences," by which he means "the general social views, myths, trends, traditions, or intellectual/moral states that pervade the self-systems of the participants and thereby condition the way they perceive a particular urgency" (*The Context of Human Discourse: A Configurational Criticism of Rhetoric* [Columbia: University of South Carolina Press, 1992], 146).

4. In a frequently cited article ("The Basic Functions of Quotation," in *Sign, Language, Culture* [ed. A. J. Greimas et al.; The Hague: Mouton, 1970], 690–705), Stefan Morawski

carefully structured arguments that he believed would speak to the needs and capacities of his audience. Sometimes he appended a verse of Scripture to a point that he had already made in his own words, while in other cases he cited the quotation first and then proceeded to explain its relevance to the intended audience. In a few places he used a biblical quotation to replace his own words, perhaps to minimize the possibility of the audience reacting negatively to his argument. When commenting on a biblical narrative, he occasionally cited a key verse from the original passage in order to underline what he saw as the central point of the story for his audience. And in certain instances he seems to have lifted a verse or phrase from Scripture simply because he appreciated the beauty and aptness of its language. Some of these references to Scripture probably came to Paul spontaneously as he was dictating his letters, but most show signs of having been carefully planned in advance.

7. To increase the chances that his audience would understand and respond to these "words of God" in the way he intended, Paul regularly adapted the wording of his quotations so as to highlight the link between the biblical passage and his own developing argument.[5] He also used various introductory formulae and exegetical comments to indicate how he intended his quotations to be understood. In these cases we have a reasonably clear indication of the rhetorical strategy that informed Paul's handling of the biblical text, though uncertainty often remains regarding ancillary aspects of the quotation. In other cases the link between the quotation and the surrounding argument is left unexplained. At times the ambiguity is only temporary; that is, the audience is left to puzzle over the quotation until its meaning becomes clear from the ensuing comments. Occasionally this uncertainty, including the associated affective response, is critical to the

---

discusses four common reasons for quotation: (1) the authority function (grounding one's position in the views of another); (2) the erudite function (presenting excerpts from a work under review); (3) the stimulative-amplificatory function (using another's words in place of one's own argument); and (4) the ornamental function (quoting for their aesthetic effect). Obviously, this list is too broad and generic to be of much use when applied to the letters of Paul.

5. For evidence that Paul adapted the wording of quotations to coincide with his own rhetorical agenda, see Dietrich-Alex Koch, *Die Schrift als Zeuge des Evangeliums: Untersuchungen zur Verwendung und zum Verständnis der Schrift bei Paulus* (BHT 69; Tübingen: Mohr, 1986), 102–98; Christopher D. Stanley, *Paul and the Language of Scripture: Citation Technique in the Pauline Epistles and Contemporary Literature* (SNTSMS 74; Cambridge: Cambridge University Press, 1992), 83–264; Vernon K. Robbins, *The Tapestry of Early Christian Discourse: Rhetoric, Society, and Ideology* (London: Routledge, 1996), 103–7.

developing argument.[6] In other cases the quotation takes the place of a direct argument, whether because its wording was deemed especially apt or because it conveyed a point that Paul was reticent to express in his own words.[7] In still other cases the link remains unclear. Though it is possible that even these latter ambiguities are intentional,[8] most rhetoricians would probably regard them as missteps in a developing argumentative strategy.

8. Paul did not quote Scripture in a vacuum. The churches in Galatia and Corinth were probably familiar with Paul's practice of arguing from Scripture as a result of his earlier visits to their communities. Subsequently, other people had also brought instruction to these churches from the Jewish Scriptures, some of which Paul believed to be wrong-headed and even dangerous.[9] At least some of Paul's quotations were designed to counter these "false teachings" and to offer alternative readings of the authoritative biblical text. His "opponents" in turn would have crafted fresh arguments from Scripture to rebut the biblical arguments put forward in Paul's letters. The outcome of these debates is, unfortunately, lost to us. But we can be sure that Paul's letters represent only one stage in a developing rhetorical situation.

Evaluating Paul's Biblical Rhetoric

If the primary purpose of Paul's quotations was to influence the beliefs and conduct of the recipients of his letters, how successful was he in this effort? In an absolute sense we can never know the answer to this question, since we have no direct testimony as to the effectiveness of any of Paul's letters (with the possible exception of his "sorrowful" letter to the Corinthians), and we have no way of separating the effects of a quotation from other aspects of Paul's rhetoric. But this need not prevent us from making relative judgments about the likely effectiveness of Paul's rhetorical appeals to the Jewish Scriptures. According to Eugene White, the primary criterion for measuring the effectiveness of a piece of rhetoric is not the actual audience response, but rather the level of congruence between the speaker/author's use of language and the various circumstantial forces that impinge

6. For example, see the discussion of Gal 3:10 in chapter 7.

7. Something like this can be seen in Gal 4:30; 1 Cor 15:55; 2 Cor 6:17–18; Rom 9:27–29.

8. For example, Paul may have wanted to leave the door open for multiple interpretations, or he may have felt that the text was clear and required no comment.

9. The reference, of course, is to those whom Paul (as part of his rhetorical strategy) calls "agitators" in Galatia and "super-apostles" in Corinth.

on the rhetorical process.[10] Chief among these forces is the ability and willingness of the audience to understand the argument and respond in the recommended manner. The effective communicator is one who takes full account of the capabilities and likely responses of the intended audience within a given rhetorical context.

From the standpoint of White's model of rhetorical communication, how well does Paul use the language of Scripture to advance his arguments? Several points can be made in support of the view that Paul was an effective rhetor in his use of the Jewish Scriptures.

1. Paul seems to have made a serious effort to frame his quotations to fit the limited capabilities of his audiences. Only infrequently does he require his addressees to supply the original context of a quotation; in most cases he includes enough explanatory comments to insure that an audience with only a modest knowledge of Scripture could grasp his essential point. The amount and type of biblical knowledge that Paul assumes in his letters to the churches of Corinth and Galatia (but not Rome) seems reasonable in light of what we know about Paul's prior contacts with these churches and the general level of literacy in the ancient world. By framing his quotations in such a way that their "meaning" could be determined from the context of his letter, Paul did his best to insure that his quotations would be understood in the manner in which he intended them.

2. Paul also demonstrates a keen awareness of his audiences' respect for the authority of the Jewish Scriptures. While there was no thought of a Christian "Old Testament" in Paul's day, the ubiquity of biblical quotations and allusions in early Christian literature shows that the ancestral Scriptures of the Jewish people were regarded as authoritative from the earliest days of the Christian church because of its origins within Judaism. Paul could therefore count on the fact that his audience would take seriously any argument that claimed to have the support of the Jewish Scriptures.[11] Though we

10. As noted in chapter 1, Eugene White identifies six factors that impinge upon the effectiveness of a rhetorical communication: (1) the potential for modification of the urgency; (2) the capacity of the readers/listeners to alter the urgency; (3) the readiness of the readers/listeners to be influenced; (4) the occasion—the immediate circumstances in which the communication takes place; (5) relevant aspects of the persuader's self-system; and (6) the persuader's real and apparent purposes in communicating (*Context,* 38–39).

11. Ross Wagner, who approaches Paul's questions from a very different methodological perspective than the one modeled in this study, likewise underlines the fundamental importance of the audience's respect for the authority of the Jewish Scriptures as the *Grundlage* for understanding Paul's biblical quotations (*Heralds of the Gospel: Paul and Isaiah "in Concert" in the Letter to the Romans* [Leiden: Brill, 2002], 92, 242, 257, 352).

might question whether Paul actually violated this trust on occasion by the way he handled the biblical text, his appeals to the authority of Scripture certainly reflect an effective strategy of argumentation.

3. Paul seems to have taken into account the possibility that the audience's attitude toward him might have influenced its response to his quotations. It probably is no accident that the four letters in which Paul quotes explicitly from the Jewish Scriptures were addressed to churches in which his apostolic authority was under suspicion. In Corinth and Galatia, some of the congregants had decided to follow another leader, or set of leaders, and were trying to induce others in the church to reject Paul and follow them. In Rome, news of Paul's "law-free" gospel had apparently raised concerns in the minds of some people about whether he could be trusted (Rom 3:8). Under these circumstances, Paul could not follow his usual strategy of issuing authoritative pronouncements and expecting them to be obeyed. He had to offer arguments in support of his position. One of his argumentative strategies was to appeal to the higher authority of Scripture. But his quotations would have been useless if his audience did not respect him as a skilled and reliable interpreter of the biblical text. Where he could count on that level of respect, as in 1 Corinthians, he simply quoted the words of Scripture to lend support to particular points. Where he feared that he had lost the audience's respect, as in 2 Corinthians and Galatians, he began his letter with arguments that would reinforce his standing as an apostle of Jesus Christ, the highest of all authorities. Only then could he quote from the authoritative Scriptures and expect to be heard.[12] Where he was relatively unknown to the addressees, as in Romans, he could not rely on his authority as an apostle, but he could be sure that they would accept the authority of the sacred text. The simple fact that Paul knew the Jewish Scriptures well enough to quote them in support of his position would have enhanced his stature in the eyes of most of the people to whom he wrote. This in turn would have increased the likelihood that they would respond positively to his arguments.

4. Finally, Paul appears to have used quotations effectively at times to shield himself from negative reactions to his arguments. By pointing to Scripture as the basis for his views, Paul was able to defuse some of the criticisms that might have been raised against his positions. In a few cases he actually uses a quotation to say something to an audience that he might have

12. The first explicit quotation in Galatians does not appear until 3:6. In 2 Corinthians, there are no quotations until chapter 4, and even those are fairly innocuous (4:6, 13).

hesitated to say in his own language. More often the quotation simply echoes a point that he has made or intends to make in his own words. What makes the quotation valuable is that it gives Paul's mostly illiterate audiences a direct encounter with the voice of God speaking in the holy Scriptures. By quoting the words of Scripture, Paul points to God as the source of the ideas or injunctions that his audience might have been tempted to reject. This was, without doubt, the most powerful element of Paul's appeals to the Jewish Scriptures, since it successfully veiled his own creative role in the argumentative process. One could argue with Paul, but who would dare to argue with God?

On the other hand, there are reasons to think that Paul's use of quotations was not an effective rhetorical strategy in every instance.

1. One potential problem arises from the diversity of Paul's actual first-century audiences. By directing his quotations toward an implied audience that possessed a certain amount of biblical literacy, Paul may have rendered some of his arguments incomprehensible, or at least obscure, to audience members who were unfamiliar with the characters or stories to which he refers (the "minimal audience"). The resultant gaps in the argument might have limited the ability of these individuals to understand and accept his position, especially if they held an unfavorable view of him already. On the other hand, the freedom with which he manipulates the biblical text to support his positions might have induced a person with a deeper knowledge of Scripture (the "informed audience") to challenge or reject some of the arguments in which his quotations were embedded. In this case, the effect of Paul's rhetorical appeals to Scripture might have been the opposite of what he intended. Fortunately for Paul, it appears that few people in his churches fit this description.

2. A second limitation on the effectiveness of Paul's quotation strategy was his relative ignorance about precisely which passages of Scripture his audiences would have known. In the case of the Corinthians and possibly the Galatians, Paul might have recalled some of the verses that they had discussed while he was with them. But he could not have known how much of his teaching they had retained or what passages they might have learned in his absence.[13] In the case of the Romans, it is even more difficult to see how

13. Though it is true that Paul kept in touch with his churches, information about the precise content of their recent Bible study sessions (if anything of the sort existed in Paul's churches) is not the sort of news that was likely to be passed on in the sporadic communications that Paul maintained with his churches.

Paul could have possessed any reliable knowledge about which biblical passages his audience would recognize. In cases where Paul assumes that his addressees will know the background of a particular quotation or biblical story, we must be open to the possibility that he misjudged the knowledge and/or capabilities of his audience. In most cases we probably have little more than his best guess as to what his audience knew, especially in his letter to the Romans. We also should not rule out the possibility that Paul sometimes got carried away in the heat of an argument and forgot about the limited capabilities of his audience.[14] The outcome would have been the same in any event: a wrong guess about the audience's knowledge of Scripture at a key stage in an argument would have interfered with the audience's understanding and acceptance of his rhetorical point. Since Paul was probably aware that his audiences had only a limited knowledge of Scripture, a safer strategy would have been to avoid unexplained biblical references altogether.

4. Finally, the effectiveness of Paul's strategy of quotation might have been compromised if he underestimated the level of distrust and/or opposition to his positions, or his authority, among the members of his churches. Addressees who respected the Jewish Scriptures might nonetheless have rejected Paul's biblical argumentation if they felt that he was no longer a credible authority. From Paul's letters we learn that there were people in both Corinth and Galatia who were seeking to diminish Paul's reputation in order to gain support for their own views, and Paul was clearly worried about their influence. In both situations he decided to write letters to counter the challenges of his opponents and to reinforce his own reputation. In both cases, however, he seems to have run into problems. Some of Paul's remarks in his letter to the Galatians suggest that his knowledge of his opponents was rather limited, yet he proceeded to launch a scathing attack against them and their teachings. Since it appears that these people had gained significant support among the Galatians, this combative strategy might well have backfired, producing a backlash against Paul that included an auto-

14. It is certainly possible that Paul directed his quotations primarily to the literate members of his churches on the assumption that they would search out, or already know, the original context of the quotation and explain Paul's interpretive activity to the illiterate majority. But the fact that modern scholars have offered such diverse accounts of Paul's engagement with Scripture suggests that ancient readers would have encountered similar problems if they had attempted to reconstruct Paul's biblical interpretations for themselves. The difficulty would have been compounded in those cases where Paul's application of a passage stands in tension with its natural sense.

matic rejection of his arguments. This is precisely the response that he encountered from some of the people who heard his "sorrowful letter" to the Corinthians. The primary purpose of 2 Corinthians was to repair the breach that resulted from this overly harsh prior letter. The relatively sparse use of quotations in 2 Corinthians could be taken as evidence that Paul was aware that the Corinthians no longer trusted him enough to listen seriously to his biblical arguments. From these two letters we might infer that Paul was not always the best judge of the way an audience might respond to his argumentation. If the tone or content of his letter had the effect of diminishing rather than enhancing his reputation with the audience, the negative reaction may well have spilled over to his biblical quotations.

In the end, of course, all of our judgments remain speculative. Even in Paul's day, no one, including Paul himself, could have anticipated exactly how the people in his churches would respond to his rhetorical use of quotations. The actual responses were probably as diverse as the membership of the churches.[15] Rhetoric is a strategic exercise that involves a significant amount of guesswork about the potential reactions of an audience, and Paul was not exempt from this limitation. Perhaps Paul was better at anticipating the responses of his audiences than his letters indicate. Perhaps he was worse. Perhaps he had good reasons for thinking that quoting from the Jewish Scriptures would enhance the effectiveness of some of his letters or arguments and not others. Perhaps he simply used whatever arguments came to mind in the moment of dictation. All that a study like this can hope to do is to trace the contours of Paul's biblical argumentation and offer reasoned judgments about the likely correlation between Paul's rhetorical uses of Scripture and the capabilities of his intended audience.

Quotations as "Sacred Play"

At the heart of Paul's strategy of quotation lies a profound respect for the authority of the Jewish Scriptures. Whenever Paul inserts a biblical quotation into an argument, he is playing directly or indirectly on his audience's high regard for the sacred Scriptures of Judaism. The words "play" and

15. This causes problems for any attempt to determine the "meaning" of a Pauline quotation. We would do better to think of Paul's quotations as poetic devices open to multiple interpretations than to argue over whether a given interpretation constitutes the "meaning" of a particular reference to the Jewish Scriptures. Richard Hays's approach is exemplary in this respect (*Echoes of Scripture in the Letters of Paul* [New Haven: Yale University Press, 1989]).

"sacred" do not often appear together in contemporary Western culture. But both words are important for understanding Paul's rhetorical use of the Jewish Scriptures.

1. For Paul, and presumably also for the members of his congregations, the ancestral Scriptures of the Jewish people were viewed as "sacred" in the sense that their content was regarded as coming directly from God through various human intermediaries. Paul was, of course, aware that the texts were actually penned by human authors; on several occasions he introduces quotations with phrases such as "David says" (Rom 4:6, 11:9), "Moses says" (Rom 10:19; cf. 10:5), and "Isaiah cries out" (Rom 9:27; cf. 9:29, 10:20, 15:12).[16] But elsewhere he indicates his belief that the words of Scripture are in fact the very words of God, written under divine guidance for the time when their full significance would at last become clear (i.e., in the era of Jesus and his church) (Rom 1:2, 3:2; 1 Cor 9:10).[17] The same idea is implied in a number of passages in which Paul speaks of the Jewish Scriptures as a whole (or a particular verse or passage) finding their true meaning and/or application in the Christian church (Rom 4:23–24, 9:23–26, 10:6–8, 15:3–4; 1 Cor 10:11, 15:54; 2 Cor 3:14–16; Gal 3:8, 16).[18] While this does not amount to a "doctrine of inspiration," it does signify that Paul held the Jewish Scriptures in high regard due to their purported divine authorship, and he certainly wrote as though he expected his audiences to share this view. For Paul, the Scriptures spoke with the authority of God, and they should be accepted as such. A quotation from Scripture should be enough to resolve any dispute.

But while we should not doubt the sincerity of Paul's belief, we must be aware that quotations from a text deemed authoritative within a religious community can also be used as tools of coercion. Only rarely does a biblical quotation add anything new to the intellectual content of a Pauline argument. Most of Paul's quotations simply reinforce a point that he has already

---

16. It is intriguing that all of Paul's references to human authors of Scripture appear in his letter to the Romans.

17. This excludes the handful of cases where Paul refers to God as the speaker in the introductory formula of a quotation in which God is in fact the "I" in the original text (Rom 9:15, 25– 26 [?], 11:4; 2 Cor 4:6). Perhaps we should add here the two passages in which Paul appends the words "says the Lord" to the end of a quotation after he has already introduced the verse with his standard formula, "it is written" (Rom 12:19; 1 Cor 14:21).

18. This is evident also in the numerous passages in which Paul applies biblical quotations directly to his own day as if they had been written exclusively for Christians or their times (e.g., Rom 11:8–10, 26; 1 Cor 14:21; 2 Cor 6:2; Gal 4:27).

made or intends to make in his own words. Even in cases where the quotation does not function explicitly as a "proof" for a Pauline argument, the introduction of a verse from the sacred Scriptures invariably adds an air of divine authority to the passage, since it shows the God of Israel standing on the side of the speaker (i.e., Paul). If the words of Scripture are in fact the words of God, then a quotation from Scripture brings the audience into the very presence of God. The quotation carries with it a numinous quality that challenges the audience to take seriously the argument in which it is embedded. The ability to adduce such divine oracles as needed would have enhanced the reputation (*ethos*) of anyone who possessed the requisite knowledge and expertise.

Thus the danger was always present that Paul (or any other Christian author) would use quotations from the Jewish Scriptures in a mercenary manner to advance his own agenda. Appeals to the sacred are one of the chief tools by which the leaders of traditional societies seek to justify the beliefs and practices of their society and evoke submission to its institutions.[19] The allure of holding such power over the consciences of others is nearly irresistible, and we have seen several places where Paul seems to have succumbed to that temptation by appealing to Scripture in support of a highly tendentious argument.[20] In fact, one could argue that nearly all of Paul's biblical quotations include an element of force, since the very act of adducing a quotation is a covert attempt to increase the audience's receptiveness to the passage in which it appears. Gillian Lane-Mercier seems to be correct in her observation that issues of power lie at the heart of the quotation process. While it is certainly possible to use quotations to advance the aims of the sacred, the danger of profanation lurks darkly among the shadows.[21]

2. Before we condemn Paul too quickly for using Scripture to advance his own interests, we should ask how seriously he expected his quotations to be taken. As Gillian Lane-Mercier has pointed out, a certain amount of

---

19. Peter Berger (*The Sacred Canopy: Elements of a Sociological Theory of Religion* [Garden City, N.Y.: Doubleday, 1967]) speaks at length about this "legitimating" role of religion in traditional societies. According to Berger, one of the primary purposes of such appeals is to hide the human origins of social beliefs and practices and thus place them beyond reasonable challenge (29–42).

20. See, for example, the discussions of 2 Cor 9:9; Gal 3:10; and Rom 2:24.

21. The very fact that the quotation process is grounded in an assertion of power would be enough to raise the suspicions of Elisabeth Schüssler Fiorenza, who insists on the importance of applying a moral critique to the rhetoric of early Christian authors (*Rhetoric and Ethic: The Politics of Biblical Studies* [Minneapolis: Fortress, 1999], 26–30, 44–55).

"play" is inherent in the practice of quotation. Did Paul really expect the Galatians to be impressed by his argument from the singular form of the Greek noun "seed" in Gal 3:16? Did he chuckle as he applied the verse about "not muzzling the ox" to himself in 1 Cor 9:9–10? Did he have doubts about whether the Galatians would accept the validity of his Sarah-Hagar allegory in Gal 4:21–31? Was he secretly glad that his hypothetical Jewish interlocutor could not respond to his use of Isa 52:5 in Rom 2:24? Similar questions could be asked about many of the Jewish rabbis cited in the midrashim and the Talmud, where playful appeals to Scripture abound. In other words, a high regard for the authority of Scripture does not necessitate a consistently "serious" attitude toward the interpretation and application of Scripture.

Though we can never be sure what was in Paul's mind, we should be aware of the possibility that Paul himself may have questioned the validity and/or relevance of some of his appeals to the Jewish Scriptures. This is not to suggest that his letters are devoid of thoughtful biblical argumentation, nor that we should give up trying to understand how Paul read the biblical text. But contemporary scholars could benefit from recognizing the persuasive purpose of most of Paul's appeals to the Jewish Scriptures. While Paul was obviously a serious student of Scripture, his letters were not written to teach biblical exegesis. They were written to address a "provoking rhetorical urgency" that Paul believed could be brought under control through the effective use of language. Quotations from the sacred and authoritative Jewish Scriptures were an important weapon in Paul's rhetorical arsenal, and he did not hesitate to deploy this weapon when he felt that it would advance his cause.

Index of Biblical Texts

Index of Authors